BEYOND AGENDAS

Beyond Agendas

NEW DIRECTIONS IN COMMUNICATION RESEARCH

EDITED BY
Philip Gaunt

FOREWORD BY
Everette E. Dennis

Sponsored by Southwestern Bell Foundation

CONTRIBUTIONS TO THE STUDY OF
MASS MEDIA
AND
COMMUNICATIONS, NUMBER 43

GREENWOOD PRESS
Westport, Connecticut • London

Library of Congress Cataloging-in-Publication Data

Beyond agendas : new directions in communication research / edited by
   Philip Gaunt ; foreword by Everette E. Dennis ; sponsored by
   Southwestern Bell Foundation.
      p.   cm.—(Contributions to the study of mass media and
   communications, ISSN 0732–4456 ; no. 43)
      Includes bibliographical references (p.) and index.
      ISBN 0–313–28863–1 (alk. paper)
      1. Communication—Research. I. Gaunt, Philip.
   II. Southwestern Bell Foundation.   III. Series.
   P91.3.B39   1994
   302.2′072—dc20   93–12978

British Library Cataloguing in Publication Data is available.

Library of Congress Catalog Card Number: 93–12978
ISBN: 0–313–28863–1
ISSN: 0732–4456

First published in 1993

Greenwood Press, 88 Post Road West, Westport, CT 06881
An imprint of Greenwood Publishing Group, Inc.

Printed in the United States of America

The paper used in this book complies with the
Permanent Paper Standard issued by the National
Information Standards Organization (Z39.48–1984).

10 9 8 7 6 5 4 3 2 1

For Jean
with thanks
for continually showing me new directions

Contents

Figures and Tables

Foreword

In an age of information, disciplined intelligence about communication is more vital than ever before. In the United States, it would seem that those who can benefit from communication research are well positioned because of the rich range and texture of available research. But, wait—that is a cursory view which, when examined more carefully, is not quite the case. True, both the quantity and quality of media and communication research in the United States and a few other information societies is extraordinarily rich. But it is also fragmented and difficult to access, not to mention understand. Few organizations, let alone individuals, have as their mission the assessment, synthesis and examination of media research output, whether in the academy, industry or other settings. The result is an ever growing body of research, embracing many topics—from individual media and media use to arcane aspects of communicators and their missions.

Any serious mapping of the communication research enterprise not only presents a mind-boggling range of topics and concerns but also employs a multitude of research methods, yielding an output that is neither comparable in any sense nor particularly understandable. Social scientists and humanists meet on the field of communication research with different motivations, interests and values, not to mention that they have different methods of extracting information.

If this diverse and fragmented condition is the case on both the national and international scenes, how does it relate to those in the academy with similar interests and passions for knowing more about mass communication and its various subfields? Here, too, there is a lack of coherence and some potential confusion, where one study has little to do with another except in the most superficial sense. People interested in the cognitive effects of media, for example, are concerned with how individuals process information but might employ one of a number of different methods to ascertain their information about this important arena for research, scholarship and policy formation. The same is true with macroresearch issues, such as media ownership and economic control. Survey researchers labor alongside critical scholars and come to sometimes similar, but most often radically different, conclusions.

While there is nothing wrong with a diversity of values, research topics and methods of scholarship, these do not add up to any coherent whole. The result is generally low status for media research. Much of the output of the academy, for example, has little influence upon scholars in fields outside of communication who are studying media or communication issues. It is not uncommon for leading economists, political scientists and sociologists who study media to do their work in a disciplinary vacuum with no reference to the rich yield and long legacy of media and communication research from such fields as mass communication, communication studies, journalism, advertising and others. At the same time, the media industries, which would be natural constituents for university-produced research, pay little attention to it, again for a variety of reasons ranging from the way topics are framed to the quality of written expression. Similarly, the policy makers in business and government who are open to intelligence from all sources have little contact with communication research generated by those in the universities.

For these reasons, and others, the Wichita Symposium, from which this collection of essays emerged, is particularly welcome. Bravely, the organizers of this important and singularly useful event assembled in one place at one time some of the preeminent leaders in communication research in the United States and elsewhere. They brought together social scientists and historians with legal scholars and critical theorists. They asked them to consider the current state of communication research (warts and all) and to project from that discussion some notions about research in the 1990s and beyond.

The result, I am told, was an inspired and intelligent exchange of old, experienced voices and new ones as well. People did more than present their personal or institutional research agendas. Instead, they related to others and urged more cooperative and integrative ventures. In the end, research is really about respect. It depends upon understanding, cooperation and integration. Without it, research is a singular fragment with little short-term or long-term value.

The Wichita Symposium solved no problems, but it did open the conduit on discussion not only to people who are dedicated to communication research as a full-time preoccupation, but also to others from related fields who are doing seminal work. With any luck, the result of this important meeting should be more cooperation, greater understanding and yes, even greater respect. While this was largely an exercise of researchers talking to other researchers, it was a setting not inhospitable to industry folk and those from settings outside universities who can also benefit from the yield of research. After all, the ultimate beneficiary of such efforts should be the public as consumers of communication and as communicators.

The Wichita Symposium broke the ice for a continued conversation about communication research that should remove barriers to cooperation and research utilization and move those who practice this craft to think more broadly about their work and how it might be used. That is already a mighty contribution, but with any luck it could be an opening for a far greater mission—that of integrating and making sense out of communication research by linking it with the curriculum of our communication and journalism schools and by making it more intelligible to potential users in the media, government and the private and nonprofit sectors.

By holding this symposium, The Wichita State University organizers, especially Vernon Keel and Philip Gaunt and their colleagues, deserve special commendation. They have rendered a service to their field and, by extension, to the public.

My only personal regret about this important meeting is that a command performance meeting in Washington, D.C., kept me from taking part.

Everette E. Dennis
Executive Director
The Freedom Forum Media Studies Center
Columbia University
New York, NY

Acknowledgments

The Wichita Symposium, which was at the origin of this collection of essays, was the result of much work by many people. But all this hard work would have been in vain without the support of the Southwestern Bell Foundation. I particularly want to recognize the efforts of Southwestern Bell Telephone's Randy Barron, James Callaway, Larry Schnieders, Shawn McKenzie and John Hull, who, right from the start, saw the need to seek fresh vantage points from which to view communication research. The generous and disinterested support provided by the foundation could be viewed as a model for the kind of partnership that can exist between the private sector and the academy.

I also want to recognize the special contribution of James Carey of the University of Illinois, Everette Dennis of the Freedom Forum Media Studies Center and David Weaver of Indiana University, who, during the early planning stages of the symposium, acted as a sort of advisory committee providing valuable advice, constructive suggestions and friendly encouragement.

The administration of The Wichita State University also deserves recognition for its institutional support. I particularly want to thank President Warren Armstrong for his personal involvement and interest in the symposium.

Vernon Keel, Director of the Elliott School of Communication, played a key role in the development of the project, not only by providing departmental support, but, above all, by acting as a one-man think tank always ready to suggest and talk through new ideas and perspectives. In fact, the whole idea for the symposium grew out of some early conversations with Vernon back in the spring of 1990. I am particularly grateful to him, too, for his insightful comments on early drafts of this volume.

Organizing an event of this nature requires a relentless devotion to detail. A lot of the detailed work was skillfully handled by Nancy Fisher, a lecturer at the Elliott School, with the assistance of a number of graduate students and the office staff, who cheerfully took on extra duties, often at the last minute. To all of these and all the other people who helped out at various times, my warmest thanks.

Finally, I want to express my gratitude to my family, especially Jean, for putting up with me during the long and sometimes frustrating months of preparation leading up to the symposium and the production of this book.

BEYOND AGENDAS

The Future of Communication Research

Philip Gaunt

In the fall of 1992, 140 leading communication scholars were invited to attend the Wichita Symposium to take a fresh look at communication in general, and communication research in particular, as we approach the twenty-first century. The symposium, "Beyond Agendas: New Directions in Communication Research," was organized by The Wichita State University's Elliott School of Communication, with the generous support of the Southwestern Bell Foundation. This volume, which has emerged from the symposium, contains essays by twelve of the world's foremost experts in a broad array of research areas. While these twelve essays are the sole work of their authors, it is appropriate to recognize the important contribution of the symposium's chairs and discussants, whose ideas represent an even broader interdisciplinary view of the whole field of communication. They are listed here with their affiliations.

Phillip Clampitt, University of Wisconsin–Green Bay

Robert Craig, University of Colorado at Boulder

James Dearing, Michigan State University

William F. Eadie, California State University–Northridge

David Eason, Middle Tennessee State University

Jean Folkerts, George Washington University

Theodore L. Glasser, Stanford University

Peter Haratonik, Hofstra University

Hanno Hardt, University of Iowa

Fred Jablin, University of Texas at Austin
David Kamerer, The Wichita State University
Chris Leland, The Wichita State University
Maxwell E. McCombs, University of Texas at Austin
Dan Nimmo, University of Oklahoma
Victoria O'Donnell, Montana State University
John D. Peters, University of Iowa
Linda Putnam, Purdue University
Ronald E. Rice, Rutgers University
Donald L. Shaw, University of North Carolina
J. Michael Sproule, San Jose State University
Federico Subervi, University of Texas at Austin
Stuart Surlin, University of Windsor, Ontario
Michael Tracey, University of Colorado at Boulder
John Wright, The University of Kansas

BACKGROUND

All areas of communication have been affected by the technological changes that have taken place over the last few decades. From E-mail and the workaday fax to intelligent networks and fiber optics, and with such mysteries as "virtual reality" just around the corner, new technologies are dramatically changing the way in which we communicate. Some of the changes have been major; others have modified communication processes in subtler ways. At the same time, it has become increasingly evident that communication itself can be an agent of social change, for better or for worse. Bad communication inevitably causes problems; good communication can sometimes solve them.

However, the convergence of communication forms and channels that characterizes the information age in which we live goes beyond engineering and hardware. Communication research needs to explore the social, cultural, intellectual and regulatory challenges arising from this new convergence. The fragmentation of society, the emergence of new communities of interest and increasingly articulate ethnic and linguistic groupings, as well as population shifts south and west, offer serious threats to social well-being and peace unless new strides can be made in understanding the communication processes involved. There is little doubt that new communication technologies will have a role to play in such phenomena. Some of them may isolate and divide people, others may encourage expanded horizons and intercultural exchanges. Together, they will be the vehicles of education and knowledge as well as a vector for a whole array of cultural symbols and social constructs.

In the past, communication research has tended to be driven by agendas, but the essays in this book seek to go beyond agendas and to explore the options that might be generated by marrying the concerns and methodologies of the various areas of the discipline within the context of convergence. Much American communication research has focused on messages and their impact on audiences, in other words *what* is communicated. In light of the changes taking place in our global society, there is now a pressing need to look at *how* information is communicated. We need to know more about meaning, intention, nonmanifest content and the locus of understanding. Is meaning conveyed in the text or the spoken word, or is it situated in the receiver? Or, is it part of a transactional phenomenon placed somewhere between the message and the receiver?

These are questions that have long been of interest to researchers, but, today, we must keep before us the fact that communication is an integral part of everyday life and that research on these phenomena is not just an academic exercise. Academics are sometimes afraid of being political or ideological and are even timid in trying to help apply their research to social problems and issues. But now might be the time to enter the arena and attempt to make the kind of recommendations that policy makers, legislators and community leaders need but are not equipped to formulate. If we want to advance our field, it is important to place communication on the national agenda, alongside education, health care, housing and security.

Today, ten years after *Ferment in the Field,* we need to go beyond agendas, beyond turf battles, beyond the conflicts of mass communication versus speech communication, professional versus liberal arts, old liberal arts versus new liberal arts, positivistic versus naturalistic. Above all, we need to remember that communication is essentially a human process, even if it is mediated by the technologies of the twenty-first century. It remains a process that affects the lives of us all. The challenge facing our field is to bridge the gap between academic concerns and human realities; to take communication out of the ivory tower into the street, the neighborhood, the school and the community at large.

The essays in this volume are presented in four parts.

PART I: HISTORICAL PERSPECTIVES

In "Looking Back, Looking Forward: A Century of Communication Study," Everett M. Rogers traces the origins of the field back to the theories of Georg Simmel at the University of Berlin and the founding of the Chicago School in 1892. Rogers looks past the widely acknowledged "four founders" of communication study (the political scientist Harold D. Lasswell, the sociologist Paul F. Lazarsfeld, the social psychologist Kurt Lewin and the learning psychologist Carl I. Hovland) to the Chicago School during its golden era, from 1925 to 1935, in order to identify its key role in launching communication study in America.

The main scholars of the Chicago School, John Dewey, George Herbert

Mead and Robert E. Park (and by assimilation Charles Horton Cooley of the University of Michigan), drew upon the theories of Simmel, and also the ideas of Marx, Darwin and Freud, to shape two important directions for communication research. The first was symbolic interactionism, a theory that recognizes the key role of interpersonal communication in personality socialization. The second was a concern with the role of the mass media in recreating a sense of community among the urban poor. What was at issue to the Chicago School was whether American democracy, formulated for the rural community, could be adapted with the help of the mass media of the period—that is, whether newspapers could help solve the social problems of the urban poor, immigrants newly arrived from the villages of Europe.

Rogers argues that the influence of the Chicago School predates that of the "four founders" and has had a more lasting effect. In particular, by introducing an interpretive approach to two-way interaction, the school has given communication a much broader view. It posits that communication makes us human, a concept that is at the core of symbolic interactionism. Its focus on mass communication as a means to create a democratic society in urban settings shaped some of the first effects research, for example, the Payne Fund studies. Finally, interpretive scholars are now relying more heavily on the ethnographic methods developed during the heyday of the Chicago School of Sociology.

In "Urban Communication: The City, Media and Communications Policy," Garth S. Jowett makes a plea for revitalizing the study of urban communication. This chapter examines the relationship between the history of the city and the emergence of specific urban communication systems. The rise of the cities resulted in the development of new forms of communication media, precipitated by the increasing need to provide a constant flow of information to meet the requirements of the urbanized population. Alphabetic writing, printing, the telegraph and the telephone were technologies that emerged to meet an increased need for communication within the urban environment. In turn, each of these systems fundamentally altered the communications infrastructure of the city. However, each communication system also required the installation of specific forms of social control. The introduction of such communication systems increasingly made local communities aware they could no longer deal adequately with national media within the confines of a locally constituted political unit. This, in turn, led to the establishment of both governmental and industry self-regulation as a response to local concerns about media power.

Jowett argues that communication studies could make a major contribution to the formulation of urban communication policy by focusing attention on specific aspects of the urban communications infrastructure. Three areas are particularly worthy of attention: first, the role of the urban environment in the shaping and dissemination of popular culture; second, the evolution of urban interpersonal communication patterns with a view to understanding how such shifts may be assessed by policy makers; and third, the historical and political reasons for the failure to develop coherent urban communication policies.

PART II: INFORMATION FLOWS AND FILTERS

Jowett's plea for urban communication policies gives priority to communicating meaningfully with others in postindustrial society. In "Achieving Dialogue with 'the Other' in the Postmodern World," W. Barnett Pearce adopts a social constructionist perspective to explore some of the implications of communication in the multidimensional, pluralistic multiverse in which we exist. The complex notion of "dialogue" within a hermeneutic interpretation of communication inevitably invites an analysis of the Other, seen not simply as *another* but one who is *other than us,* one whose evaluative and interpretive criteria may be very different from ours. In one sense, the ethnographic approaches of early sociologists confronted us with the existence of the Other. In a deeper and more circular sense, the postmodern notion of reflexivity shows that we are changed by the process of communication, thus confronting "otherness" in ourselves.

The shift from the strictures of modernity to "new paradigm" approaches to communication theory requires new metaphors. One of the metaphors advanced by Pearce is that of media as a place, a new type of place with specific characteristics that comprise the infrastructure of social interactions. The ramifications of this metaphor provide an intriguing research perspective, but Pearce goes on to speculate that new directions in our field may depend more on the underlying temperament of the researchers or the grammars of their discourse, represented by the intersection of three continua. The first is the quest for certainty on one end and the exercise of curiosity on the other. Taken to an extreme, the quest for certainty would lead to silence; the exercise of curiosity, on the other hand, envisions that the conversation will continue. The second continuum is the distinction between a vision of a monistic social world, which seeks universal, unifying frameworks, and a vision of a pluralistic social world, which attempts to engage skillfully and wisely with unique and never fully predictable events. The third continuum opposes participant knowledge and spectator knowledge. By merging the three continua, positivism is clearly seen to fall in the cube defined by the quest for certainty by theorists functioning as spectators who believe that the social world is monistic. A more valuable approach for our field is defined by the exercise of curiosity by "practical" theorists functioning as participants in a social world conceptualized as pluralistic.

Continuing the theme of information flows and filters, Doris A. Graber in "Failures in News Transmission: Reasons and Remedies," argues that the manner of news presentation in the American press does not meet the information-processing capabilities and interests of average American audiences. Commonly used news presentation techniques, especially on television, make all learning extraordinarily difficult and memorization of details highly unlikely. Audiences are overwhelmed by an overabundance of undigested facts and contradictory statements. Subject matter selection is influenced by a set of outworn myths about the essential political knowledge required for effective citizenship in a democratic society. Therefore, much of what is currently presented is unnecessary and more confusing than enlightening. Though most people are interested in the causes and consequences of major political events, such information is not always provided.

Graber suggests that the way in which television news stories are framed provides an obstacle to understanding. The heavy insistence on facts, the lack of interpretation and explanation, the fact that stories are often too short and too crammed with detail, and the absence of "stopping points" in news programs, often run counter to the information-processing capabilities and cognitive frameworks of television audiences. There is no absolute way of structuring stories to meet the needs of all audiences at all times, but more attention must be paid to the idiosyncracies of particular audiences, the political context at the time and the focus of audience interest and attention. The training of political journalists should be designed to provide them with more expertise in political analysis as well as a better understanding of human information processing in general. Much more experimental research on news framing formats is needed so as to allow reporters to tailor stories to suit the cognitive frameworks of their audiences.

While news stories, news framing and news formats can strongly influence our behavior as citizens in a democratic society, Jeremy Tunstall in "Television Producers and Genres," suggests, at least implicitly, that man is not made of news alone. He further suggests that the senior producers of television series form a strategic research site from which might emerge important new information about how and why programs are made and aired. A cross-national study comparing series producers in different countries would be particularly valuable. One major difficulty, however, is the confusion that arises over the meaning of such basic terms as "network," "schedule" or even "series." Another key television term, "producer," has a wide range of meanings even within national systems. Hollywood television, for example, recognizes several different types of producer: executive producer, supervising producer, senior producer, producer and co-producer.

In describing his own work on London-based producers, Tunstall argues that *genre* would make a better basis for cross-national comparison than would "network" or "prime time." An analysis of only prime time in the United States, for example, would miss a lot of what is happening. A number of U.S. genres air either on network, but out of prime time, or on genre-specific cable channels. A genre such as documentary, for example, appears on network prime time in Britain but not in the United States. However, the U.S. system does offer documentary on PBS and elsewhere. A genre-based comparative approach would allow a genuine documentary-to-documentary comparison. The different channel locations in different national systems would be part of the comparison. Tunstall's suggested study, although difficult to do, would produce valuable information about areas of production and programming that have often been neglected in favor of news analysis.

"Obstacles to Internal Communication among Subsidiary and Headquarters Executives in Western Europe," by Maud Tixier, completes the discussion of information flows and filters. Based on two years of ongoing research in fifteen countries (the twelve nations of the European Community, Switzerland, Sweden and Austria) on executives transferred from one European country to another, this chapter examines how their preferred communication styles diverge or converge and what impact this situation has on the development or use of new technologies. The study first takes a look at national cultures and identifies a number of national characteristics that can influence communication: religion, upbringing and attitudes toward work, money and success. Within these main categories are to be found differing notions of time and flexibility. With regard to communication, these factors may determine preferences for written or oral, formal or informal, long or short, implicit or explicit, clear or ambiguous, soft or aggressive communication styles. Ingrained linguistic structures may also dictate certain levels of discourse, encouraging or suppressing brevity, discursiveness, humor, directness, familiarity and even different forms of logic.

Tixier presents evidence suggesting that the countries of southern Europe favor a centralized style of management, that Great Britain and Germany prefer a consensual style, while Denmark, the Netherlands and Sweden lean toward participative management. Such characteristics may help to explain why certain countries are more or less advanced in terms of adoption of new communication technologies, but Tixier is careful to point out that a more important influence may be availability and supply. In sum, this chapter, like that by Jeremy Tunstall, speaks to the need for more focused research on intercultural communication.

PART III: POLICY AND SOCIAL OUTCOMES

"New Directions in Communication Research from a Japanese Perspective," by Youichi Ito, covers three main areas: mass media effects, international information flows, and development and communication. In the first area, two new Japanese models are introduced. The first, *joho kohdo,* or information behavior model, assumes that people extract information not only from the mass media but also from non–mass media sources. If information transmitted by the mass media is congruent with information extracted from the environment and direct experience, then the credibility of the mass media will be maintained.

The second model, which is tripolar in structure, assumes that when two of the three major components of social consensus formation, that is, the mass media, government policies and public attitudes, agree with each other, then a climate of opinion *(kuuki)* develops and places pressure on the third component to comply. The power of *kuuki* is influenced by the degree of homogeneity within each component.

With regard to international information flows, Ito argues that the world order is extremely changeable and that, as a result, imbalances in information flows may be quickly reversed. Discussions about cultural imperialism, media imperialism or the New World Information Order should take this changeability into consideration. On the other hand, the "world language order" remains very stable, which is why the Japanese Kyodo News Agency is little more than a national news agency while Agence France Presse (AFP), whose budget is less than half of Kyodo's, remains an international agency. Thus, the dependency theory may be more applicable to international politics based on language hegemony than on the changeable fields of military, economic or technological influence.

These studies are related to a third area, development and communication. Once again, Ito draws upon the Japanese experience to present a model of development and communication based upon three factors present in Japanese social history: (1) a view of the world as a hierarchy of competing human groups, (2) well-educated masses and (3) a set of ethical rules governing intergroup competition and collectivism. As in the other areas covered, Ito proposes some fresh perspectives from which to approach future research.

The notion of public debate hinted at by Youichi Ito is central to the argument presented by Ellen Wartella in "Communication Research on Children and Public Policy." The main thrust of Wartella's argument is that while both the historical record and current events dictate that communication research and scholarship *can* make a difference in children's media, they usually do not. Changing this situation demands nothing less than a complete redirection of research and scholarship as well as a transformation of our attitudes toward them, a step that requires us to put aside our "paradigm debates" and emphasize the public nature of our enterprise.

Wartella analyzes three current issues that have attracted considerable public attention. They are the Children's Television Act of 1990, the case of Whittle Communication's Channel One daily news program in schools and the 1992 battle over funding for public television. These public issues underscore the intense public interest in the role of communication in modern life, but, all too often, communication research is not a part of the debate.

The nature of communication scholarship, its politics and its impact, is predicated upon how we approach our research and, perhaps more important, how we relay it in the public arena. A lot of scholarship never makes it to the public arena because scholars are often ignorant about how to act as public intellectuals and advocates for a particular point of view.

In conclusion, Wartella argues that we need to ensure that our work has a pragmatic commitment. We need to think about which public we are addressing in our research: the public at large, those media audiences we often study, public policy makers at the federal and state levels, communication practitioners or other cultural elites who write or talk about communication. To approach communication scholarship today without an understanding of the political commitments inherent in our line of research, in the kind of issues that are studied and in the potential uses of that research, is incredibly naive. We can no longer claim timidity as public scholars.

The issues that we study tomorrow may be very different. Jennings Bryant ponders the important question of *how* we study them in his chapter "Will Traditional Media Research Paradigms Be Obsolete in the Era of Intelligent Communication Networks?" Intelligent networks will enable us to receive all the media services to which we have become accustomed, along with many new ones, over a single electronic information utility. No one knows at present what form this advanced communication network will take or what the ownership, control or operational patterns will be. However, planning future telecommunications systems without taking full advantage of the predictive potential of telecommunications theory would leave the discussion to policy makers, who in the past have not seen the need for theory and research until it was too late, and to engineers, who typically are more concerned with the technical possibilities of a system than with its human potential.

Given an almost unlimited choice of both entertainment programming and information resources, what will individuals select? With the interactivity made possible by intelligent networks, what impact will individuals have on the information they choose to select either for entertainment or learning or problem solving? Intelligent networks are designed to be personalized, but how much control will individuals want to exercise, or be allowed to exercise by network designers?

The complexity of human telecommunications behavior in the new media environment will require that theories be constructed and research conducted from extremely diverse epistemological and metatheoretical perspectives. Bryant suggests that as we think about creating theory regarding advanced communication networks, it would be wise not to retreat from the kind of intellectual pluralism that our diverse interdisciplinary heritage provides, particularly those perspectives offered by interpersonal and organizational communication. Certainly, we need to create our *communication* theories of intelligent communication networks, but we should continue to incorporate the thoughtful work of others with vastly different theoretical perspectives in technology, policy making, political science, economics, First Amendment and cultural studies and, of course, consideration of effects at the individual level of analysis.

PART IV: FUTURE DIRECTIONS

Turning to the shape of the future, in his provocative chapter "Everything That Rises Must Diverge: Notes on Communications, Technology and the Symbolic Construction of the Social," James W. Carey views our world, in recast Teilhardian terms, as a noosphere without an Omega Point and encircled by a telecommunications belt. At this moment in our history, despite the convergence of communication technologies, the forces that represent divergence remain stronger than those in favor of homogenization. Divisions within our cities are too strong. Cultures show remarkable strength in absorbing and modifying external influences. As a result of conflict between these forces we are having a social meltdown. The question remains: What is going to replace what we had before?

Much of what we had before was framed by the phenomena taking place at the time of the foundation of the Chicago School. The closing of the frontier and the creation of a national network by the railroads created a new physical ecology, out of which grew a new symbolic ecology and, ultimately, an ecology of the media. Although the "great audience" was forged by the media, and national collectivities emerged, diversity was not destroyed; it was just pushed into new places. This was the end of a metanarrative, that of Lincoln and rural America. Today, as we reach the end of a long Kondratieff cycle, many of the constructs forged at the turn of the century—what Carey terms the "mantras" of race, class and gender—have dissolved into Burke's "thingless names" or "nameless things."

At this fleeting moment of balance between the forces of heterogenization and homogenization, we must recover a public space for citizenship, but, Carey concludes, we can only do that if we are able to identify and describe the social differences being produced and reproduced in what we often naively call the information society.

In another chapter turned toward the future, "Informing the Information Society: The Task for Communication Science," Denis McQuail focuses on three related topics: an interest in media and social change, a discussion of "communication science" and the importance of a critical approach to the media in terms of the welfare of society. Any attempt at understanding changes that are taking place both in the production and the delivery of communication and in organized media systems raises wider questions about conditions and trends in contemporary societies. Among these questions, the future role for public communication policy and the continued relevance or not of any strong version of public interest in communication remain high on the agenda.

As we enter a stage of development described as an "information society," it is appropriate to view public communication as the "nervous system" of such a society and as playing an essential role in the enhanced self-reflexivity of a postmodern world. For the same reasons, the emerging discipline of communication science has the opportunity to acquire a renewed direction and purpose and to fulfill a task that is at the same time social-normative, theoretical and practical.

Without appropriate communication policies, viewed not as an instrument of political control or social surveillance but as the expression of value choices within a self-reflexive monitoring process, the information society faces three serious threats. The first is the unequal distribution of information, which can lead to the emergence of an information underclass. The second is the potential risk of an increasingly unidimensional society, with much more choice for the few and cultural poverty for the many. The third is information chaos, which makes it difficult to learn from the public information resources of society.

In the final chapter, "Communication Research in the 1990s: New Directions and New Agendas?" David H. Weaver argues that the new media of communication, as well as an array of new services provided through the existing media, offer more choices and more interactive opportunities for receivers. This increases the importance of studying how people construct beliefs, opinions and ideas from mediated communication. At the same time, the convergence of communication technologies and the appearance of the same content forms and genres in a variety of media also make it more difficult to study the uses and effects of particular media or the production of media content.

Several new directions in communication have already appeared, in particular a shift from the quantitative methods of the logical positivist approach to the qualitative methods of the interpretive or naturalistic approach. There is also a growing awareness of communication influences other than those produced by the traditional news media, accompanied by a movement away from the study of direct effects of media messages to an analysis of how people construct meanings from a variety of messages. Finally, a trend toward more fine-grained content analysis indicates a growing emphasis on how issues are covered rather than what subjects or events are reported, especially in "framing" studies.

Weaver concludes his review of the field by calling for more use of multiple methods, especially a combination of quantitative and qualitative; more studies combining several levels of analysis; more holistic studies that analyze sources, messages and receivers concurrently; more studies over longer periods of time; and additional concepts, theories and approaches that will stimulate and reenergize communication research. The main task ahead of us is to determine which of many new research directions now emerging will be the most useful for furthering our understanding of communication processes. The problem is not a dearth of new ideas and directions, but rather a surplus. Winnowing that surplus without throwing out useful approaches from the past is the great challenge of the next decade of communication research.

CONNECTIONS

From this set of essays, and from the comments and suggestions of the chairs and discussants of the symposium, a number of important themes and connections emerge, with some intriguing implications for the future of communication research. Not surprisingly, at a time when many of our public institutions are being closely scrutinized, many of the issues raised concern public agendas, public debate, public communication and public interest. These are themes that connect many areas of research in our field, whether they focus on the uses and effects of mass media or on the construction of meaning by the various components of our society. This insistence on seeking social outcomes from our research goes back to the Chicago School, but it appears to be gaining renewed attention a century later. Communication has changed radically in the intervening years. Today, as communication continues to evolve in an era of rapid technological change, we need to understand how public agendas are formed, how public communication can further the public interest and how communication research can contribute to the public debate.

Society, whether viewed as a national entity or as a local, urban subculture, or, again, as discrete communities of interest, is held together—or not, as some would argue—by communication. Within this society, however it is defined, communicating with the Other is more than mere interaction; it may be the key to survival. Investigating the Other has long been a classic problem in anthropology. From a structuralist perspective, understanding the Other involves entering the Other's culture and exploring that culture's symbols and meanings. In a more modern, or rather postmodern interpretation, accepting and exploring the differences between us and the Other transforms the social world in which we live, both culturally and politically. In an even broader interpretation, the collective Other may represent diverse ethnic, economic, geographic, linguistic and intellectual groupings. Identifying the Other in ourselves may further illuminate the process of self-reflexivity. Communicating with the Other, then, must take place at various levels: intrapersonal, interpersonal, intercultural and international. The shift in perspective required to understand and communicate with the Other, or any set of Others, has far-reaching implications for communication research.

This "decentering" of focus, to use another postmodernist term, may imply that we give more emphasis to the interpretation of meanings and to the various social, cultural and political factors that influence interpretation, and less emphasis to the production and delivery of messages, except as they contribute to the construction of meaning. It may even imply, as British communication scholar Raymond Williams suggested at the Future of Communications Studies Conference in London twenty years ago, that we abandon the notion of *mass* communication altogether. There is little doubt that if we know more about how meanings are constructed then we will be better qualified to formulate and convey meaningful messages. We may even be in a better position to use new technologies in an ethical and socially responsible way. The potential of the new technologies with which we will have to contend is still unknown. There is an urgent need to explore this potential before they are upon us.

At another, interconnected level, a greater understanding of meaning will contribute to the dialogue required to build social consensus about public issues. In a networked society, the mass media may continue to play a major role in building social consensus, but so will other forms of public communication, silent or otherwise. Part of the public debate may depend on "silent" databases, bulletin boards and other computer linkages. Once again, how will the collective Other process and interpret these public information resources? What segments of society will have access to them? Such considerations suggest increased research into rights, responsibilities, ethics and public policies. Because of the reach offered by new technologies, such research will need to be international as well as domestic and may require the formation of multinational research teams, possibly funded by transnational corporate entities. The question of public policies for communication is one that is problematic in the United States because it may appear to conflict with First Amendment principles. However, in view of the potential inequalities of access and consumption in an information society, and the real dangers of creating a two-tiered culture in this as in many other areas, it may become necessary to consider some form of carefully controlled regulation similar to that which is prevalent in many other countries. This perspective points to a need for systematic comparative research.

Other comparative research perspectives are appropriate at both the macro- and microlevels. One concerns information gatherers and processors inside corporate, educational, legislative and political organizations. The way in which information is selected and shaped can have a considerable effect on decision making, the formation of public agendas and the formulation of public policy. At a time when nations are becoming increasingly interdependent, both economically and politically, a better knowledge of communication processes in other cultures may greatly improve intercultural exchanges. Another, micro-level perspective concerns the use of language in communication. A comparative rhetorical and structural analysis of the mechanisms of different languages may shed some interesting new light on how meanings are constructed. In this regard, some of the less obscure premises of deconstructionist thought might help us to isolate meanings and create parallels between our language and that of others.

These are some of the themes that emerge from this volume: the social relevance of communication research; the need to consider a wide variety of ''others'' in our society; the importance of dialogue and public debate in the formation of social consensus and policy; the legalities and ethics of applying new technologies; and, at the root of all these concerns, the construction and interpretation of meaning by individuals and communities. *Taken together, these issues represent not an agenda but a set of interrelated perspectives that cut across all the various areas of our field.* In the absence of any grand, universal theory of communication, the desirability of which is still open to debate, this set of perspectives does nevertheless provide a clear and unifying direction for the future.

Several lines of inquiry suggest themselves to follow this direction. Despite the convergence of communication forms and channels, the social world remains split into diverse and constantly shifting groups. In order to understand how and why individuals within these groups construct meaning, it is not enough to observe them from afar. It is necessary to enter the streets, neighborhoods, churches, ethnic communities, professional bodies, gangs even, to participate in their activities and share their discourse. Such ethnographic approaches may seem antiquated, but they may be the only way of finding out about communication processes in social groupings that may otherwise remain "invisible." Description—thick or otherwise—of these phenomena would provide essential basic data on which to build further analysis.

By the same token, structural and rhetorical analysis of messages delivered and interpreted by various segments of society would lead to a greater understanding of communicative exchanges within and among these segments. In this respect, the comparative analysis of messages and meanings in different languages, which is a well-established field of inquiry in linguistics, might have a valuable contribution to make to communication research, not only in intercultural studies but also in such areas as symbolic interactionism and coding and decoding.

With regard to mediated and public messages, documentary analysis is indicated to track the formation of public agendas through the mass media, congressional debate and other public forums. This should be supported by in-depth interviews and surveys of policy makers, legislators, legal scholars, editorialists, editors, public affairs practitioners and cultural figures, so as to explore further the relationship between public issues and the social, political, cultural and legislative context in which they appear. Here, new methods of issues forecasting will need to be developed, probably by combining content analysis, focus groups and modified computer modeling techniques.

The impact of future technologies of communication will continue to be a problem because it is not possible to observe phenomena that do not already exist. However, the intelligent use of experimentation should make it possible to simulate the probable effects of projected technologies, most of which go through fairly lengthy development stages before being introduced. Comparative study of technological developments in other cultures may also provide valuable insights into public acceptance and usage of emerging technologies not already available in the United States. While the issue of official policies governing various aspects of communication remains problematic, for the reasons stated above, further comparative study will reveal how other countries have come to terms with governmental and—perhaps more important for the future—with intergovernmental communication policies. It is only a matter of time before this issue rises to the top of the public agenda. We would do well to be prepared.

In more general terms, as a reflection of what is taking place in society, communication research will probably need to shift some of its emphasis away from mass communication to other forms of public communication, and to abandon some of the more ponderous quantitative procedures in favor of more naturalistic and evaluative methods, particularly in comparative settings. Much is to be gained, too, from combining research methodologies hitherto associated with specific subareas of our field. Because of the complexities of investigating communication processes in increasingly differentiated segments of our society, because of the reciprocal tensions generated by the convergence of technologies and the divergence of specific communities, and because of the unknowns surrounding emerging technologies, our research should seek greater depth rather than width. This will involve more emphasis on individual rather than mass phenomena as well as longer studies over longer periods of time.

These directions, however, have some important implications for the future of our field within the academy. It should be pointed out that some of these implications were identified by doctoral students attending the Wichita Symposium and they, more than many others, represent the future of communication research. The need for deeper studies over longer periods of time conflicts with traditional requirements for tenure and promotion. Despite protestations to the contrary, many university administrators and tenure and promotion committees are more impressed by quantity than real quality. As a result, young scholars have sought to produce short, quick studies, often based on standard statistical procedures. This is not an indictment of either individuals, schools or universities, or even of the tenure and promotion process in general. This is just the way the game has been played for a long time. Furthermore, the desperate need to publish and the sheer number of publication submissions have pressured some journals into requiring shorter and shorter studies.

But let us stop and consider for a moment. If the realities of our field—and possibly other applied fields in the social sciences and the humanities—require longer, deeper, more complex studies, should not tenure and promotion requirements be somewhat different? Could it be that, in a few specific areas of the academy, some of our oldest university traditions have in fact become counterproductive to good and useful scholarship? If doing genuinely useful research means that we have to become involved in public policy and public debate, should this not be recognized by university administrators, and should not the university rewards system be modified to reflect this?

Given the nature of university administrations, some of these outcomes might appear to be unrealistic. What can we do, as communication researchers, to improve our chances of achieving these changes? First, we need to take stock of who we are and what we do. This might require us to do some research on the social relevance of our work and the contribution we can and do make to the public debate, not only about communication issues per se but about many other areas involving communication. In this respect, as communication is so central to all forms of human endeavor, it is important for us to reach out across the academy and develop interdisciplinary research initiatives with colleagues in areas such as psychology, anthropology, political science, sociology, history, urban affairs, minority studies, education and even modern languages. Second, while we should think about how we do our research and what we do our research on, we must also give consideration to what we do with our research once it is completed. There will always be ample room for pure research in our field, but as communication touches so many practical aspects of our lives, we should be careful to write our research in such a way that it will be accessible to nonacademic audiences. If we can do all this and truly become outspoken advocates of our chosen field vis-à-vis the academy, the public, the media and policy makers, then we may well succeed in placing communication on the national agenda.

Part I

HISTORICAL PERSPECTIVES

2

Looking Back, Looking Forward: A Century of Communication Study

Everett M. Rogers

The purpose of this chapter is to describe the influence of the Chicago School on communication theory and research. The Chicago School was important because it represented the first flowering of social science in America, serving as the intellectual beachhead for important European theories, particularly those of the German sociologist Georg Simmel. Chicago gave a strong empirical dimension to the social science study of social problems in the United States. The Chicago School was amelioristic and progressive and pragmatic, seeking to improve the world by studying its social problems. *The Chicago School investigated whether American democracy, born in a society of rural communities, could survive in the crowded immigrant slums of a rapidly growing city.* Chicago scholars formed a theoretical conception of personality socialization known as "symbolic interactionism" that centered on human communication. The Chicago School also cast the mold for future mass communication research on media effects through studies of the foreign language press and the Payne Fund studies of the effects of films on children.

Here we trace the development of the Chicago School, stressing its impacts on communication study. While primary attention centers on Robert E. Park, the most influential member of the Chicago School and the scholar who pioneered research on mass communication, other Chicago scholars such as Charles Horton Cooley, John Dewey and George Herbert Mead also placed communication at the center of their conception of human behavior. First, however, we question the overly simplistic conception of the history of communication study that I call the "four founders myth."

THE FOUR FOUNDERS MYTH

The myth of the four founders began with Bernard Berelson's (1959) attack on the field and was emphasized by Wilbur Schramm (who is *the* founder, if ever there were one). Berelson (1959), in his "God-is-dead" presidential address to the American Association for Public Opinion Research, claimed that Lasswell, Lewin, Lazarsfeld and Hovland were losing interest in communication research, and that the field was thus "withering away." Wilbur Schramm (1959) disputed this field-is-dying assertion, but he popularized the four founders myth in his writings over the next three decades (Schramm, 1980, 1981, 1985).

The four founders myth is not totally incorrect. These four scholars did indeed play important roles in launching communication research. But there were many other founders, several of equal or greater influence in shaping communication study: Wilbur Schramm, Robert E. Park, Theodor Adorno, Claude E. Shannon, Norbert Wiener and Robert K. Merton. Further, the four founders in turn had "founders," that is, individuals who influenced their thinking about communication. For example, Harold Lasswell was strongly influenced by Freud, and Robert E. Park built on the theories of Simmel. So are Freud and Simmel also founders of the field of communication?

Why did Bernard Berelson and Wilbur Schramm select their seemingly arbitrary "four founders" in 1959? The "four founders" did their most important research and writing in the 1930s, 1940s and 1950s, about the time that the field of communication study was emerging as a distinct body of scholarly work in America. But the myth of the four founders does not distinguish between forerunners and founders. Scholars like Georg Simmel, Robert E. Park, George Herbert Mead, Kurt Lewin, Harold D. Lasswell, Carl I. Hovland, Norbert Wiener and Claude E. Shannon conducted what we consider communication research by today's standards. They were *forerunners,* scholars who made an important intellectual contribution to a new field of study, but who did not identify themselves with the new field, nor did their students, nor did they institutionalize the new field by establishing university departments bearing the name of the new field (Ben-David and Collins, 1966). *Founders* are not formally trained in a new field of study, but they conduct research in it and educate the first generation of scholars in the new field.

Our field's chief founder was Wilbur Schramm, who not only institutionalized communication study at Iowa, Illinois and Stanford in the form of institutes for communication research, but also wrote the textbooks that defined the field in the 1950s and taught dozens of the first Ph.D.–holders in communication. Paul F. Lazarsfeld was more a forerunner than a founder. He did conduct mass communication research from 1935 to 1960, but he identified himself as a sociologist and his disciples' work as sociology. Lasswell, Lewin and Hovland also were definitely forerunners, not founders. They did not give up their primary identification with political science, social psychology and psychology, respectively. So the next time that someone tells you that the four founders established the field of communication study, tell them about the Chicago School.

GETTING STARTED ON THE MIDWAY

The first classes on the Midway campus of the University of Chicago were offered just over one hundred years ago in September 1892. The University of Chicago was an important part of several major phase-changes that took place in American higher education about a century ago. At that time, the 400 or so colleges and universities in the United States focused mainly on providing an undergraduate education in the liberal arts. The European model, beginning with Harvard, founded in 1636, was Cambridge and Oxford, and, to a lesser extent, such other ancient universities as Paris, Bologna and Padua. But Johns Hopkins University was founded in Baltimore in 1876, modeled on the German research universities of Göttingen and Berlin. The primary focus was on teaching graduate students to conduct research. The role of the professor was to carry out scholarly investigation, and, through an apprenticeship arrangement, teach research skills to doctoral students.

This research mission required considerable resources, more than could be obtained from student fees. So the first generation of American research universities turned to wealthy businessmen who had created fortunes in oil and railroads and steel during the several decades following the Civil War. These robber barons' names identify these research universities: Johns Hopkins, Clark, Stanford, Vanderbilt, Carnegie and Mellon. The richest man of the day was John D. Rockefeller of the Standard Oil Company. He funded the first twenty years of the University of Chicago to the tune of $35 million, a sum that would be roughly equivalent to a half billion in today's dollars. Further, in the 1920s and 1930s one of Rockefeller's foundations, the Laura Spelman Rockefeller Memorial, awarded $3.4 million to the University of Chicago to fund social science research. And the Rockefeller Foundation in the 1930s, 1940s and 1950s funded the research of each of the main figures in communication study: Harold D. Lasswell, Paul F. Lazarsfeld, Kurt Lewin, Carl I. Hovland, Norbert Wiener, Wilbur Schramm and Gregory Bateson. *The launching of communication study is the story of consuming the Rockefeller millions.* We are a scientific field built on oil.

Chicago was America's second largest city, with almost 1.1 million people, when the University of Chicago was founded. It had an exceptional degree of cultural diversity. In 1900, half of its 1.7 million people were foreign-born (Bulmer, 1984, p. 13), and many others were the offspring of foreign-born parents. When the great German sociologist Max Weber visited Chicago in 1904, he said: "The whole tremendous city . . . is like a man whose skin has been peeled off and whose intestines are seen at work" (Weber, 1926, p. 286).

Chicago was characterized by a tremendous in-migration of European villagers, who struggled with poverty, crime and other social problems.

The University of Chicago started relatively late (256 years after Harvard) but it had a meteoric academic rise, in part due to the ample funding from John D. Rockefeller. Rockefeller did not give his generous gift in a generous way. Instead, he dribbled it out in small chunks over several decades (Goodspeed, 1916/1972). Rockefeller was a devout Baptist, and he wanted to be sure that his new Baptist university in Chicago would be successful. In each of its early years, as the university overspent its annual budget and seemed about to fall into bankruptcy, Rockefeller would step in to save it. Finally, he said "no more." But by then, he had contributed $35 million, the largest gift ever made at that time.

The University's Baptist leaders hired as their president William Rainey Harper, then 35 years old and a Hebrew professor at Yale University. A shrewd bargainer, Harper said he would come to Chicago if Rockefeller would donate an additional $1 million for divinity and graduate education. Rockefeller agreed, thus beginning the unique relationship between the go-getting young university president and his wealthy donor (Goodspeed, 1916/1972). Harper's new university was wildly successful. Harper had a keen eye for academic talent, and he was a very persuasive salesman as he went after the top scholars in each field. He typically doubled a professor's salary if he would join the Chicago faculty. By 1900, eight years after the university's founding, the University of Chicago was considered one of the top U.S. universities in academic quality.

FOUNDING THE DEPARTMENT OF SOCIOLOGY

President Harper recruited Albion W. Small, then president of Colby College, a small Baptist institution in Waterville, Maine, to join the Chicago faculty. Small had studied history and political economy at the University of Berlin and at the University of Leipzig from 1879–81 and then earned his Ph.D. degree from Johns Hopkins University in 1889. He also was an ordained Baptist minister, thus fitting perfectly the University of Chicago's twin demands for scholarly excellence and religious appropriateness.[1] Small pioneered in teaching a sociology course at Colby College, and he had written an introductory sociology textbook. He told President Harper that he wanted to be head of a sociology department at Chicago.

Small, who translated and published the main writings of Georg Simmel, wanted his department to be the American outpost for German sociology.[2] The Chicago School was to extend German sociological theories and apply them to investigating the urban social problems of the city. The sociological investigations in Chicago's slums tested how U.S. democracy could be adjusted to function more effectively in the new urban milieu of turn-of-the-century America. In the first issue of the *American Journal of Sociology* (which he founded and edited), Small insisted that sociology should not be a "do-nothing" social science. Instead, he wanted it to do good.

Simmel's theoretical perspective, which Robert E. Park reflected in his research and writing, can be summarized in five main points.

1. Society, the core concept of sociology, exists through communication among individuals

2. All human communication represents some kind of exchange that has reciprocal effects on the individuals involved

3. Communication occurs among individuals who stand at varying degrees of social distance from each other

4. Human communication satisfies certain basic needs, such as for companionship or aggression, or to pursue income, education or other desired goals

5. Certain types of communication become patterned with time, and thus represent culture and social structure, which provides stability to society

The decision to establish a department of sociology at the University of Chicago traces to President Harper's policy of appointing particular persons because he thought them outstanding, rather than because he had a definite idea about sociology (Diner, 1975). Had President Harper hired a different scholar (as indeed he tried to do) instead of Small, sociology at Chicago would have been subordinated in a department of political science. Thus, by accident, Chicago had the first sociology department in the United States.

The University of Chicago completely dominated early sociology. By 1909 (seventeen years after its founding), Chicago offered 100 of the 1,000 sociology courses then taught at 200 U.S. universities. From 1895 to 1915, Chicago awarded thirty-five of the first ninety-eight U.S. doctorates in sociology (Hinkel, 1980, p. 13), and, from 1915 to 1935, Chicago graduated sixty Ph.D.s. Eleven of them were among the first twenty-seven presidents of the American Sociological Society. By 1929, one-third of all students in sociology in the United States were at the University of Chicago. They got their Ph.D. degrees there, and then spread out to teach at other universities. They sent their star students back to Chicago to study for their doctorates. Many sociology departments in other U.S. universities thus became virtual "farm clubs" for Chicago.

Also, the leading books in sociology were written at Chicago: for example the influential textbook edited by Robert E. Park and Ernest Burgess, *Introduction to the Science of Sociology* (1924), and W. I. Thomas and Florian Znaniecki's *The Polish Peasant in Europe and America* (1927/1984), reporting the first empirical study in sociology, a classic volume that coined the concept of attitude.

GEORG SIMMEL AND CHICAGO SOCIOLOGY

Georg Simmel (1858–1918) was born in Berlin, studied at the University of Berlin, and taught at that university for most of his academic life. He was the consummate metropole, holding intimate salons in his home for the leading philosophers, artists and intellectuals of his day. Influenced by the evolutionary theory of Charles Darwin and Herbert Spencer, Simmel taught and wrote about social evolution, urban social life and the ecology of the city. The Chicago School served as a kind of empirical laboratory for his theoretical conceptualizations. Among Simmel's important books are *The Stranger,* which inspired Robert E. Park's concepts of social distance and the marginal man, and *The Web of Group-Affiliations* (Simmel, 1955), which led to network analysis. Simmel saw the central problem of sociology as the understanding of human socialization (Spykman, 1966, p. 40), a viewpoint carried forward by George Herbert Mead and John Dewey of the Chicago School, which they formulated into symbolic interactionism. Simmel directly influenced the Chicago School in a variety of ways. For example, Robert E. Park enrolled in courses from Simmel, including one in sociology at the University of Berlin, and later, when Park taught at Chicago, he was a conduit for Simmel's theoretical perspectives on human ecology, race relations and the study of social problems.

DEWEY, MEAD AND PARK

The flowering of social psychology and sociology at Chicago was the work of an amazingly few key scholars: John Dewey, George Herbert Mead, Robert E. Park and a distant colleague, Charles Horton Cooley at the University of Michigan (see Figure 2.1). What did these important American scholars have in common?

They were born around the time of the Civil War, and they all shared a small-town upbringing. They were Protestant and moralistic in background, but through their scientific training they sought to become objective observers of social life. They were ameliorative, interested in attacking social problems by understanding them more accurately. They were optimists, and felt that social progress was needed in order for American democracy to flourish in an urban setting beset with social problems.

They all had a University of Michigan/University of Chicago connection. John Dewey taught Cooley and Park at the University of Michigan. Cooley influenced Mead regarding his concept of the self. Dewey brought Mead with him from the Michigan faculty to Chicago. The four scholars were linked in an interpersonal network of intellectual influence and of intersecting careers.

They stressed the subjectivism of human communication,[3] that the receiver of a message interprets it in a way that is idiosyncratic to that individual (rather than exactly as the source had intended).

The early Chicago School was empirical, but not very quantitative, depending mainly on ethnographic methods. Park said that statistical methods were "parlor tricks," and it was not until the 1930s that Chicago sociology began to utilize statistical methods for the analysis of quantitative data.

John Dewey taught in the Department of Philosophy at Chicago from 1893 until 1904, when he left in anger for Columbia University. He was an exponent of pragmatism, the philosophy that interpretation of the meaning of beliefs should be made in terms of their practical effects, and of progressive education (based on his famous dictum: "Teach the whole child").

George Herbert Mead, also in the philosophy department, taught a course in advanced social psychology in which most sociology doctoral students enrolled. His book *Mind, Self and Society* (Mead, 1934) was compiled posthumously by one of Mead's students, Charles W. Morris, from his classroom notes taken during Mead's class in 1927 (Farr, 1983). Mead argued that an individual's personality was formed through communication with other people, as self-images develop by means of interaction with others.

Robert E. Park was at Chicago from 1913 to 1935, the "glory years." He was the scholar who best exemplified the Chicago School, and he can be considered the first student of mass communication.

The Chicago sociologists concentrated on the study of deviant subcultures, members of various down-and-out groups in Chicago: gangs (Thrasher, 1927/1963), hobos (Anderson, 1923/1961), slum residents (Zorbaugh, 1929), suicides (Shonle, 1926), ghetto residents (Wirth, 1926/1929) and "taxi-dancers" (Cressey, 1929/1972). The Chicago sociologists wanted to study a social problem up close, mainly by ethnographic methods such as observation and in-depth interviews, although they also gathered quantitative data of an aggregate nature, such as rates of prostitution or of juvenile delinquency in different parts of the city. A Chicago doctoral student typically chose a social problem for dissertation study, carried out the investigation, and then published a book about it with a lengthy introduction by Robert E. Park. The Chicago School was a dense network of scholars carrying out research in one city about its social problems. Optimism, positivism and reform marked the Chicago School. Now we take up each of the four main Chicago scholars in more detail.

JOHN DEWEY AND PRAGMATIC PHILOSOPHY

John Dewey (1859–1952) was "the most widely known and influential philosopher this country has ever produced" (Haworth, 1960). In his productive academic career, he published 36 books and 815 articles and papers, unfortunately written in a dull style (Eastman, 1941). "Dewey, in short, is the path not taken by American mass communication research" (Peters, 1989). Most modern communication scholars do not recognize John Dewey as one of their forefathers. His work lies too far over the horizon for them to recognize his influence, and indeed many of his ideas are only indirect ancestors of contemporary communication study. Communication, to Dewey, was the means for getting people to be full, participating members of society (Peters, 1989). Dewey made a famous remark that "Society not only continues to exist *by*

Figure 2.1
Intellectual Influences on, and from, the Chicago School

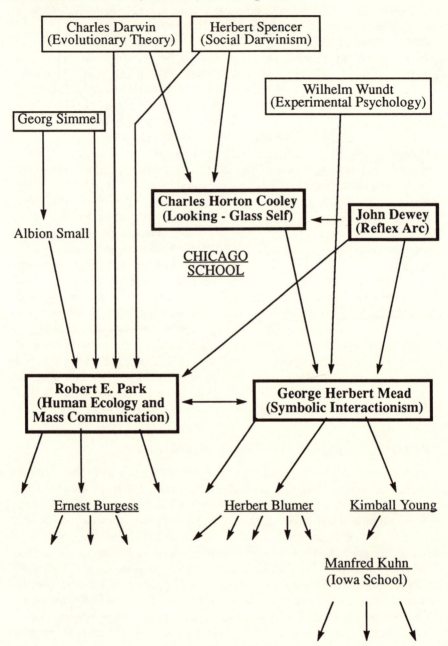

transmission, *by* communication, but it may be fairly said to exist *in* transmission, *in* communication.''

Dewey was involved in Jane Addams's Hull House at 800 South Halsted Street, located north of the University of Chicago in a crowded slum of European immigrants. Addams was a reform-minded young leader who organized Chicago intellectuals to help the underclass, often through meetings at Hull House that provided a facility for elites to come to the slums to live and observe the problems of the underdog. Hull House grew to cover an entire city block by the mid-1920s, when it had 70 residents who provided services to 9,000 women, men and children per week.

During his decade (1894–1904) at the University of Chicago, Dewey mainly contributed to the psychology of self. Dewey's famous article on ''The Reflex Arc Concept in Psychology'' (Dewey, 1896) drew on William Wundt's[4] idea of the gesture, and was later expanded by his Chicago colleague, George Herbert Mead. The main tradition of psychology when the Chicago School got underway was individual-centered, without much attention to an individual's social relationships. Stimulus-response (S-R) theories predominated. Dewey, Mead and other Chicago scholars questioned the oversimplification represented by the S-R model, claiming that an individual's interpretation of the stimulus was also involved in determining the response. So the S-R model became a stimulus-interpretation-response model, with meanings (derived via interaction with others) as an important component. Note the important shift here from intrapersonal psychology to communication relationships as explainers of behavior.

Dewey's 1926 lectures at Kenyon College expressed his concerns about American democracy. These lectures, published as Dewey's *The Public and Its Problems* (1927), argued that agricultural settlements in early America were the basis for community and for democracy. As the United States was transformed by the Industrial Revolution into an urbanized mass society, Dewey doubted that American democracy could survive unless certain elements of the rural community could be restored. Dewey stated: ''The Great Society created by steam and electricity may be a society, but it is no community'' (1927, p. 98). He thought that the restoration of a sense of community was possible, however. ''Till the Great Society is converted into a Great Community, the Public will remain in eclipse. Communication can alone create a great community'' (Dewey, 1927, p. 142). He hoped that the mass media (for example newspapers) could again connect people with each other in the metropolitan society, so that democracy could survive. Dewey's pondering about how American democracy could adapt to urban life was an issue carried on by his Chicago School colleagues George Herbert Mead and Robert E. Park.

GEORGE HERBERT MEAD
AND SYMBOLIC INTERACTIONISM

George Herbert Mead (1863–1931) was born in Hadley, a small town in Massachusetts, where his father was a Congregational minister. While a student at Oberlin College in Ohio, where he received his bachelor's degree, Mead began to question religious dogma, and to be troubled by self-doubts about his religiosity. Given that the field of philosophy and of Christian beliefs were closely tied in that era, Mead's religious questioning posed difficulties for his intended future as a philosophy professor. Mead studied for one year at Harvard University with William James, the noted pragmatist, whose children he tutored. Then he enrolled at the University of Leipzig with Wilhelm Wundt, specializing in the theory of the gesture. Mead believed that the act is the basic unit of social science, because of its symbolic significance. The act is social because it is interpreted by another individual. After teaching in Ann Arbor for several years, Mead moved from the University of Michigan to Chicago in 1894, where he taught for the next thirty-seven years, until his death in 1931.

An important concept for Mead was *role-taking,* the ability of the self-individual to act socially toward himself/herself, as toward others. Mead conceived of the mind as social, as developing through communication with others. His theory stated that individuals get to know themselves through interaction with others, who communicate to them who they are. Charles Horton Cooley, an early sociologist at the University of Michigan, had coined the term, "the looking-glass self," to denote an individual's self-conception as constructed by imagining how others reflect one's image to oneself. But Cooley did not offer an explanation of how the self was formed. That explanation was provided by Mead, who argued that one is not born with a self, nor does one develop instinctively. Instead, said Mead, the self is developed through a social process of interaction with others (Faris, 1970, p. 96). The individual internalizes the interpretations and meanings of various others, particularly early in life, to create a "generalized other," which is built up of the averaged expectations of many other individuals. The generalized other is those expectations of others with whom one interacts and who become a general guide to one's behavior. Gradually, an individual learns to act not just in relation to the expectations of a few specific people, but in terms of how other individuals in general would expect one to behave.[5] The essence of the self is reflexivity, the capacity to see oneself as an object of one's own reflection.

ROBERT E. PARK AND CHICAGO'S GOLDEN ERA

Park has been called "perhaps the single most influential person in American sociology" (Boskoff, 1969, p. 94). He launched the scholarly study of four important social science topics: mass communication, race relations, human ecology and collective behavior. Robert E. Park (1864–1944) came from a rural, Protestant background. He was born on a farm in Pennsylvania, but grew up in Red Wing, Minnesota, on the Mississippi River, where he was fascinated by the Scandinavian families who also lived in the town. Park attended the University of Michigan, where he was one of John Dewey's protégés. He enrolled in six philosophy courses offered by Dewey. "Park took from Dewey a life-long interest in the role of communication as a force for integrating society and in devices for communication, especially the newspaper and the telephone" (Matthews, 1977, p. 5). Park graduated from Michigan in 1884 and then worked as a newspaper reporter in Minneapolis, Detroit, Denver and New York. Park was an investigative reporter and a reformer. For example, when a diphtheria epidemic broke out, Park plotted the diphtheria cases on a city map, in order to identify the probable source of infection—an open sewer (Park, 1929, p. 5).

In 1892, Park learned that John Dewey, his former philosophy professor at Michigan, was starting a new publication called *Thought News*. Dewey's partner in this activity was a shadowy figure, Franklin Ford, who had edited a financial journal, *Bradstreet's,* in New York. Professor Dewey was utterly fascinated by Ford, a kind of snake-oil salesman. *Thought News* was intended to link the expertise of university scholars with newspaper audiences by providing useful information about long-term social trends. Dewey introduced Park to Franklin Ford, and Park joined their visionary publishing venture. The copy for the first issue of *Thought News* was written in April 1892, but was never published. Park's experience with *Thought News* changed the course of his life (Raushenbush, 1979, p. 18). From then on, Park was interested in the relationship of the press to public opinion, a topic that he was to pursue in his doctoral dissertation a decade later in Germany.

In 1898, Park quit newspaper work for graduate study: "I went back to the university and spent altogether seven years at it—at Ann Arbor, Harvard, and in Germany. I did this because I was interested in communication and collective behavior and wanted to know what the universities had to say about it" (Park, quoted in Raushenbush, 1979, p. 28). At the turn of the century, no university provided the scholarly study of communication. So Park, the former newspaperman, studied philosophy, which at that time included what we today call psychology and social psychology. In the fall of 1898, at age 34, Park and his growing family moved to Harvard, where he obtained an M.A. degree in philosophy. Harvard did not give him what he was looking for, so Park moved with his wife and children to Germany, where he registered at the Friedrich-Wilhelm's University of Berlin. In the spring of 1900, he took Georg Simmel's course in sociology, the only course on this topic in which Park would enroll, which gave Park the fundamental point of view for the study of the newspaper and society (Park, 1929, p. 8). After completing his Ph.D. degree, Park returned to the United States, to work as an assistant to Booker T. Washington at the Tuskegee Institute, in Alabama. As a white scholar at a black university, Park gained insight into the life of poor black people in the South.

At age 51, in 1913, Park began teaching at Chicago. The Chicago School was already a growing concern. The University of Chicago had given thirty Ph.D. degrees in sociology before Park arrived in 1913. Another seventy-seven doctorates were awarded by 1934, when Park retired to emeritus status (Faris, 1970, pp. 135–140). Park elevated the department into international prominence, forging a type of empirically based social science that the world had not previously known.

Social Disorganization

The Chicago research program on the city included historians, political scientists, economists, anthropologists and geographers, as well as sociologists. "Park was the natural, if never the official, leader of this very energetic movement" (Hughes, 1964). The Chicago School was, to a certain extent, a school of social sciences. The pragmatic and progressive nature of empirical research at Chicago infected anthropology, social psychology, philosophy and political science, as well as sociology. The research focus on the urban problems of the city of Chicago was encouraged by the Local Community Research Committee, and its successor, the Social Science Research Committee, funded mainly by the Laura Spelman Rockefeller Memorial between 1923 and 1932 (Park, 1939/1982).

Park's interest in urban life, sparked by Georg Simmel, concentrated on the disruptions and social disorganization of urban life, especially among new European immigrants, who faced extreme difficulties in adjusting to daily existence in the rapidly growing, crowded city of Chicago in the 1913–35 period. For example, Chicago was estimated to have 30,000 "hobos" (the word used in the 1920s for what are today called "homeless men"). Many of Chicago's hobos were concentrated in the Madison-Halsted Street area, in what was called "Hobohemia." Nels Anderson, a Chicago doctoral student who was personally acquainted with the hobo life-style, in 1921 began to conduct informal interviews with individuals in Hobohemia in order to collect their life histories. He played the role of a hobo, emerging daily from Hobohemia to attend his classes on the Midway campus. Park told Anderson: "Write down only what you see, hear, and know, like a newspaper reporter." Anderson's dissertation research was funded by a grant of $300 of Rockefeller money, administered by Park. He described the Chicago urban world of the hobos, who were viewed as outcasts by society. Park and his colleague Ernest Burgess approved Anderson's dissertation, Park edited it into book form, added a preface and six days later sent the manuscript off to the University of Chicago Press. *The Hobo* was the first volume in the Sociological Series of the university press. Many more were to follow—a total of eighty-four books on various social problems were published.

The Chicago sociologists found that each succeeding wave of European immigrants that poured into the city's slums experienced the same severe social disorganization. With time, as these populations prospered and migrated into higher-status residential areas, their rate of social disorganization declined (Faris, 1970, p. 57). Slums were a kind of informal school for urban living. However, European Jews, who had lived in urban ghettos for 500 years, did not experience an equivalent degree of social disorganization when they migrated to America (Wirth, 1926/1929). The Chicago slums were socially disorganized, but they were not unorganized. Such institutions as the family, school and church typically broke down in a slum, but other forms of organization, such as teenage gangs, flourished. The gangs attracted the children of foreign-born immigrants and often channeled these young people into more serious types of crime (Faris, 1970, p. 77).

Park elaborated the concept of *social distance,* the perceived lack of intimacy between two or more individuals or other categories.[6] Park derived this concept from Simmel's idea of the stranger, and one of Park's students, Emory Bogardus, developed a social distance scale.[7] Park also adopted his "marginal man" from Simmel's concept of the stranger. A *marginal person* is one who lives between two worlds, but does not belong to either. An example would be the child of an immigrant to America who rejected his parents' language and culture, but did not consider himself to be a full-fledged member of American society either. Robert E. Park and his Chicago students not only studied social distance and marginality, but Park insisted that his students become objective and detached observers of what they studied.[8]

Defining the Meaning of Sociology

The Chicago School, especially under Park's leadership, defined the meaning of sociology in two important ways. European sociology, prior to Chicago, had been theoretical and abstract in nature. Chicago sociology was grounded firmly in data. So after Chicago, sociology, and the social sciences more generally, were based in the empirical world.

The other redefinition of sociology at Chicago was to free it from a primarily normative concern, replacing this orientation with an emphasis on objectivity and a corresponding disdain for the applied field of social work. Many of the early figures in American sociology were Protestant ministers or their sons, motivated to solve social problems out of a social gospel concern. Sociology had been defined as "do-goodism," a viewpoint established by Albion Small at Chicago. Park redefined this conception of the field. He told the doctoral students in his classes, often in profane terms, that they could study any social problem, but they should do so independently of their own moral values. For example, a Chicago sociologist might conduct an investigation of prostitution, but the scholar's abhorrence of this profession should not affect how the research was conducted, the findings obtained, or how they were interpreted. And from time to time, Park would growl his standard reproof at a Chicago doctoral student: "You're another one of those damn do-gooders" (quoted in Raushenbush, 1979, p. 96).

Park separated sociologists from social workers. In 1920, a School of Social Service Administration was created at the University of Chicago to train social workers. A general pattern was set at Chicago, which was to be followed elsewhere in the United States: Social work was defined as a woman's field, whereas sociology was mainly for male scholars. Social amelioration was the province of social work, leaving sociology free from concern with direct solutions to social problems. Intellectual hostility marred the relationship between sociology and social work at Chicago, and elsewhere (Diner, 1975). The applied and interventionist nature of sociology during the early years at Chicago ended in 1920, with American sociologists becoming increasingly uncomfortable with the reform of social problems.

The founding fathers of American sociology at the Chicago School were indeed *fathers,* not mothers. Men dominated the new discipline. At Chicago, only 13 (12 percent) of the 112 Ph.D. degrees in sociology granted through 1935 were awarded to women (these data are based on a listing of Chicago Ph.D.s in sociology provided by Faris, 1970, pp. 135–140). These female sociologists tended to teach in women's colleges or in schools of social work.

Thus, under Robert E. Park, the Chicago School, grounded as it was in the European theories of Darwinian evolution and Simmel's interactionism, defined the new field of sociology as: (1) empirical, (2) value-free and detached from its social applications and (3) a male activity.

Park's Communication Research

Park felt that his prior work as an investigative newspaper reporter was good preparation for his career in sociology. "Sociology, after all, is concerned with problems in regard to which newspaper men inevitably get a good deal of firsthand knowledge. . . . One might say that a sociologist is merely a more accurate, responsible, and scientific reporter" (Park, 1939/1982). Park's newspaper experience greatly aided his later sociological investigations of social problems in the city. He has been called the "first theorist of mass communication" (Frazier and Gaziano, 1979).

Robert E. Park's (1925) study of the immigrant press came about as the result of national concern with the possible disloyalty of European immigrants in the United States, generated by America's 1917 entry into World War I. Would the millions of German Americans be loyal to the United States or to Kaiser Wilhelm? Would they spread propaganda and engage in sabotage? On the other hand, how could the civil rights of immigrants loyal to the United States be preserved? The Carnegie Corporation sponsored ten studies of immigrants, with Park directing a study of the foreign-language press. He found that such newspapers (in Yiddish, Polish, German, etc.) mainly helped the recent immigrant learn how to survive and adjust in North America. Little newspaper content encouraged loyalty to the foreign homeland. The foreign-language newspapers in America were gradually working themselves out of their role by aiding the assimilation of their immigrant audience into American culture.[9]

THE PAYNE FUND STUDIES OF THE EFFECTS OF FILM

When a new mass media technology diffuses in America, it often is accepted first by children and teenagers. *The heavy use of a new communication technology by youth typically sets off adult concern, which leads to scholarly research on the effects of the new technology, and, occasionally, to actions by policy makers.* The main interest of parents and policy makers concerns the effects, particularly the potential negative effects, of the new communication technology (Wartella and Reeves, 1985). The Payne Fund studies were a prototype for this pattern of using children as litmus paper for a medium's effects.

When film began to attract large audiences in the United States in the late 1920s, a coordinated program of thirteen investigations of the effects of movies on American children was financed by a foundation called the Payne Fund. The purpose was to determine the possibly harmful effects of film viewing on children and youth. Most of the scholars conducting the Payne Fund research were faculty at the University of Chicago, with several at Ohio State University and a few at other universities. The Payne Fund studies were organized by W. W. Charters, director of the bureau of educational research at Ohio State University. He asked Robert E. Park to participate, but Park was about to leave on a trip to China. So Park got his Chicago colleague Herbert Blumer involved.[10] In all, the Payne Fund studies represent one of the largest scientific programs ever conducted on media effects. Tens of thousands of children and youth served as respondents during the 1929–32 study period.

The Payne Fund research showed that U.S. children went to the movies about once a week, and that 72 percent of feature films dealt with the themes of crime, sex and love. The movies frequently showed the use of tobacco and liquor (this during Prohibition). Understandably, parents were concerned about the effects of these films on their children. In one Payne Fund study, for example, a sample of children were asked whether they had bad dreams after viewing a violent film. Many responded that they did. *The 1929 Payne Fund studies probably were the first communication research on media effects.*

CHICAGO'S DECLINE

The influence of the Chicago School fell off rapidly about the time that Robert E. Park retired. Why? Chicago created its own competition when its Ph.D. graduates left to teach at other universities. Many other good schools of sociology, such as Columbia University, caught up with Chicago. American sociology moved away from a focus on crime, prostitution, poverty and other aspects of social disorganization. Chicago eventually shifted from its stress on qualitative ethnological methods to a quantitative and statistical approach. But the shift occurred only after several years of conflict. Chicago began to look somewhat old-fashioned to the rest of American sociology. While Chicago sociology was interpretive and broadly humanistic, after the 1930s American sociology became highly quantitative and statistical, a turn away from the Chicago School's approach. Sociological research became more abstract and concerned with the generalizability of the research findings. The situated community studies of Chicago sociology were replaced by variable analysis of sociological concepts.

THE CHICAGO SCHOOL
AND COMMUNICATION RESEARCH

The conventional viewpoint of the history of communication research is that it emerged in the 1920s, 1930s and 1940s as social scientists from several disciplines began to conduct empirical research on propaganda[11] (Lasswell, 1927/1938/1971), and on radio's effects on its audiences (Lazarsfeld and Stanton, 1942). Earlier mass communication research dealt with the larger issue of the role of the mass media in a healthy democracy. These roots of mass communication research go back to scholars of the Chicago School, as well as to Walter Lippmann, the influential news analyst who wrote the important book, *Public Opinion* (1922/1965). Both the Chicago scholars and Lippmann considered communication to be the essence of human relationships. "There is more than a verbal tie between the word common, community and communication" (Park and Burgess, 1924/1969, p. 36). *To the Chicago School, communication was much more than just the exchange of information; communication created and maintained society* (Belman, 1975, pp. 170–175).

The Chicago School provided a more unified theory of communication's place in society than did the so-called four founders of communication study, who became prominent after Chicago declined in the late 1930s. The Chicago School's perspective is rarely cited by communication scholars today. Peters (1986) suggests that Lasswell, Lewin, Lazarsfeld and Hovland were elevated to founder status because they succeeded in the new form of methodologically sophisticated, quantitative, funded research. These four "founders" narrowed the focus of communication study to an individualistic, short-term paradigm that explained mass media effects. In contrast, the Chicago School dealt with the broader issue of the role of community and mass communication in a democratic urban society.

Robert E. Park conducted the first mass communication research on newspaper content, audiences and ownership structure. In his 1922 book, *The Immigrant Press and Its Control*, Park raised research questions that are highly relevant today (Rogers, 1986, p. 79):

1. How does media content influence public opinion? (This is the agenda-setting process.)

2. How are the mass media influenced by public opinion?

3. Can the mass media bring about social change?

4. How are individuals linked to the mass media through interpersonal networks?

"Communication was a fundamental human process to the Chicago sociologists, although other than Robert E. Park they did not point the specific directions that future communication research was to take. Perhaps this is one reason why the relationship of the Chicago School of Sociology to the modern discipline of communication science has been so little appreciated, and most often ignored by other observers tracing the history of communication research" (Rogers, 1986, p. 79). Perhaps in the future, communication scholars will accord more attention to the Chicago School, and to the important history of our field that occurred *before* the era of Lasswell, Lazarsfeld, Lewin and Hovland, a time in which the social scientific roots of communication study were getting established at Chicago. One useful lesson from the Chicago School is to study the intercultural communication behavior of urban minority populations. Less than half of the population in America's largest cities (New York, Los Angeles, Detroit, Atlanta and San Francisco) is white. How can communication study continue to ignore the racial diversity of urban communication?

The experience of the Chicago School also guides us to the interpretive approach to communication study, which emphasizes the subjective meanings that an individual gains from a communication message. The interpretation of a message is usually studied by relatively less structured, more qualitative research methods, but an interpretive perspective and qualitative methods are not exactly identical. Interpretive research tends to be inductive, moving from the empirical level to the theoretical level. Theory defines the directions of research, but is usually not used to derive specific hypotheses for testing.

Ethnomethodology consists of data-gathering methods that allow respondents to provide data in ways that are structured by the respondent, rather than by the investigator. Such ethnographic data ideally reflect the respondents' point of view, and capture the respondents' constructions of reality. The interpretive approach has certain weaknesses, such as the difficulty of managing and summarizing the large amounts of qualitative data in the form of field notes and transcripts that usually are obtained by an interpretive scholar. The richness of interpretive data causes data-reduction problems for interpretive scholars.

During the past decade or so, mass communication researchers have studied how individuals "read" media messages. Investigations of television viewers, for example, show that the individual is an active interpreter of the message content, not just a passive recipient. Often both quantitative and qualitative data-gathering methods are utilized by the investigator in order to understand how individuals interpret the media messages. These television viewing studies go a step beyond the Lazarsfeld type of media effects research in that the newer studies ask how television characters are interpreted by the viewer, and thus how effects are mediated. For example, consider older female viewers of the U.S. television series "Dynasty." If they perceive the heroine, Alexis Carrington Colby, as a successful, powerful older woman, they may gain increased self-esteem. But if older female viewers perceive Alexis as an unattainable ideal, they may feel more depressed and helpless. Here we see how an audience member's perceptions and interpretations of media messages mediate their effects.

In a strange way, and one that contemporary interpretive scholars do not recognize, they have returned to the research perspectives used by the Chicago School seventy years ago.

NOTES

1. Actually, since its founding, the University of Chicago has never been very Baptist.

2. Simmel was the dominant European influence on the Chicago School. Small had been a fellow student with Simmel at the University of Berlin in 1880, and they maintained a friendship via correspondence and personal visits (Christakes, 1978).

3. The Chicago School stressed the importance of individuals' perceptions as explanations of behavior. W. I. Thomas (1927/1984, p. 9) proclaimed: "If men perceive a situation as real, it is real to them in all of its consequences."

4. Wundt founded experimental psychology at the University of Leipzig around 1880.

5. Thus Mead's generalized other solved the problem created by Cooley's theory of the looking-glass self, which implied that an individual would have as many selves as there are people with whom the individual interacts. Mead said that we generalize the many others.

6. Park utilized the concept of social distance in his analyses of race relations. He argued that the greater the social distance between two individuals, the less they influence each other reciprocally (Coser, 1977, p. 360).

7. The Bogardus scale indexed, for instance, whether a white Caucasian perceived himself as closer to an individual of Chinese descent than to a black American (Bogardus, 1926, 1933).

8. Although Park emphasized that a scholar should gain the subjective point of view of a respondent, by empathically and imaginatively participating in the life of the respondent, in order to gain a real understanding of social actions, Park often quoted William James's "On a Certain Blindness in Human Beings," which argued that each of us is likely to misunderstand the meaning in other people's lives (Park, 1950/1974, p. 21).

9. More recently, in the 1980s and 1990s, foreign-language media in the United States have again become important, especially Spanish-language television, because of the large numbers of immigrants from Latin America.

10. Park later carried out a similar study of film effects on Chinese children in Hong Kong.

11. Propaganda analysis helped get research on mass communication off the ground in the 1920s and 1930s, but then was largely forgotten (Sproule, 1987), or else lost its

identity in the plethora of media effects studies that came to dominate the field of mass communication.

REFERENCES

Anderson, N. (1923/1961). *The hobo: The sociology of the homeless man.* Chicago: University of Chicago Press; New York: Phoenix Books.

Belman, S. L. (1975). *The idea of communication in the social thought of the Chicago School.* Ph.D. Thesis. Urbana: University of Illinois at Urbana-Champaign.

Ben-David, J., & Collins, R. (1966). Social factors in the origins of a new science: The case of psychology. *American Sociological Review, 31*(4), 451–465.

Berelson, B. (1959). The state of communication research. *Public Opinion Quarterly, 23*, 1–5.

Bogardus, E. S. (1926). Mutations of social distance. *Journal of Applied Sociology, 11*, 77–84.

Bogardus, E. S. (1933). A social distance scale. *Sociology and Social Research, 17*, 265–271.

Boskoff, A. (1969). *Theory in American sociology: Major sources and applications.* New York: Thomas Crowell.

Bulmer, M. (1984). *The Chicago School of sociology: Institutionalization, diversity and the rise of sociological research.* Chicago: University of Chicago Press.

Christakes, G. (1978). *Albion W. Small.* Boston: Twayne.

Coser, L. A. (1977). *Masters of sociological thought: Ideas in historical and social context* (2nd ed.). New York: Harcourt Brace Jovanovich.

Cressey, P. (1929/1972). *The taxi-dance hall: A sociological study in commercialized recreation and city life.* Chicago: University of Chicago Press.

Dewey, J. (1896). The reflex arc concept in psychology. *Psychological Review, 3*, 357–370.

Dewey, J. (1927). *The public and its problems.* Chicago: Swallow Press.

Diner, S. J. (1975). Department and discipline: The department of sociology at the University of Chicago, 1892–1920. *Minerva, 12*(4), 514–533.

Eastman, M. (1941, December). John Dewey. *Atlantic Monthly, 168*, 671–685.

Faris, R.E.L. (1970). *Chicago sociology, 1920–1932.* Chicago: University of Chicago Press.

Farr, R. M. (1983). Wilhelm Wundt (1832–1920) and the origins of psychology as an experimental social science. *British Journal of Social Psychology, 22*, 289–301.

Frazier, P. J., & Gaziano, C. (1979). *Robert Ezra Park's theory of news, public opinion, and social control. Journalism Monographs*, no. 64.

Goodspeed, T. W. (1916/1972). *A history of the University of Chicago: The first quarter century.* Chicago: University of Chicago Press.

Haworth, L. (1960). The experimental society: Dewey and Jordan. *Ethics, 71*, 27–40.

Hinkel, R. C. (1980). *Founding theory of American sociology, 1881–1915.* Boston: Routledge & Kegan.

Hughes, E. C. (1964). Robert E. Park. *The Sociological Eye, 2*, 543–549.

Lasswell, H. (1927/1938/1971). *Propaganda technique in the World War.* New York: Knopf; New York: Peter Smith; Cambridge, MA: MIT Press.

Lazarsfeld, P. F., & Stanton, F. N. (Eds.). (1942). *Radio Research, 1941*. New York: Duell, Sloan & Pearce.

Lippmann, W. (1922/1965). *Public Opinion*. New York: Harcourt, Brace; New York: The Free Press.

Matthews, F. H. (1977). *Quest for an American sociology: Robert E. Park and the Chicago school*. Montreal: McGill-Queen's University Press.

Mead, G. H. (1934). *Mind, self and society*. Chicago: University of Chicago Press.

Park, R. E. (1925). The immigrant community and immigrant press. *American Review*, 143–152.

Park, R. E. (1929). Life history. Unpublished paper, University of Chicago Library, Department of Special Collections, Ernest W. Burgess Papers, Box 1F, Folder 1.

Park, R. E. (1939/1982). Notes on the origins of the Society for Social Research. *Journal of the History of the Behavioral Sciences, 18*(4), 337–338. Originally published in *Bulletin of the Society for Social Research, 1*, 1–5.

Park, R. E. (1950/1974). *Race and culture*. New York: The Free Press. Later published in E. C. Hughes, C. S. Johnson, J. Masuoke, & L. Wirth (Eds.), *The collected papers of Robert Ezra Park, Volume 1* (pp. 11–149). New York: Arno Press.

Park, R. E., & Burgess, E. W. (1924/1969). *Introduction to the science of sociology*. Chicago: University of Chicago Press.

Peel, J.D.Y. (1971). *Herbert Spencer: The evolution of a sociologist*. New York: Basic Books.

Peters, J. D. (1986). Institutional sources of intellectual poverty in communication research. *Communication Research, 13*(4), 527–559.

Peters, J. D. (1989). Democracy and American communication theory: Dewey, Lippmann, Lazarsfeld. *Communication, 11*, 199–220.

Raushenbush, W. (1979). *Robert E. Park: Biography of a sociologist*. Durham, NC: Duke University Press.

Rogers, E. M. (1986). *Communication technology: The new media in society*. New York: The Free Press.

Rogers, E. M. (1993). *A century of communication study*. New York: The Free Press.

Rogers. E M., & Chaffee, S. H. (1992). Communication and journalism from Daddy Bleyer to Wilbur Schramm: A palimpsest. Paper presented to the Association for Education in Journalism and Mass Communication, Montreal.

Schramm, W. (1959). Comments on Berelson. *Public Opinion Quarterly, 23*(1), 6–9.

Schramm, W. (1980). The beginnings of communication research in the United States. In D. Nimmo (Ed.), *Communication yearbook 4* (pp. 73–82). New Brunswick, NJ: Transaction Books.

Schramm, W. (1981, April 14). There were giants in the earth in these days. Les Moeller Lecture, School of Journalism and Mass Communication, University of Iowa, Iowa City.

Schramm, W. (1985). The beginnings of communication study in the United States. In E. M. Rogers & F. Balle (Eds.), *The media revolution in America and Western Europe* (pp. 200–211). Norwood, NJ: Ablex.

Shannon, C. E. (1949). The mathematical theory of communication. In C. E. Shannon & W. Weaver (Eds.), *The mathematical theory of communication* (pp. 29–125). Urbana: University of Illinois Press.

Shonle, E. (1926). *Suicide: A study of personal disorganization*. Ph.D. Thesis. Chicago: University of Chicago.

Simmel, G. (1955). *The web of group-affiliations*. Translated by K. F. Wolf & R. Bendix. New York: The Free Press.

Sproule, J. M. (1987). Propaganda studies in American social science: The rise and fall of the critical paradigm. *Quarterly Journal of Speech, 73,* 60–78.

Spykman, N. J. (1966). *The social theory of Georg Simmel*. New York: Atherton Press.

Thomas, W. I., & Znaniecki, F. (1927/1984). *The Polish peasant in Europe and America*. New York: Knopf; Urbana: University of Illinois Press.

Thrasher, F. M. (1927/1963). *The gang: A study of 1,313 gangs in Chicago*. Chicago: University of Chicago Press.

Wartella, E., & Reeves, B. (1985). Historical trends in research on children and the media; 1900–1960. *Journal of Communication, 35,* 118–133.

Weber, M. (1926). *Max Weber: Ein Lebensbild*. Tubinger, Germany: J.C.B. Mohr.

Wirth, L. (1926/1929). *The ghetto: A study in isolation*. Ph.D. Thesis. Chicago: University of Chicago. Later published as *The ghetto*. Chicago: University of Chicago Press.

Zorbaugh, H. W. (1929). *The Gold Coast and the slum: A sociological study of Chicago's Near North Side*. Chicago: University of Chicago Press.

3

Urban Communication: The City, Media and Communications Policy

Garth S. Jowett

> It is in the city that man developed philosophy and science, and became not merely a rational but a sophisticated animal. This means, for one thing, that it is in the urban environment—in a world which man himself has made—that mankind first achieved an intellectual life and acquired those characteristics which most distinguish him from the lower animals and from primitive man.
>
> —Park, 1929, p. 1

> The City is the nerve center of our civilization. It is also the storm center.
> —Strong, 1968, p. 127

In this chapter I want to examine the relationship between the history of the city and the emergence of urban communication systems. Specifically, in the first part I examine the nature of urbanization in the United States and the role technological communication networks played as an integral part of this historical process. In the second part I want to make a case for the revitalization of the subfield of urban communication studies both as a significant, but neglected area of intellectual inquiry, and also more importantly to provide salient information on the current nature and state of urban communication that will be of direct application to policy makers coping with one of the most serious problems in modern American society.

The Reverend Josiah Strong's views of the American city, stated so forcefully in his book *Our Country: Its Possible Future and Present Crisis* (1885), have a powerful resonance for a large section of the public in our own times. While Strong's concern for the increasing influence of the city on American life was motivated by his fear of the increasing importance of Roman Catholicism, which flourished in the burgeoning urban areas in the late nineteenth century, he also saw the city as a place where all human evils were concentrated:

Socialism not only centers in the city, but is almost confined to it; and the materials of its growth are multiplied with the growth of the city. Here is heaped the social dynamite; here roughs, gamblers, thieves, robbers, lawless and desperate men of all sorts, congregate; men who are ready on any pretext to raise riots for the purpose of destruction and plunder; here gather foreigners and wage-earners; here skepticism and irreligion abound; here inequality is the greatest and most obvious, and the contrast between opulence and penury the most striking; here the suffering the sorest. As the greatest wickedness in the world is to be found not among the cannibals of some far off coast, but in Christian lands where the light of truth is diffused and rejected, so the utmost depth of wretchedness exists not among savages, who have few wants, but in great cities, where, in the presence of plenty and of every luxury men starve. . . . Under such conditions smolder the volcanic fires of a deep discontent. (Strong, 1968, p. 128)

These were not unique sentiments, although in all fairness it must be pointed out that the great American cities of the late nineteenth century also had many admirers, who saw in their flamboyant boosterism and chaotic energy the symbol of the distinct social and cultural break between the Old World and the New.

The progressive urban reformer Frederic C. Howe (1968), as an example, saw the city as "the hope of democracy," and wrote in 1914: "The city is the hope of the future. Here life is full and eager. Here the industrial issues, that are fast becoming dominant in political life, will first be worked out. In the city, democracy is organizing. It is becoming conscious of its powers. And as time goes on, these powers will be exercised to an increasing extent for the amelioration of those conditions that modern industrial life has created" (p. 240).

These two contrasting positions are not unreconcilable, for the city can assume a myriad of shapes and guises, and the urban milieu has always been all things to all people. For more than 6,000 years of recorded history humankind has argued over what is the most natural and humane state of human social interaction. Is it the singular, simple, independent life-style of our nomadic ancestors, still practiced by many tribal cultures in our own world; or will the interdependent, complex urbanized life that an increasing percentage of the world's population continues to choose for itself allow humans to fulfill their true destiny? The choice is fast becoming moot, for it is currently estimated that by the year 2000 more than 80 percent of the world's population will live in what can be defined as urban areas of 20,000 or more residents (Huth, 1978, p. 12).

THE CITY AND THE DEVELOPMENT
OF COMMUNICATION SYSTEMS

The rise of the city from the first primitive permanent settlements of nomadic hunters of the Neolithic period almost 10,000 years ago to the modern megalopolis such as São Paulo, Mexico City or Tokyo, where the population can exceed 15 million, has been the source of fascination and historical speculation. Why did our ancestors decide to forego their tents and build permanent housing and domesticate their animals? What was the attraction in giving up nomadic independence for the interdependent and specialized urban life-style? What exactly is the function of cities? How has urbanization changed the nature of human interaction? These and other questions about the advantages and disadvantages of urbanism have received a great deal of attention from anthropologists and historians for many decades.

Cities have always intensified the pace of life. There is no doubt that cities are places where a wide variety of resources are produced, exchanged and controlled. Lewis Mumford (1961), in his great idiosyncratic study of urban history, pointed out that "the rise of the city, so far from wiping out earlier elements in the culture, actually brought them together and increased their efficacy and scope. . . . What happened . . . with the rise of cities, was that many functions that had been heretofore scattered and unorganized were brought together within a limited area, and the components of the community were kept in a state of dynamic tension and interaction" (p. 31). The agglomeration of these diverse economic, social and cultural elements into the earliest urban systems created a synergy that fundamentally transformed the nature of human interaction. Nowhere is the product of this synergy more obvious than in the variety of communication media and interactive systems that have evolved to meet the needs of an increasingly complex urban environment. As Richard Meier (1962) noted: "Cities were evolved primarily for the facilitation of human communication" (p. 13).

In every culture, East and West, the rise of cities resulted in a concomitant development of new communication media, precipitated by the increasing need to provide a constant flow of information to meet the requirements of the urbanized population and the new systems of commerce that resulted from the increased urban interaction. While the flow of information within the urban area may have been subjected to a variety of political controls, a constant stream of official information was necessary to maintain internal coherence. Governments had to make laws and decrees known, proclamations had to be disseminated and commercial information was the lifeblood of an entrepreneurial society.

The development of the major forms of communication can be directly attributed to the needs of the cities. The first systematic alphabetic writing forms originated in Sumer in the fourth millennium B.C. in response to the needs of the public economy and administration (Gelb, 1963, pp. 61–71). Such writing systems were more flexible than the pictographic or hieroglyphic forms favored by the priestly class, and were easily learned and transportable. Such communication systems, according to Harold Innis (1951), favored expansion of trade and military conquest.

By the Middle Ages, the cities of medieval Europe served as moral centers dominated by the political power of rulers and the culture of the Roman Catholic church. They also were major foci for trade and the development of proto-manufacturing centers, where workers could achieve an economy of scale which exceeded that of workers scattered throughout the outlying countryside. It was in the intellectual and economic conditions fostered in these medieval cities that the printing press was developed by combining indigenous and imported technologies to meet the urgent demand for all types of written records and the increasing need for the widespread dissemination of information (Eisenstein, 1979; Febvre and Martin, 1976).

The great seaports and trading centers, such as Venice, London and Antwerp, were the sites where the first commercial newsletters, the forerunners of the modern newspaper, flourished. The unprecedented growth of cities in the eighteenth and nineteenth centuries, fueled by the engines of international commerce and extensive industrialization, created a need for specialized communication systems such as the optical telegraph developed by the French engineer Claude Chappé, which by 1844 stretched between 29 French cities through 500 stations covering more than 3,000 miles (Fabre, 1963, p. 74). The electric telegraph, and especially the telephone, were also inventions that owed their genesis to the urban environment. The introduction of these two communication technologies forever altered the temporal-spatial dimensions between distant urban centers as well as contributing to reducing the feelings of isolation that permeated the rural areas (Pred, 1973, 1980; Thompson, 1947; Fischer, 1992; Rakow, 1992).

By the twentieth century, newspapers and magazines, motion pictures, radio and then television had all been spawned and nurtured in urban centers, spreading out to bring urban culture to the far-flung countryside. The rapid expansion of urbanization and urban culture into what had been relatively isolated rural society was one of the dominant concerns of social theorists at the turn of the century (Bramson, 1961; Brantlinger, 1983; Giner, 1976). This concern was manifested in the emerging "mass society" theory, which Daniel Bell in 1960 suggested was, with the exception of Marxism, "probably the most influential theory in the western world today" (p. 21).

THE TELEGRAPH AND THE TELEPHONE:
INTERCONNECTING THE NATION

The nexus of transportation and communication has always been integral to the economic and cultural development of the United States. The only way this continental nation could be held together was, in James Carey's phrase, to use "the word and the wheel" (1989, p. 5). Thus, through massive engineering projects to build roads and bridges, combined with a great deal of emphasis on the power of a free press, literacy and education, it was hoped to bind the nation together in both a social and cultural unity. While the earliest forms of communication—the first colonial newspapers and the postal system—were modestly successful in this binding role (Brown, 1989), by the middle of the nineteenth century new forms emerged that had even greater potential for encouraging both cultural unity and cultural standardization.

The introduction of the telegraph in 1844 forever separated the concept of "communication" from that of "transportation." No longer did messages have to be physically transported from one location to another. This separation also allowed the concept of "communications" to be associated with a wider range of specific activities related to the interchange of information as well as the provision of entertainment. It was in this sense that the various media of communication emerged as new economic forces in their own right. As James Carey (1989) has noted: "the telegraph was a new and distinctively different force of production that demanded a new body of law, economic theory, political arrangements, management techniques, organizational structures, and scientific rationales with which to justify and make effective the development of a privately owned and controlled monopolistic corporation" (p. 205).

Soon after its introduction the telegraph began to have a major influence on the structure of American commerce, the gathering and dissemination of news, while also significantly altering the very shape of urban environments. The advent of the telegraph precipitated the process of decentralizing the manufacturing and administrative sectors of American businesses, a practice that was later greatly accelerated by the telephone. Companies could now consider widening the scale of the distribution of their goods and services as control of a national sales force was now feasible. Telecommunications also facilitated the centralized location of American businesses in urban downtowns, where they could be in close proximity to their suppliers and customers. As Pred (1973, 1980) has shown, the economic dominance of cities was even further enhanced by the introduction of the telegraph. The telegraph was also the first of the urban-based communication systems to generate an entire discourse on what changes the introduction of such systems of information dissemination would create in the social and cultural life of the nation (Czitrom, 1982, pp. 3–29).

The telephone continued the process begun by the telegraph of increasing the centrality of the urban areas. In fact, the telephone precipitated two somewhat contradictory changes in the structure of cities. On the one hand, telephones allowed the decentralization of manufacturing facilities from corporate headquarters and encouraged the development of suburbia and exurbia; but on the other hand, it also allowed the congregation of businesses into central downtown locations. The telephone also altered the shape of the urban skyline, because without telephonic communications large-scale office buildings above six stories were not really viable. The number of stairwells and elevators needed to accommodate the hand-carried message traffic would simply have taken too much valuable space.

The telephone, more than any other form of communication, provided an internal coherence to the disparate components that fell under the control of urban administrative units. It brought together the various interdependent agencies such as the schools, the fire and police departments, emergency services and health agencies into a cohesive and manageable form of city government. With the completion of a transcontinental telephone service in 1914, the spatio-temporal dimensions of the nation had been fundamentally reformulated. Perhaps the most significant social contribution of the telephone was its role in diminishing the problem of rural isolation (Fischer, 1992; Rakow, 1992). While other factors such as streetcars, improved roads and automobiles have also contributed to the increased efficiency and ease of modern communication, the telephone was the most ubiquitous and central of all modern communication systems.

Colin Cherry, one of the great pioneers in the development of communication theory and history, noted that the development of the telephone exchange was possibly more important than that of the telephone itself. He pointed out (Cherry, 1977, p. 114): "It was the exchange principle that led to the growth of endless new social organizations, because it offered *choice* of social contacts, on demand, even between strangers, without ceremony, introduction, or credentials, in ways totally new in history." Alexander Graham Bell's vision of a vast interconnected system linking individuals and services is in the process of being realized in our modern world, but, except for the telephone and cable television, the vast world of telecommunications is still relatively invisible to the general public.

MEDIA POWER AND SOCIAL CONTROL: A BRIEF HISTORY

Starting in the midnineteenth and through the first half of the twentieth century the introduction of national magazines, motion pictures, radio and then television all contributed to diminishing the differences between urban and rural culture in the United States. It was in the urban centers on the eastern seaboard that the first national communication systems were developed. The physical format and editorial style of the New York penny press of the 1830s had gradually spread to other urban centers across the country. The development of national magazines in the period just before the Civil War, and their revitalization after 1867, can be considered the first national popular media helping to shape a national agenda for social and political issues and contributing to the standardizing of cultural practices (Tebbel, 1969).

In their seminal study of the community *Middletown* (Muncie, Indiana) conducted in 1925, the sociologist Robert S. Lynd and the social psychologist

Helen Merrell Lynd emphasized the importance of the new forms of communication in helping to end social and cultural isolation in the United States. They noted the increasing ubiquity of a nationwide media-created culture, and commented that "indeed, at no point is one brought up more sharply against the impossibility of studying Middletown as a self-contained, self-starting community than when one watches these space-binding leisure-time inventions imported from without—automobile, motion picture, and radio—reshaping the city" (Lynd and Lynd, 1929, p. 271).

It was, however, the motion picture, more than any other previous form of popular communication, that established a national consciousness and emphasized the increasing cultural power of the cities (Jowett, 1976; May, 1980; Sklar, 1975). It was also the motion picture that emphasized the difficulties that individual communities would now experience in trying to cope with the introduction of a wide range of ideas and values from outside of their previously closed cultural systems. While printed material was relatively easy to control, the ubiquity of the movie house in even the smallest communities and its unprecedented attraction, especially to young children, proved to be an enormous challenge to those whom Henry May (1959, p. 30) has called the "custodians of culture." With the unexpected social and cultural impact of the motion picture—later reinforced by the introduction of radio in the 1920s and then television in the 1950s—cities, towns and suburbs were made aware that they could no longer deal adequately with the national media solely within the confines of a locally constituted political unit. As Seymour Mandelbaum has noted (1986): "Control of the national media required complex alliances outside the boundaries of the local polity" (p. 138).

The impotence of local communities in the face of these new national media led concerned citizens to turn to larger political units such as state and national authorities for solutions to the problems of media control. Thus in 1915 the Supreme Court in *Mutual* v. *Ohio* denied motion pictures the protection of the First Amendment, and for the next thirty-seven years the motion picture became the only communications medium in the history of the United States to be subjected to systematic legalized prior censorship (Jowett, 1989). Similarly, the United States government established the Federal Radio Commission in 1927 (which became the Federal Communications Commission in 1934), ostensibly to control legally the technological aspects of broadcasting, but the inference was strong that such control extended to content as well.

Meanwhile the motion picture industry, much like baseball had done in the wake of the 1919 World Series scandal, created a national trade association in 1921 to establish and enforce a series of self-regulatory mechanisms to prevent further inroads of federal control, particularly the creation of a federal motion picture censorship bureau. The radio and television industries each followed suit with their own codes of conduct. While self-regulation rather than official government censorship was considered the "American way" to respond to pressure from local communities, in the long run these industry-driven mechanisms have failed to satisfy these concerns, and the issue is as alive in 1992 as it was seventy years ago (Jowett, 1990; Montgomery, 1989).

The rise to prominence of the mass media in the twentieth century was, and is, a unique historical event, which facilitated the creation of specific types of social interaction ("media audiences") on a scale of magnitude never experienced before. The true historical significance of this development has seldom been systematically evaluated, and is, as yet, little understood and even less appreciated. The capability to reach large, heterogeneous audiences relatively instantaneously has engendered a uniquely modern form of public culture, created by and disseminated through the various mass media organizations. This modern "mass culture" transcends individual urban systems, linking both urban and rural inhabitants to form a national media culture, which exists as a separate layer atop the layers of traditional regional variations in cultural practices. This multilayered sandwich of cultural practices is a distinct feature of modern mediated societies, where the politics and geography that previously delineated social and cultural boundaries have been overpassed by the electronic media.

Modern cities are information-intensive social entities and serve as major command centers for the collection and dissemination of information. In many ways these activities define the essential nature of the city today, where a large part of commercial activities is concerned with what can be called "information processing" (Strover, 1987, p. 2). Beninger (1986) in his detailed study has traced the development of various control mechanisms in response to shifts in industrial and bureaucratic procedures from the early nineteenth century to today. He notes that because of the increasing complexity of the postindustrial society there will be an incremental reliance upon the "technologies of control" (p. 429), and that the chief instrument for such control will be the various technologies of telecommunications. The prime locus of such telecommunications control centers still lies in the cities of the nation, where the wide range of telecommunications activities can achieve economies of scale because of the large number of potential clients for their services. In many ways communication systems are the modern equivalent to the variety of transportation services that developed the infrastructure of the United States in the nineteenth century. As such, their impact on the future shape of this country will be at least as great as that of the automobile in the early part of this century.

This brief overview of the interrelationship between the growth of cities and the development of various communications systems merely scratches at the surface of the subject. In this summary I have tended to deal with mediated communication systems, because this is the area that I personally know best. However, there are many other facets of this fascinating and complex history that are of equal importance in unravelling the mystery of how we as human beings have communicated with each other and our environment throughout recorded history.

THE STUDY OF URBAN COMMUNICATIONS:
A MODEST PROPOSAL

In this chapter I am concerned with the state of our cities, and more particularly with the study of the communication infrastructure of cities, and what we as scholars and practitioners in the field of communication can and should be doing to understand and explicate the urban communication process. Ultimately, of course, the objective is to move beyond esoteric academic explication into playing a substantive role in the mysterious realm of the policy maker. I feel that with the vast intellectual and methodological resources of our various disciplines, we can make a major contribution to increasing understanding of the complex process of urban communication and thereby actively assist in making or reformulating relevant policies in the urban polity. For too long the various fields of interest that constitute the amorphous academic discipline of "communication studies" have stood on the sidelines of urban studies, and the subject of "urban communication" has all but disappeared or never realized its potential.

It is somewhat of an academic mystery why, despite our inexorable move toward becoming an almost totally urbanized (and suburbanized) nation, we lack a comprehensive theory about the nature of the urban communication infrastructure. Richard L. Meier (1962) in his pioneering, and still singular, study, *A Communications Theory of Urban Growth,* was prescient when he told us:

It is no overstatement to assert that people in urban areas are preoccupied with communications. . . . It has been possible to depict urban communications as a system for some time, but the exercise has not been undertaken because no particular advantages were foreseen. Now, however, the situation has changed. An assessment of trends in communications rates suggest that cities face some unprecedented crisis in the not-too-distant future. It can be shown that an increase in the communications rate is a prerequisite of socio-economic growth, but overloading of communications channels causes distress and disorganization. Changes in the patterns of human interaction so as to reduce communication stress will be required if the welfare of urban residents is to continue to improve. (Pp. 1–2)

Meier's work was difficult, provocative and tentative, but he did suggest some useful parameters for establishing a theoretical framework for the study of communications as an integral part of the urban environment.

Unfortunately, few, if any, scholars have been brave enough to venture beyond Meier's initial explorations by creating competing theories of the role of communication in the urban superstructure. The most innovative work in this field has been done by geographers, particularly those interested in the question of the dissemination of information. The work of Everett Rogers on the "diffusion of innovations" is also provocative (see Pred, 1973, 1980; Rogers, 1983).

As a result the field of urban communication has remained an academic back-water, spawning the occasional monograph or scholarly article, but never at-tracting the sustained attention devoted to other areas of interest such as media effects, organizational communication or new communication technologies ("telematics").

In the years since Meier's contribution there have been some important his-torical studies that have illuminated the way in which the shift in the dominant forms of communication technologies have influenced the growth of interaction between urban areas (Pred, 1973, 1980), and the impact of specific electronic communications technologies on the shape of the American urban environment (Fischer, 1992; Marvin, 1989; Nye, 1990). What we lack, however, are more intensive studies of a particularist nature such as Mandelbaum's study *Community and Communications* (1972), which explored the role of communications in social integration, urban educational policy and urban planning in the early years of cable television, and Greenberg and Dervin's study *Use of the Mass Media by the Urban Poor* (1970), which provided much useful base informa-tion about the relationship between class, ethnicity and media usage. We also need more specific studies of the urban press, such as Morris Janowitz's study of *The Community Press in an Urban Setting* (1952); Jack Lyle's *The News in Megalopolis* (1967); and, most recently, Tichenor, Donohue and Olien's *Community Conflict and the Press* (1980).

The time has now come for us to focus our collective expertise in a coherent and sustained manner on the study of communications in the urban environ-ment. This, of course, cannot be done in geographic isolation from the rest of the nation. Such a concentration must invariably involve examining the entire communications infrastructure of the country—urban, suburban, exurban and rural—but a focus on the complexities of communications both in, and emanat-ing from, our cities will reap rich intellectual and policy-related rewards.

There is, however, a considerable semantic problem that must first be over-come. After talking to pioneers in the field of urban communication I have come to realize that for a variety of political and cultural reasons the term "urban" no longer has the ring of urgency and problem-solving potential attached to it that it did back in the 1960s and early 1970s. In fact, quite the opposite is true, and from a political perspective the word "urban" is now a synonym for "liberal failure." Today the term has assumed the connotations of low socioeconomic status, or lost inner-city youth, or even more specifically African-American youth. Each of these is certainly encompassed in the notion of "urban," but there is also a wide range of other concepts and social groups within the totality of the urban infrastructure.

While more politically correct terms such as "cultural and ethnic diversity" and "multiculturalism" may now be in fashion, nevertheless I believe that we should revitalize the historically and sociologically accurate idea of "urban" regardless of the red flag that it may wave in the face of jaded politicians or overly sensitive academics. (It has been suggested to me that the term "local" communication would be politically acceptable as well as being more descriptively accurate.) While we play semantic games, we cannot ignore the fact that the cities are the major source of our most dynamic cultural shifts, as well as the site of our most troubling racial problems. So despite whatever may currently be politically correct, there is still an urgent need to study why our urban communications infrastructure appears to be so dysfunctional, and the source of so many of our society's ills.

THE STUDY OF URBAN COMMUNICATION: MODELS FOR THE FUTURE

In a 1977 collection of readings (Arnold and Buley, 1977), one of the few books that have attempted to focus the various subdisciplines within communication studies on the subject of urban communication, the editors noted that the Executive Committee of the Association of Departments and Administrators of Speech Communication had recently taken a specific position on the study of urban communication. Fifteen years later it is worth recalling that their resolution called for "the development of urban communication curricula and programs be undertaken and that steps also be taken to develop study in problems of urban communication continuing with action caucuses at future SCA meetings" (Arnold and Buley, 1977, p. vii). The Arnold and Buley collection of original and reprinted material still stands as an isolated example of an attempt to create a holistic approach to the subject of urban communication, which, for whatever reason, never really took hold.

In the remainder of this chapter I would like to suggest some specific areas of urban communication that are worthy of further study. These are by no means the only subjects that need attention; I have focused on these because they pique my intellectual curiosity. However, these topics are not just intellectual exercises, for each area is of vital significance to urban policy makers. Research into these topics will greatly assist the formulation of sound policy options.

The Role of the City in the Formation of Popular and Mass Culture

It is no secret that there is an enormous academic interest in the general field of cultural studies. However, despite the plethora of articles and books on the wide range of cultural studies, there has been very little systematic attention paid to the specific role played by "the urban" in the process of the production, dissemination and consumption of cultural products. Iain Chambers (1986), in one of the few books that explicitly acknowledges the urban role in this process, has noted: "It is in the city that contemporary popular culture—shopping and video arcades, cinemas, clubs, supermarkets, pubs, and the Saturday afternoon purchase of Saturday night clothes—has its home" (p. 17). As modern mass culture winds its way throughout society, it leaves the clear stamp of its urban origins.

The cultural encroachment of the city into the countryside is not a new phenomenon. What is new, however, is the extent to which a particular set of urban values and symbols (what I call the "urban ideology") is being adopted by a large section of American youth, whether they live in the city, the country, the suburbs or small midwestern communities. A good place to start might be to try to define exactly what are modern urban values. Using a multiple-methodology approach, we could measure and analyze the extent to which such an urban ideology is coming to dominate social interaction at every level and in all communities. It would be only natural in such an intellectual exercise to consider the role of the various mass media in the production and dissemination of this urban ideology. This is an example of an intellectual exercise that has very clear implications for policy makers.

Urbanism and Shifts in Interpersonal Communication

In this chapter I have not spent much time discussing the field of interpersonal communications because that is not my own area of expertise. Yet, as a communication historian, there is one topic that I have always been interested in, and about which I have never satisfied my intellectual curiosity. Clearly there have been numerous changes in the manner in which humans have communicated with each other, and the shift in the codes of interpersonal conduct through the ages has been historically documented (unfortunately, not necessarily from a communication studies perspective). Essentially I want to know more about the nature of these changes in interpersonal communications over time, and how such changes fundamentally altered the communications infrastructure of societies. What role did the various mediated communications systems, such as the telegraph, telephone and the mass media, play in this historical process? I have read both Harold Innis (1951) and Marshall McLuhan (1962, 1964) on this subject; these two metacommunications philosophers merely whet my appetite for a more sustained and clearly expounded examination of these issues. However, particularly in the twentieth century, we need to know how such changes in interpersonal communication codes have affected our entire communications infrastructure. It would be an important intellectual contribution to the fields of history and communication studies, as well as a major consideration for policy makers, if we understood with greater clarity the significance of such changes.

The Failure to Develop a Coherent Urban Communications Policy: The Mandelbaum Thesis

As communication technologies begin to play an ever larger role in our cities, there is a need to develop coherent urban communications policies that will help to shape the cities of tomorrow. Seymour J. Mandelbaum (1986), one of the few scholars in North America to try to combine the fields of history, communications and urban planning, has noted that "communication is not usually treated . . . as part of the local technical infrastructure of urban life" (p. 132). His explanation for this lacuna is worth quoting at some length:

Specialized urban polities, such as sewer and water districts, have been organized around components of the physical infrastructure. General-purpose governments in a variety of very profound ways have treated infrastructural decisions . . . as important elements of intergroup relations. . . .

Not so in the communication field! City polities have been deeply concerned with the flow of information. Schools—institutions for intergenerational communication— dominate local budgets and a great deal of city politics. . . . The history of motion picture distribution and of libraries has been marked by repeated city attempts to control access to messages. New waves of immigrants reinvigorate old local disputes over the dominance of the English language in civic discourse. . . . Virtually all city governments operate substantial telecommunication facilities for the use of police and fire-fighting forces. . . .

It is . . . precisely the density of the local communication policy field that leads me to wonder about the absence of a synthetic image and politics. Why were debates surrounding the design of schools not generalized to shape urban radio and television? Why were persistent discussions of intergroup communication not transformed into a program for urban telephony? Why did the tradition of analytic comment on the implications of changes in the metropolitan press not generate a significant local political agenda? (P. 133)

Mandelbaum (1986) suggests that there are three basic barriers that have inhibited the development of urban communication policies to match the other areas of the physical urban infrastructure (pp. 134–136). First, historically there was no real forum in which urban communication policy issues could be discussed at the local level. Much of this has taken place at the federal or intraindustry level. Second, First Amendment issues have inhibited policy making, especially in the areas of content of communications. Third, there has been a basic conceptual deficiency in understanding the nature of communication systems.

Mandelbaum (1986) analyzes each of these barriers and concludes that they are far from being insurmountable. He suggests that much of the blame can be placed on the social philosophies of both liberals and conservatives vying for political and cultural control in the cities. Liberal critics have insisted that competent adults should have a free choice among an ever-expanding array of messages without the fear of censorship or restrictions; conservative critics, in contrast, "have argued for the moral salience of social groups; for the quality of community life rather than individual choice as the measure of value" (p. 138). The result of this division was that "neither urban theorists nor practitioners developed a synthetic notion of an urban communication infrastructure. Nor did they build professions and institutions which embedded that notion within the political structure of U.S. cities'' (p. 138).

The Mandelbaum Thesis, as I call this fine historical analysis, is worthy of extensive testing. Researchers could trace the various attempts that have been made to establish coherent urban communications policies, ranging from the rules and regulations governing nickelodeons and other forms of entertainment, to the complex political negotiations surrounding the awarding of cable television franchises. How much were these policies subjected to either liberal or conservative pressure? Most important, what can current policy makers learn from these mistakes? The key question is: How can a city benefit from having a cohesive urban communication policy? The Mandelbaum Thesis provides a solid platform for beginning a systematic program of urban communications policy research.

In this chapter I have offered a brief history of the relationship between urbanization and the development of certain communication systems. Admittedly, my aim has been to rekindle an interest in a field that has not received the systematic attention that I believe it deserves. It is a field with rich intellectual opportunities awaiting the scholars who wish to accept the challenge. I have also suggested some specific areas for further study, but there is an infinite number of other topics well worthy of consideration. Our cities are in trouble, and we as communication scholars should lend our expertise to solving one of the most troublesome problems of our generation.

REFERENCES

Arnold, W. E., & Buley, J. L. (Eds.). (1977). *Urban communication: Survival in the city*. Cambridge, MA: Winthrop Publishers.

Bell, D. (1960). *The end of ideology*. Glencoe, IL: The Free Press.

Beninger, J. R. (1986). *The control revolution: Technology and economic origins of the information society*. Cambridge, MA: Harvard University Press.

Bramson, L. (1961). *The political context of sociology*. Princeton, NJ: Princeton University Press.

Brantlinger, P. (1983). *Bread and circuses: Theories of mass culture as social decay*. Ithaca, NY: Cornell University Press.

Brown, R. D. (1989). *Knowledge is power: The diffusion of information in early America, 1700–1865*. New York: Oxford University Press.

Carey, J. W. (1989). *Communication as culture: Essays on media and society*. Boston: Unwin Hyman.

Chambers, I. (1986). *Popular culture: The metropolitan experience*. New York: Methuen.

Cherry, C. (1977). The telephone system: Creator of mobility and social change. In I. de Sola Pool (Ed.), *The social impact of the telephone* (pp. 112–126). Cambridge, MA: MIT Press.

Czitrom, D. J. (1982). *Media and the American mind: From Morse to McLuhan*. Chapel Hill: University of North Carolina Press.

Eisenstein, E. L. (1979). *The printing press as an agent of change.* Cambridge, England: Cambridge University Press.

Fabre, M. (1963). *A history of communications.* New York: Hawthorn Books.

Febvre, L., & Martin, H. J. (1976). *The coming of the book: The impact of printing, 1450–1800.* London: NLB.

Fischer, C. S. (1992). *America calling: A social history of the telephone to 1940.* Berkeley: University of California Press.

Gelb, I. J. (1963). *A study of writing.* Chicago: University of Chicago Press.

Giner, S. (1976). *Mass society.* New York: Academic Press.

Greenberg, B. S., & Dervin, B. (1970). *Use of the mass media by the urban poor.* New York: Praeger.

Howe, F. C. (1968). The city: The hope of democracy. In A. Strauss (Ed.), *The American city: A sourcebook of urban imagery* (pp. 239–240). Chicago: Aldine.

Huth, M. J. (1978). *The urban habitat: Past, present and future.* Chicago: Nelson-Hall.

Innis, H. A. (1951). *The bias of communication.* Toronto: University of Toronto Press.

Janowitz, M. (1952). *The community press in an urban setting.* Chicago: University of Chicago Press.

Jowett, G. S. (1976). *Film: The democratic art.* Boston: Little, Brown.

Jowett, G. S. (1989). "A capacity for evil": The 1915 Supreme Court mutual decision. *Historical Journal of Film, Radio and Television, 9*(1), 59–78.

Jowett, G. S. (1990). Moral responsibility and commercial entertainment: Social control in the United States film industry. *Historical Journal of Film, Radio and Television, 10* (1), 3–31.

Lyle, J. (1967). *The News in Megalopolis.* San Francisco: Chandler Publishing.

Lynd, R. S., & Lynd, H. M. (1929). *Middletown.* New York: Harcourt, Brace & World.

McLuhan, M. (1962). *The Gutenberg galaxy: The making of typographic man.* Toronto: University of Toronto Press.

McLuhan, M. (1964). *Understanding media: The extensions of man.* Toronto: University of Toronto Press.

Mandelbaum, S. J. (1972). *Community and communications.* New York: Norton.

Mandelbaum, S. J. (1986). Cities and communication: The limits of community. *Telecommunications Policy, 10*(2), 132–140.

Marvin, C. (1989). *When old technologies were new: Thinking about electric communication in the late nineteenth century.* New York: Oxford University Press.

May, H. (1959). *The end of American innocence.* New York: Knopf.

May, L. (1980). *Screening out the past: The birth of mass culture and motion picture industry.* New York: Oxford University Press.

Meier, R. L. (1962). *A communications theory of urban growth.* Cambridge, MA: MIT Press.

Montgomery, K. C. (1989). *Target: Prime time: Advocacy groups and the struggle over entertainment television.* New York: Oxford University Press.

Mumford, L. (1961). *The city in history.* New York: Harcourt, Brace & World.

Nye, D. E. (1990). *Electrifying America: Social meanings of a new technology.* Cambridge, MA: MIT Press.

Park, R. E. (1929). The city as a social laboratory. In T. V. Smith & L. White (Eds.), *Chicago: An experiment in social science research* (pp. 1–19). Chicago: University of Chicago Press.

Pred, A. R. (1973). *Urban growth and the circulation of information: The U.S. system of cities, 1790–1840.* Cambridge, MA: Harvard University Press.

Pred, A. R. (1980). *Urban growth and city systems in the United States, 1840–1860.* Cambridge, MA: Harvard University Press.

Rakow, L. F. (1992). *Gender on the line: Women, the telephone and community life.* Urbana: University of Illinois Press.

Rogers, E. M. (1983). *Diffusion of innovations.* New York: The Free Press.

Sklar, R. (1975). *Movie-made America.* New York: Random House.

Strong, J. (1968). Perils—Our city. In A. Strauss (Ed.), *The American city: A sourcebook of urban imagery* (pp. 127–134). Chicago: Aldine.

Strover, S. (1987). *Urban telecommunications: The policy planner's dilemma.* Austin: Center for Research on Communication Technology and Society, University of Texas.

Tebbel, J. (1969). *The American magazine: A compact history.* New York: Hawthorn Books.

Thompson, R. L. (1947). *Wiring a continent: The history of the telegraph industry in the United States, 1832–1866.* Princeton, NJ: Princeton University Press.

Tichenor, P. J., Donohue, G. A., & Olien, C. N. (1980). *Community conflict and the press.* Beverly Hills, CA: Sage.

Part II

INFORMATION FLOWS
AND FILTERS

4

Achieving Dialogue with "the Other" in the Postmodern World

W. Barnett Pearce

The title of this chapter names what I believe to be the primary post–Cold War challenge for communication theory and research. The facts of cultural pluralism, international interdependence in economics and politics, and the enduring strengths of ethnicity and religion have been undeniable for some time. However, the Cold War legitimated framing these issues in a particular way, often referred to as the "National Security Discourse" (see Weiler and Pearce, 1992). This discursive framework contained little space for "dialogue"; in fact, it structured a set of values and practices that made "dialogue" appear weak, soft, appeasing, unpatriotic and—worst of all—a losing strategy in a "winning-is-everything" context.

Now that the Cold War is over, the legitimation for "national security" as a transcendent metanarrative has dissipated, and we can explore new, more prosocial agendas. In this chapter, I weave a number of questions around this central theme. The most specific question asks whether it is possible to engage in dialogic communication in the mass media. This question presupposes a more reflexive concern: who are "we" who ask it, and in what form of communication should we speak? Not surprisingly, these questions are related, as the "we" who are theorists and researchers are also part of the "we" who might achieve dialogue with "the Other" in a postmodern world. At the end of this chapter, I conclude that dialogue can only be known in dialogue, and I hope that those who weave their way through the intervening text will see this as a reflexively orienting statement, not just a tautology.

A FOCUS ON FORMS OF COMMUNICATION

> The great tragedy of this age is not that men are poor—all men know
> something of poverty; not that men are wicked—who is good? Not that
> men are ignorant—what is truth? Nay, but that men know so little of men.
> —DuBois, 1982, p. 264

Franklyn Haiman and I recently argued about the appropriate response to racist "hate speech" (Haiman, 1991; Pearce, 1991a). He strongly affirmed the need for "more speech"; I equally adamantly called for "better speech." As I see it, his position demands belief that there is something inherent in communication, per se, such that if one has "enough" of it, good things will happen. On the other hand, I took the position that there are different *forms* of communication with strikingly different social effects. "More speech" may or may not result in less racism; the process of communication contains within it the seeds of all the vices as well as virtues known to humankind. Only with care (or luck) does "more speech" mean "better speech."

Haiman and I disagree less about the desirable consequences of open discussion than in our assessments of what is the greatest danger we face when making policy decisions about communication. For Haiman, the clear and pressing danger is the restriction of information and participation in public dialogue resulting from censorship of any kind; for me, the devil that I wish to fight consists of boring, debilitating, oppressive patterns of communication.[1]

Like DuBois, I am impressed by the sometimes low correlation between the amount of communication and the extent to which we know the persons with whom we converse. We can converse incessantly and still remain ignorant of our fellows. That this is possible says something about our concept of communication. Dictionary definitions focus on the transmission of information from one place or one mind to another. If this concept of communication is employed, then there should be a direct correlation between more communication and more information. However, an older and more comprehensive concept derives from the etymology of communication: the process of "making common."

In this chapter, I draw upon the "social constructionist" approach to communication (Pearce, 1989). This approach shows us as "inside" the process in which things—including ourselves—are made common. In this view, communication activities are—let's play with metaphors—the "containers" in which we live, move and have our being; the "social ecologies" in which "we" are formed and that we affect by our actions; the extrasomatic "wombs" of social relations in which we are nourished but from which we are never ejected; and the "systems" of which we are components.

The social constructionist approach to communication focuses on "forms" of the activities in which we are involved.[2] Although we do not have a very rich or rigorous vocabulary for describing forms of communication, some set of distinctions is crucial for the argument I am building. Here, I choose the familiar differentiation of "monologue" and "dialogue."

DIALOGUE

The distinction is a qualitative one inhering in the form and quality of the interaction among participants in the communication, not so much in the specific acts that each performs. For example, in monologue questions are asked to gain a speaking turn or to make a point; in dialogue, questions are asked to invite an answer. In monologue, one speaks in order to impress or impact on others; in dialogue, one speaks in order to take a turn in an interpersonal process that affects all participants.

Martin Buber (1967, p. 113) defined "genuine dialogue" as an encounter "where each of the participants really has in mind the other or others in their present and particular being and turns to them with the intention of establishing a living mutual relation between himself and them." He distinguished this "genuine dialogue" from two counterfeits: "technical dialogue," in which "objective understanding" is the sole goal; and "monologue disguised as dialogue," which he characterized as "strangely tortuous and circuitous ways" in which "they imagine that they have escaped the torment of being thrown back on their own resources." Anatol Rapoport (1967, pp. 90–91) differentiated (strategy-driven) monologists from (conscience-driven) dialogists.

The basic question in the strategist's mind is this: "In a conflict how can I gain an advantage over him?" The critic cannot disregard the question, "If I gain an advantage over him, what sort of person will I become?" For example, he might ask what kind of a nation the United States might become if we succeeded in crushing all revolutions as easily as in Guatemala. With regard to deterrence, the critic might ask not, "What if deterrence fails?" (everyone worries about *that*) but, on the contrary, "What if deterrence works?"[3]

According to Rapoport, three characteristics differentiate the forms of thinking of the those habituated to monologue and dialogue:

1. Strategists conceive action in terms of its effects on objects or other people; dialogists conceive action in terms of its effects on themselves. This is similar to Buber's observation that the "I" of "I-thou" is not the same as the "I" of "I-it."
2. Strategists can only begin to work when values are given or assumed; for dialogists, determining what values are is a principal preoccupation.
3. Strategists assume that objective facts are to be ascertained; dialogists take into consideration our perspective and actions as determining what are—or what seem at this moment to be—the facts of any matter.

My own struggles with this topic led me to propose two distinctive characteristics of dialogue: putting one's own resources at risk, and not treating the other like a native (Pearce, 1989). The first is straightforward: unlike monologue, dialogue involves the risk that you will be changed by the encounter.[4]

The second characteristic of dialogue is more complex. The meaning of an act is not exhausted by the (mechanical or reflex) effect it produces on us. Communication is a hermeneutic exercise in which we ensconce acts within a web of evaluative and interpretive criteria. However, the question is whose criteria—our own or those of the other person? If we treat the other like a native of our own culture, we hold them accountable to our standards. While this practice may seem to embody the Golden Rule, it is at the same time the most vicious form of cultural imperialism. If we treat the other as *not* a native, we at least open a space for their act to derive its meaning from their evaluative and interpretive criteria; by developing a certain kind of binocularity, we entertain the possibility that what they meant by what they did and said may be very different from what we would have meant had we said or done it.

DIALOGUE *WITH "THE OTHER"*

> Few issues have expressed as powerful a hold over the thought of this century as that of "The Other." . . . It is difficult to think of a second theme that so sharply marks off the present—admittedly a present growing out of the nineteenth century and reaching back to it—from its historical roots in the tradition . . . the question of the other cannot be separated from the most primordial questions raised by modern thought.
> —Theunissen, 1984, p. 1

I enclosed "the Other" in quotes in order to distinguish one who is simply *an other* from one who is *other than us*. Where the former recognizes plurality ("the class of persons like myself has more than just me in it"), the latter recognizes alienness and diversity ("the persons who are not me are, in some important ways, not *like* me").

Ways of dealing with "the Other" have emerged as a central issues in philosophy, and dialogue has been offered by some as a crucial element in philosophical method. For example, Richard Rorty embraced the hermeneutic perspective as a way of dealing with others without reducing them to a common foundation, and Richard Bernstein reasoned his way to "an engaged fallibilistic pluralism" in which there is a moral "*task* to seek out commonalities and points of difference and conflict" among those who are "the Other." This task is less concerned with its "product" (e.g., some level of agreement) than its "process," which Bernstein identified as "a dialogical response where we genuinely seek to achieve a mutual reciprocal understanding—an understanding that does not preclude disagreement" (Bernstein, 1992, p. 337). Dialogue necessarily involves the risk that we will be changed by encounter with the Other. Dialogue involves "increase in self-knowledge . . . challenge to prior conceptions . . . opportunity for misunderstanding . . . risk of personal confusion and disruption . . . possibilities that meaning will be deformed . . . [and] danger that understandings will prove incommensurable" (Gunn, 1992, p. 11).

Ironically, the social need for dialogue is greatest in just those situations in which it is most difficult. It is most needed and most difficult when we encounter "the Other." "Our capacity to live peaceably with each other depends upon our ability to converse intelligibly and reason coherently. But this ability is weakened by the very differences that make it necessary. The more we need it, the weaker it becomes, and we need it very badly indeed" (Stout, 1988, p. 3).

Is dialogue more difficult than monologue? Is it more fragile? Does it require a greater array of enabling circumstances (something along the lines of the old adage, "it takes two to make peace but only one to make war")? At any rate, three temptations often seduce us into various forms of monologue: (1) Encounter with others perceived to be like us tempts us to act on the basis of habit, memory and scripts, neither attending to or attempting to express our own particularities or those with whom we communicate. Tsujimura (1987), noting that "Japanese tend to be taciturn or untalkative," referred to:

Japan's racial and linguistic homogeneity. It is a matter of course that people can understand each other easily with few words if they are monolingual and monoracial. In this sense, the United States represents the opposite extreme: a high level of diversity and verbosity. . . . Such conditions force people to overcome a variety of difficulties created by language barriers, different life-styles, and different ways of feeling and thinking in order to understand one another. Thus, Americans have no choice but to fully explain and exhaust their words; the social context in which they live often requires it. (P. 119)

The dangers in such monologues are easy to spot. In fact, Japanese are not all alike, and they continue to have great difficulty in acknowledging diversity. They do not seem to have an available discourse in which to discuss the plight of the indigenous Ainu and the conscripted Koreans who live in Japan, and there is no process by which a foreigner can "become" Japanese. Dialogue requires a certain kind of "mindfulness"; a willingness to foreground one's own assumptions and vocabulary, not as a neutral instrument for the formation of messages, but as an inherently biased and biasing framework for communication.

(2) Encounters with the alien other pose the temptation to treat the other as "wholly other," so alien that we need not even try to communicate with them. We treat their social worlds as *incomparable* with our own, thus escaping the moral obligation to take them into account as "subjects" with evaluative and interpretive criteria of their own. A further temptation is to project our desires and fears onto the other, seeing them as the embodiment of those aspects of ourselves that we would disavow. "Othering" has become one of those new vices, long practiced but until recently nameless, by which one group projects

"onto others, and almost inevitably socially marginalized others, what we most fear or desire, despise or despair of achieving, in ourselves" (Gunn, 1992, p. 11). Edward Said (1979, pp. 7–8), speaking specifically of "Orientalism," argues that "othering" is an expression of certain hegemonic cultural forms, in this case, "the hegemony of European ideas about the Orient, themselves reiterating European superiority over Oriental backwardness."

(3) The converse temptation is to treat the other as only superficially different from us, "just like us" under the veneer of exotic custom or differently pigmented skin, thus denying the "otherness" of the other. "We are handicapped by our history. The most common forms of communication in our social worlds, those into which we are co-opted as infants and make our own through experiential learning, do not deal well with the other. Monocultural communication excludes the other, and both traditional and modernistic communication—in radically different ways—subsumes the other in our own evaluative and interpretive criteria" (Pearce, 1989, pp. 96–155). How can we do better? Where can we find better models?

DIALOGUE WITH "THE OTHER" *IN THE POSTMODERN WORLD*

> We have met "the others," and they are us.
> —After "Pogo," by Walt Kelley

As Will Rogers said about blushing, only a certain genre of academic writers apologizes for using the term "postmodern"—or need to! I am using "postmodern" to assert that certain pretensions of modernity have been demonstrated pernicious, and to denote a certain "constellation" (to use Bernstein's [1992] preferred metaphor) of beliefs and practices. The crucial transitional move is from traditional society's belief in a totalizing "grand narrative" and past modernity's belief in a nonideological playing field over which our minds can move unimpeded if equipped with the right "method" (a belief discredited by Michel Foucault, Theodor Adorno, Thomas Kuhn, Richard Rorty and Richard Bernstein, among many others), to an image of a multidimensional, pluralistic (in William James's term) multiverse in which our minds have multiple interests (as Jürgen Habermas showed us), in which we are embodied (as Mark Johnson has argued) and ecologically integrated (as Gregory Bateson noted so provocatively), and which is constituted rather than represented by our communicative activities (in ways elucidated by Rom Harré, John Shotter, Kenneth Gergen and other "social constructionists").

The discovery of other cultures as viable ways of being human is one of the most significant discoveries of the twentieth century. Compare the state of anthropology at the beginning and end of the century: one hundred years ago, anthropologists were thoroughly ethnocentric, identifying their task as that of studying "primitive cultures." Today, anthropologists are boldly experimenting with the frontiers of written and visual inscription, trying to put "into our ways of saying what they are up to" (Geertz, 1973) or achieving "interlocution" among the anthropologist and those studied (Clifford, 1988). The ethnography of communication movement (see Carbaugh, 1990) has taught us, if nothing else, that the peoples of different cultures engage in fundamentally different forms of communication.

However, cultures are neither static nor homogeneous. Among other things, this means that "the Other" is not necessarily exotic or removed in time or space from ourselves.

Speakers have far more resources at their disposal than the single set of forms and stylistic conventions of a single "language." In fact, every national language is teeming with sublanguages, each with its own conventions. Wherever significant social differentiation occurs in life, there too will begin to form a new sublanguage. In any society of any complexity, therefore, numerous such sublanguages always coexist, challenge one another, and become grist for the verbal mill of those who master their conventions. What we are describing, of course, is the state of *heteroglossia,* which Bakhtin takes to be the primordial linguistic state for human beings in society. (Schultz, 1990, pp. 34–35)

If all societies have always been heteroglossic, why are so many critics so excited about the concept just now? There is something new under the sun that makes traditional ways of dealing with heteroglossia no longer sufficient: the mass media of communication. Taking a social constructionist approach, I see communication as gamelike patterns of social interaction in which we are participants. From this perspective, the media of communication are the enabling infrastructures of those gamelike patterns; they have the same relationship to patterns of communication as the board to a game of chess, the deck of cards to a game of poker, and the gridiron to a game of football.

This perspective on media is consistent with Walter Ong's (1982) analyses of the transformations of society (that is, clusters of gamelike patterns of interactions) by successive developments of "new media." For example, writing is not just another way of encoding and transmitting messages, it structures new patterns of social interaction. In an oral society, knowledge was incarnate in persons and only learned in social conversation with a particular other person; in a print society, knowledge is often encoded in books and libraries, and learned while reading silently alone.

The electronic media of communication do not simply provide new means of transmitting messages, they comprise an infrastructure that enables a different set of events and relationships to occur. I have a whole shelf of books written by people who have tried to assess the effects of the new media; let me add yet another idea: the media as a new "place."

The phrase "in the media" refers to what happens when, for example, a government program or scandal enters a public space in which it is commoditized and sold in newspapers, television, magazines, and so on. The use of the term recognizes that something is different when information gets "in the media." What does "in" mean in this context, and, in this phrase, what is "the media"?

All societies set aside places for certain kinds of action. Some places distinguish between what Mircea Eliade called the "sacred" and the "profane"; others are specific to important or trivial events. Such places include churches, restaurants, courts, legislatures, theatres, concert halls, the public square or shopping malls, private homes and bus stations. Think of "the media" as a place; a new type of place with specific characteristics that comprise the infrastructure of social interactions. What kind of place is it?

"The media" as a place consists of many media. Newspapers, magazines, broadcast radio, television, audio- and videocassettes, electronic databases, faxes and the like are all mixed up. Each medium uses the others as content. This place jumbles together, in a seamless whole, the most important and the most banal of events: "America's Funniest Home Videos" occurs in the same place as live coverage of the bombing of Baghdad; Madonna and Bill Moyers simultaneously offer advice about the meaning of life on different channels but in the same place.

The media is heteroglossic. Whorf's MIT alumni would find it a strange new world; Bakhtin (1984) would recognize it in an instant and call it "carnival."

"The media" is a place with unique dimensions. In terms of physics, it has no location and is largely irrelevant to distance. Time is the most important dimension, and is fractured into many splinters: print freezes time, translating the spoken word to a lifeless artifact that has the capacity to be resurrected by a reader; video- and audiotape creates a continuous present, permitting the juxtaposition of nonsimultaneous events, a kind of ersatz immortality in which all moments are one; and the broadcast media create time as a commodity, to be divided, sold and consumed. It also has distinct moral dimensions: Its art consists of occluding the reality of its presence. The camera shows something other than itself; actors train so that they can appear to be "natural." Pretense is the substance of the construction of "the media" as a place; the media is inevitably a liar.[5]

Gamelike patterns of interaction are enabled and structured by the physical and moral dimensions of the media, but they are not solely determined by them, any more than games of chess or football are determined by the board or gridiron. The "scoring" in these games is primarily a function of political and economic forces. In the United States, the games played in the media are primarily economic: "information" as well as "art" has become a commodity to be bought and sold; the lines between news and entertainment are increasingly permeable. The value of a "product" is determined by its popularity (that is, the audience who will consume it) either directly as in purchasing a tape or disk or indirectly by constituting themselves as an audience for commercial messages for some other product. Among other things, this has transformed the notion of a "public space" for reasoned debate about, for example, public policies into a commercial space dominated by the hawking of wares.

"The media" is a new place in our society, and clearly, that place owes more to the bazaar than to the church, legislature or classroom. In the search for metaphors that capture the essence of this place, I think of a county fair, with the din of competing shills seeking to entice momentary curiosity and separate the unwary from their money. "The media" is not a very noble place; perhaps it should not be.

As a place, "the media" eliminates the geographic and social barriers that have always kept "others" apart. In this way, it exacerbates the need for dialogue by reminding us of and perhaps confronting us with "the Other." On the other hand, the physical and moral dimensions of "the media" are not conducive to dialogue.

The paradigm case of dialogue is oral conversation (see Ong, 1982). It is in the moments of interaction that "gaps" appear between the participants. These gaps are not objects of contemplation but aspects of sensuous human activities. The creation of the social world is continuous; the specific responses within particular contexts to the utterances of another with an utterance of our own creates a unique, nonrepeatable event that becomes part of our shared world—this is the manner in which we make common our social worlds.

The enabling infrastructure of oral speech facilitates interpersonal relationships (conversing involves one's whole self, not just the intellect; it responds to the interlocutor as an embodied person, not a disembodied text) and the development of co-constructed episodes in which each successive act is deeply enmeshed in an undulating, serpentine narrative. Print or manuscript media clearly do not facilitate these forms of social interactions. The facilitations and impediments of "the media" as a place in contemporary society is very complex; it seems to have facilitated the development of less formal styles of speech and demeanor but not dialogue.

Ethnography confronted us with the existence of "the Other"; using a variety of literary devices, a cluster of writers have insisted that "otherness" is not arranged in discrete groups but is distributed throughout even our own society; and the emergence of the new "place"—"the media"—has dissolved the distinctions among places, juxtaposing differences in a carnival of heteroglossia. All of these stress the existence of the Other.

The notion of reflexivity shows that we are changed by the process of communication, thereby confronting "otherness" in ourselves. This is the significance of my paraphrase of philosophy according to Pogo: if we are *inside* processes of communication and shaped by them, and if communication processes are mutable, contingent on the interaction of what happens in them and between that and the material conditions in which they occur, then what we do at a given instant enters into an ongoing process that shapes who we are subsequently. We are, in a very literal sense, continually in a process of inventing ourselves (Harré, 1980, 1984; Shotter, 1984; Gergen, 1982).

We act both out of and into social contexts. These contexts are not isomorphic with the perceptions or intentions of any of the participants, and so these contexts are encountered as (and are) objectively real. If this process is frozen in time, it looks like a circle, with reciprocal causality between what occurs (the objective contexts) and the people who act (subjectivity). If the process is seen in temporal motion, it looks like a spiral that bends into strange shapes and trajectories depending on what happens. If we can resist conceptual vertigo long enough to track this process, *at least in principle* we always run the risk of encountering ourselves having been changed by the process into something alien to our selves.

This risk is not necessarily greater in dialogue than in other forms of communication: The unintended consequences of strategic or monologic patterns are well known. However, the chance, even likelihood, of encountering ourselves as alien to what we are/were is acknowledged explicitly in dialogue, where we deliberately—perhaps courageously, perhaps reluctantly—put our resources "at risk."

ACHIEVING DIALOGUE WITH "THE OTHER" IN THE POSTMODERN WORLD

> . . . polyphonic truth . . . avoids both the "anything goes" form of "relativism" (i.e., individual subjectivism) *and* the monolithic form of official (dogmatic) scientific ideology . . . both relativism and dogmatism equally exclude all argumentation, all authentic dialogue, by making it either unnecessary (relativism) or impossible (dogmatism). Polyphony as an *artistic* method lies in an entirely different plane.
> —Schultz, 1990, p. 43

"The media" as a new place with distinctive physical and moral dimensions comprises a major part of our social milieu, and these dimensions seem inimical to dialogue. Can dialogue be done "in the media," or must we reserve other places for that form of communication? Are there clever strategies that permit dialogue (or reasonable approximations) in the media? What insidious forms of monologue-disguised-as-dialogue should we identify and critique? I have just enough experience with such questions to appreciate their difficulty (see Narula and Pearce, 1986), and thus will leave them to more capable hands.

Who are "we" who seek to achieve dialogue? What are our interests and assumptions? How do these assumptions and interests prefigure what we learn and do? How does our way of working reconstruct the prejudices embedded in those assumptions and interests?

I want to focus on this second set of issues, for two reasons. First, my experience as a communication theorist has been one of continual discovery of the intellectual prosthetics with which I feel my way about. These self-reflexive discoveries constitute the lived experience of a theorist who actually learns things—as opposed, I guess, to one who simply confirms hypotheses. I find it a profoundly humbling form of life, and I distrust the knowledge claims of those who do not seem to share it.

Second, I am struck by the synonymy between what communication theorists and researchers *do* and *what they study*. "Modern science is based on the discovery of a new and specific form of communication with nature—that is, on the conviction that nature responds to experimental interrogation. . . . Nature cannot be forced to say anything we want it to. Scientific investigation is not a monologue" (Prigogine and Stengers, 1984, pp. 5–6). If we are in dialogue with nature, it answers our questions, *but only in the terms in which we asked those questions.* Our interests and assumptions shape the inquiries we make and the interpretations of the data. Ironically, a major part of our ability to be sensitive to "the Other," whether that Other is physical reality, the data produced by an experiment or survey, or another person, stems from our reflexive awareness of our own involvement in the process by which they are "constructed" in our experience (Millar, 1992).

I am increasingly struck by two observations about our involvement in the co-construction of knowledge. (1) William James noted that the work that academics do is prefigured primarily by their temperaments (his famous distinction between "tough-minded" and "tender-minded") rather than their schools of thought. (2) Ludwig Wittgenstein noted that our "forms of life" as well as the "language games" in which we engage are prefigured by the "grammars" of our language; the "conceptual necessity" embedded in a "drop of grammar," he wrote, contains whole "clouds of philosophy."

Is it possible that our disciplinary battles about research and theoretical agendas have less to do with specific methods or formulations than with the underlying temperament of the researchers or the grammars of their discourse? Perhaps so: The cube produced by the intersection of three continua seems useful as a way of teasing out some important distinctions (see Figure 4.1).

Temperaments of theorists range from those who want to be right and those who hope "to be interested and perhaps even interesting, or at least not boorish" (Gunn, 1992, p. 16). For convenience, call this a difference between the quest for certainty on the one hand and the exercise of curiosity on the other. If taken to an extreme, the quest for certainty would lead to silence—a time when all questions are finally answered without fear of contradiction. The exercise of curiosity, on the other hand, envisions that the conversation will continue, becoming ever richer and more complex.

Clouds of philosophy embedded in drops of grammars differentiate those who believe that our social worlds contain stable forms from those who find them unfinished, inherently unpredictable, pluralistic places. Call this a distinction between presumptions of monistic and pluralistic social worlds. The first leads to a quest for "all-embracing schemas, universal unifying frameworks . . . vast structures in which there should be no gaps left open for spontaneous, unattended developments, where everything that occurs should be, at least

Figure 4.1
Temperaments and Grammars for Social Theory and Research

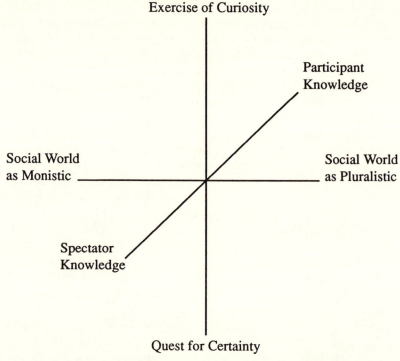

Exercise of Curiosity

Participant
Knowledge

Social World
as Monistic

Social World
as Pluralistic

Spectator
Knowledge

Quest for Certainty

in principle, wholly explicable in terms of immutable general laws'' (Hausheer, quoted in Prigogine and Stengers, 1984, p. 2). The second leads to an attempt to engage skillfully and wisely with unique and never fully predictable events.

Another distinction in the grammars of social theorists focuses on their perspective. The etymology of ''theory'' is ''spectator.'' A theorist in this sense is an observer rather than a participant. By implication, the world observed by a theorist is ''out there,'' objective and distant, and theory takes the form of statements representing that external reality. Using Aristotle's terms in the *Nicomachean Ethics,* others have argued that our social worlds, and communication processes in particular, are better described as *poiesis* (this is Rorty's [1989] sense of the ''strong poet''), or *praxis* (Shotter, 1990; Cronen, in press). If the ''stuff'' of social theory is *praxis,* then theory takes the form of practical wisdom rather than epistemology. Let this distinction be called ''participant'' versus ''spectator'' knowledge.

Positivism clearly falls in the cube defined by the quest for *certainty* by theorists functioning as *spectators* who believe that the social world is *monistic.* I do not believe that much of interest about achieving dialogue with ''the other'' in the postmodern age has come, or is likely to come, from this sector. In my judgment, the relatively unexplored perspective that holds the most promise is defined by the exercise of *curiosity* by "practical theorists" functioning as *participants* in a social world conceptualized as *pluralistic*. Working within this temperament and this grammatical form establishes a distinctive notion of what a communication theorist is up to: to put our beliefs—as well as all forms of social existence—to the test of determining to what extent they render the experiences of ordinary life "more significant" and "more luminous" and thus "make our dealings with them more fruitful" (Gunn, 1992, p. 93). This shows that what we are doing is a form of *praxis* that must be evaluated by criteria other than the extent to which it reduces the "Cartesian Anxiety." Working out the implications of this move suggests new criteria for evaluating research, new concepts of communication and new ways of engaging with particular instances of communication.[6]

CONCLUSION

The discerning reader will note that I have been building to the conclusion that "dialogue" is not an objective thing "out there" that we ought to study or facilitate without being affected by it. Recall my argument with Haiman; just as "more speech" does not necessarily mean better race relations, so "more research" does not necessarily mean "more knowledge" (whatever that might mean) or even "more wisdom." If the social world is pluralistic and heteroglossic, then the sustained use of any set of research prosthetics will impose their own biases on the knowledge that we create. If so, as Clifford Geertz and James Clifford might be heard as arguing, one criterion for evaluating research methods is their ability to discern their own horizons and voices that speak languages other than their own.

The times demand that we find ways to institutionalize dialogue as the *form* (not the content) of the metanarrative in postmodern society. My answer to the question of how we are to achieve this does not look like what the "old paradigm" would recognize as an answer. I do not believe that there is a (monologic) plan to be strategically implemented. However, by engaging with the processes we are interested in studying, and doing so in a way that has the quality of dialogue, we can, as Gunn (1992, p. 16) put it, "be interested and perhaps even interesting, or at least not boorish."

NOTES

1. Note that my emphasis is on participating in patterns of communication that are boring, and so forth, rather than on what those patterns "produce" or on their "effects." I am struggling to find a way of talking about communication as gamelike patterns of social interactions in which we are enmeshed, rather than as a process or thing somehow different from its effects, as if these were outside communication patterns.

2. Different levels of explanation are required to understand a system as a whole and

to understand its component parts. A category scheme that indexes *all the utterances* in a social system may tell us very little about the *form* of communication in which those utterances occur. To make matters even more complex, most human utterances are simultaneously part of multiple forms of communication. See Pearce, Cronen, and Conklin, 1979.

3. When Rapoport posed this question during the Cold War, it seemed absurd in the context of the National Security Discourse. Given the difficulty we now face in defining what "the new world order" might be, the absurdity is that circumstances find us so ill prepared to answer it. Of course, the point is not simply to ask different questions but to take a different perspective, in this case, punctuating situations not as a linear process of "how can I get what I want" but as an ecological system in which "my wants" both emerge from and are affected by the network of relationships within the system, including my own actions.

4. Jerry Falwell, president of Liberty Baptist College, celebrated monologue as the dominant communicative form. When criticized for allowing arch-humanist Senator Edward Kennedy to address his students in 1984, Falwell explained: "If one liberal Pied Piper can come to Liberty Baptist College and in one speech steal away the spiritual and intellectual loyalties of our students, then I and this college's faculty have not done our job. If, on the other hand, we have done our job, then guest lecturers of any persuasion will only sharpen the defensive skills of our students." Columnist Anna Quindlen criticized Vice President Dan Quayle's selection of the Southern Baptist Convention's annual meeting as the site to defend his comments about "family values." Such preaching to the converted, she said, "does not enlarge human understanding." Rather, it "practice[s] the politics of exclusion as a road to re-election" (*Chicago Tribune*, June 16, 1992, p. 19).

5. I wrote this in early June 1992. Ross Perot's campaign strategy had been announced but had not commenced. It described itself as using television so that the candidate can go "directly" to the people without "mediation." This use of terms attests to the success that television, as a medium of communication, has achieved in disguising itself. In the op/ed pages, "the media" now refers to a profession—journalists—who intrude, for good or ill, between the candidate and the electorate. Has Alice gone through the looking glass yet again?

6. Shotter (1990) and Cronen (in press) do not agree about the shape of what they both call "practical theory," but both provide excellent discussions of what is involved. Shotter would dispense with "theory" in favor of a toolbox of concepts; Cronen would transvalue and redefine virtually all of the technical terms in a theorists' vocabulary and transform the criteria by which research is evaluated. Chen and Pearce's 1991 exploration of the place of case studies in our discipline contains a systematic attempt to identify what "rigorous methods" in social constructionist research might look like, and Pearce (1991b) discusses what might be the case if theorists successfully resisted the temptation to engage in monologues with other theorists.

REFERENCES

Bakhtin, M. (1984). *Rabelais and his world*. Translated by H. Iswolsky. Bloomington: Indiana University Press.

Bernstein, R. J. (1983). *Beyond objectivism and relativism: Science, hermeneutics and praxis*. Philadelphia: University of Pennsylvania Press.

Bernstein, R. J. (1992). *The new constellation: The ethical-political horizons of moder-nity/postmodernity.* Cambridge, MA: MIT Press.

Buber, M. (1967). Between man and man: The realms. In F. Matson and A. Montagu (Eds.), *The human dialogue: Perspectives on communication* (pp. 113–118). New York: The Free Press.

Carbaugh, D. (Ed.). (1990). *Cultural communication and intercultural contact.* Hills-dale, NJ: Lawrence Erlbaum Associates.

Chen, V., & Pearce, W. B. (1991). Even if a thing of beauty, can a case study be a joy forever? Paper presented to the Speech Communication Association, Atlanta, Georgia.

Clifford, J. (1988). *The predicament of culture: Twentieth-century ethnography, litera-ture and art.* Cambridge, MA: Harvard University Press.

Cronen, V. E. (in press). Coordinated management of meanings: Practical theory for the complexities and contradictions of everyday life. In J. Siegried (Ed.), *The status of common sense in psychology.* Norwood, NJ: Ablex.

DuBois, W.E.B. (1982). Quoted in S. B. Oates, *Let the trumpet sound: The life of Martin Luther King, Jr.* New York: New American Library.

Geertz, C. (1973). *The interpretation of cultures.* New York: Basic Books.

Gergen, K. J. (1982). *Towards transformation in social knowledge.* New York: Springer Verlag.

Gunn, G. (1992). *Thinking across the American grain: Ideology, intellect and the new pragmatism.* Chicago: University of Chicago Press.

Haiman, F. S. (1991, October 30). Why hate speech must be heard. *Chicago Tribune.*

Harré, R. (1980). *Social being: A theory for social psychology.* Totowa, NJ: Lit-tlefield, Adams.

Harré, R. (1984). *Personal being: A theory for individual psychology.* Cambridge, MA: Harvard University Press.

Leeds-Hurwitz, W. (1992). Social approaches to interpersonal communication. *Commu-nication theory, 2*(2), 131–139.

Millar, F. E. (1992). Toward understanding the relevance of reflexivity and the rele-vance of reflexive understanding. Paper presented to the Central States Commu-nication Association, Cleveland, Ohio.

Narula, U., & Pearce, W. B. (1986). *Development as communication: A perspective on India.* Carbondale: Southern Illinois University Press.

Ong, W. J. (1982). *Orality and literature: The technologizing of the word.* London: Routledge.

Pearce, W. B. (1989). *Communication and the human condition.* Carbondale: Univer-sity of Southern Illinois Press.

Pearce, W. B. (1991a). A modest proposal for putting "hate speech" in its place. Unpublished paper.

Pearce, W. B. (1991b). On comparing theories: Treating theories as commensurate or incommensurate. *Communication Theory, 1,* 159–164.

Pearce, W. B., Cronen, V. E., & Conklin, R. G. (1979). On what to look at when studying communication: A hierarchical model of actors' meanings. *Communica-tion, 4,* 195–220.

Prigogine, I., & Stengers, I. (1984). *Order out of chaos: Man's new dialogue with nature.* New York: Bantam.

Rapoport, A. (1967). Strategy and conscience. In F. Matson and A. Montagu (Eds.),

The human dialogue: Perspectives on communication (pp. 79–96). New York: The Free Press.

Rorty, R. (1979). *Philosophy and the mirror of nature*. Princeton, NJ: Princeton University Press.

Rorty, R. (1989). *Contingency, irony and solidarity*. Cambridge, England: Cambridge University Press.

Said, E. W. (1979). *Orientalism*. New York: Random House.

Schultz, E. A. (1990). *Dialogue at the margins: Whorf, Bakhtin and linguistic relativity*. Madison: University of Wisconsin Press.

Shotter, J. (1984). *Social accountability and selfhood*. Oxford, England: Basil Blackwell.

Shotter, J. (1990). *Knowing of the third kind: Selected writings on psychology, rhetoric and the culture of everyday life*. Utrecht, The Netherlands: ISOR.

Stout, J. (1988). *Ethics after Babel: The languages of morals and their discontents*. Boston: Beacon.

Theunissen, M. (1984). *The other*. Cambridge, MA: MIT Press.

Tsujimura, A. (1987). Some characteristics of the Japanese way of communication. In D. L. Kincaid (Ed.), *Communication theory: Eastern and Western perspectives* (pp. 115–126). New York: Academic Press.

Weiler, M., & Pearce, W. B. (1992). Ceremonial discourse: The rhetorical ecology of the Reagan administration. In M. Weiler and W. B. Pearce (Eds.), *Reagan and American public discourse* (pp. 11–42). Tuscaloosa: University of Alabama Press.

5 ⎯⎯⎯⎯⎯⎯⎯⎯⎯⎯⎯⎯⎯⎯⎯⎯⎯⎯⎯⎯⎯⎯⎯⎯⎯

Failures in News Transmission:
Reasons and Remedies

Doris A. Graber

THE SCOPE OF LEARNING DEFICIENCIES

When social scientists test what people learn from the mass media, the results deserve to be called "dismal." A comparison of the public's political knowledge in the 1940s and 1950s with knowledge levels in 1989 even shows a decline in knowledge when educational levels are held constant (Carpini and Keeter, 1991). The decline was particularly noticeable for items of current information such as the names of incumbent public officials. These are surveillance items that people learn from regular attention to media, rather than items that they learn in school early in life.

If democracy, as most Americans interpret it, means that interested members of the public should be politically knowledgeable so that they can judge and influence what governments do, the current situation seems to bode ill. If the current scope of public ignorance about salient political matters is due wholly or partly to failures in news transmission, communication scholars need to devote more attention to diagnosing the nature of the problems and to suggest remedies.

Since most American news media enterprises are privately owned and controlled, one can argue that they are not obligated to be handmaidens to democratic governance. In refutation, it should be pointed out that the mass media are the only institutions capable of conveying large amounts of current information to a wide audience. The need to safeguard the nation's political health therefore thrusts responsibility for the public's civic enlightenment on them (Gurevitch and Blumler, 1990). The public needs properly selected and presented information about the public policy issues confronting officials. News stories must permit people to form sensible opinions and to relate them to particular political tasks such as political discussions, transmission of information to public officials, voting and other political activities. The media, privileged in the United States by the First Amendment, and benefiting everywhere from the willingness of public officials to supply them with news materials, must provide adequate political information because no other institution currently can.

However, the depressing news about political ignorance must be put into perspective. While most people earn low scores when they are asked political questions during surveys, it is also a well-established fact that most people do possess a large fund of usable political knowledge. Samuel Popkin (1991), for example, reminds us:

It is certainly true that most citizens do not know many of the basic facts about their government, but assessing voters by civics exams misses the many things that voters *do* know, and the many ways in which they can do without the facts that the civics tradition assumes they should know. . . . The focus on voters' lack of information about many political issues underestimates just how much information they pick up. . . . It focuses on what voters don't know instead of on what they do know, who they take their cues from and how they read the candidates. (Pp. 20–21)

The kinds of questions that produce the dismal scores are inappropriate for discovering the respondents' fund of knowledge. For example, questions that call for free recall of specific details rarely tap more than a fraction of the knowledge that emerges when questions provide cues that assist in memory searches. Though people remember visual information better than verbal data, they are rarely asked about the content and meaning of the visuals. Few studies test comprehension of the story or information gained through reasoning beyond the bounds of the main story line. It seems fair to question the wisdom of excluding comprehension as an essential element in learning tests. Similarly, why does the ability of visuals to stimulate reasoning and knowledge remain unexplored and underrated while the ability for rote memorization of detail is deemed high-quality learning?

Popkin's findings, as well as other studies, indicate that people learn about some aspects of politics but fail to learn about others (Graber, 1988; Rosenberg, 1988; Page and Shapiro, 1992; Popkin, 1991). Judging from the kinds of information that people do absorb, it apparently is not primarily a question of subject matter. For instance, people do learn about some economic issues even when they do not learn about others that are of similar relevance. They can commit names and numbers to memory, even though they frequently fail to do so. One clue to this puzzle of hopscotch learning is supplied by research that shows that people attend selectively to information. The old hypodermic theories that equated exposure with automatic learning are incorrect, even when exposure is heavy. Average television viewers who watch four hours of television daily are exposed to 35,000 commercials a year, many of them repeated over and over again. Yet they store only very few of these in memory.

What then is the chief difference between the political information people learn and the information they do not learn? It is my contention that *how* an issue is framed and presented determines not only whether it will or will not be covered by the media, but also whether it will be noticed and learned and whether it potentially influences people's opinions and ultimately, in a multistep process, generates governmental action.

To assess the causes of information transmission failures, I therefore want to focus on the framing of mass media messages, which are the raw material for learning about current politics. The questions about framing that need to be addressed are very familiar to professional educators of adults, whose messages must produce learning—which means understanding, insight and some mastery of factual data. For example, when professors prepare materials intended to inform students about some aspect of politics, the first question to be considered is ''What do they need to know about this subject?'' The answer requires determining the purposes to be served by learning. They may range from passing an academic test, to becoming well-informed, effective citizens, to achieving expert status in a particular area of knowledge.

The second question—which also partly shapes the answer to the first—relates to the capacities and interests of the audience. What is their education and experience level? How are they likely to process information? What interests them? Once the information base into which the audience will incorporate the new information is known, as well as audience members' goals and motivations for learning, specific questions about appropriate framing can be answered. These questions relate to the content of the message, its ability to capture the audience's attention and entice them to process the information, and its suitability for enabling the audience to store the message for retrieval and use when needed.

Like professional educators, journalists do not generally attempt systematic answers to questions about appropriate message framing. There is too little concern about what political information average media audiences need to know to perform adequately the political tasks that most citizens undertake. Despite an extensive literature that has been used effectively by advertisers and campaign consultants, journalists understand too little about human information processing, including what makes stories attractive and easy to absorb. News story framing has been done largely intuitively and haphazardly, guided by considerations that often have nothing to do with effective information transmission.

What evidence can I adduce to support these charges? To make my case, I will first present data that illustrate some glaring inadequacies of framing. Then I will briefly intersperse findings from information-processing research that show that framing deficiencies are barriers to learning. These findings are based on the rich crop of recent information-processing studies, including my own research, which has entailed intensive interviews with news audience members whose routine media sources were content-analyzed, and on experiments where audience learning was tested immediately after exposure to selected news stories (Conover and Feldman, 1984; Gamson, 1992; Iyengar, 1991; Graber, 1988, 1990; Neuman, Just, and Crigler, 1992). Next, I will address the controversial question about knowledge requirements for effective citizenship in our times. I will conclude with a discussion of possible remedies.

FRAMING THE NEWS: PRINCIPLES AND PROBLEMS

I am using the term "framing" quite broadly to encompass not only the context in which a story is embedded, which determines the meanings it is likely to convey, but also the basic principles that are used in telling news stories. My main focus is on the relation between framing, broadly construed, and learning from the framed information. I am only indirectly concerned about the ideological implications of particular framing and the sociology of news construction. As sociologists like William Gamson, André Modigliano and others have pointed out, when news framing refers to the practice of focusing on a particular meaning to classify, organize and interpret information, it deals with the construction of ideologies. The merits and consequences of these ideologies are beyond the scope of this chapter. The fact that some are more readily learned than others is germane (Gamson and Modigliano, 1989). Similarly, when framing affects causal thinking, as Iyengar (1991) has demonstrated, it is important to consider that some causal linkages may arouse more interest and produce more learning than others.

What are the basic principles of news framing and why do they produce learning difficulties? To discover how news stories are framed, one can either examine a representative array, or one can ask news personnel how they go about framing stories. One can also be less enterprising and rely on the reports of other scholars. For the research reported here, I have used all three approaches and found that they yielded compatible answers.

As any beginning journalism student knows, the basic principles of news framing are to cover the who, what, where, when, why and how elements of a given situation in an attractive story format. Attractiveness, as Reuven Frank reminded his staff when he was executive producer for NBC's nightly news programs, requires that: "Every news story should, without any sacrifice of probity or responsibility, display the attributes of fiction, of drama. It should have a structure and conflict, problem and denouement, rising action and falling action, a beginning, a middle and an end. These are not only the essentials of drama; they are the essentials of narrative" (Epstein, 1973, pp. 4–5).

To find out to what extent these principles are actually applied by newspeople in framing television news, which is the most widely used source of news, I undertook a two-pronged study. Informal interviews were conducted with more than fifty television news personnel responsible for various aspects of news production. My assistants and I asked them about their approaches to framing specific news stories and their reasons for choosing these approaches. These informal probes were followed by intensive interviews with five news directors who were working for major network organizations. All had college-level teaching experience and were therefore skilled in articulating their news-framing criteria. We had discovered that many experienced directors without teaching experience found it difficult to explain the factors and calculations that entered their choices. Each of the directors in the intensive interview setting was presented with identical sets of fifteen hypothetical news situations and asked how he or she would cast these stories audiovisually. The open-ended responses and follow-up answers to interviewer probes were tape-recorded.

We also examined the audiovisual framing in 350 political news stories broadcast on local and national news on the major networks. Roughly half of the sampled stories were videotaped during a single two-week span to allow for comparisons among the treatments given to the same story by different news organizations. The remainder of the stories were randomly chosen. We eliminated feature stories from the analysis because their above-average length and often highly dramatic presentation make them atypical. Likewise, we did not code stories running for less than twenty seconds because their brevity mitigated against learning. That left 209 stories for detailed analysis.

For each framing plan described by a news director, and for each of the actual news stories, we noted the presence of information that identified *who* the important actors in the story were, *what* factual situations were described or depicted in the story, and whether it contained information about *where* and *when* the reported event had occurred or was expected to occur. We also searched for information about causes and likely consequences of problems, analyses of stages in the development of problems, or indications of the problem's pervasiveness. Such information would answer the important *why* and *how* questions and would provide the essential framing that gives meaning to news stories.[1]

"The Facts, Madame, Only the Facts!"

The basic trends revealed by the findings were similar for the news directors' framing plans and for the analysis of actual news framing. As Table 5.1 shows, the *who, what, where* and *when* questions were covered quite well. More than 90 percent of the stories had substantial amounts of specific information from which viewers could construct plausible scenarios of various incidents. The directors' scores for including relevant data were nearly 100 percent. If so, why don't audiences grasp these facts and report them when questioned?

The answer lies in human information processing. News audiences do not generally attempt to memorize facts. Rather, they use facts as raw materials for the extraction of meaning and then dismiss the factual data from memory.

Table 5.1
Factual Elements in Stories

Source	Who	What	Where	When	Why	How	Context	N
T.V.	98%	100%	95%	94%	53%	34%	65%	209
Lab	100%	100%	99%	100%	37%	31%	65%	75

T.V. = stories videotaped from broadcasts; Lab = stories suggested by news directors.

This has been referred to as "on-line processing" (Graber, 1988; Lodge, Stroh, and Wahlke, 1990). They search for the main idea, rather than specific details. In fact, too much detail becomes confusing, rather than enlightening, particularly when stories provide few clues to the meaning of the facts and their relevance (van Dijk, 1988; Graber, 1988; Popkin, 1991). Similarly, the media's emphasis on conflict may be misleading, and presenting widely different positions on unfamiliar issues may confuse and occasionally repel audiences.

In the television stories that we sampled, the weakest coverage of key story elements was in news about the economy's health, fiscal policies and business news. These are pocketbook issues of direct concern to most people; adequate data for meaning construction are essential. Unfortunately, they are also areas in which both journalists and their audiences generally are knowledge-poor. Obviously, it is difficult to transmit adequate information and to process it when neither message senders nor receivers are knowledgeable.

Meaning construction hinges on the nature of the frames, which serve as a users' guide by suggesting particular meanings. Such frames may be supplied by the media or they may be retrieved from each person's store of personal and collective memories. As van Dijk (1988) has noted, "understanding is essentially relative to personal models and goals, on the one hand, and socially shared goals, frames, scripts, attitudes, or ideologies on the other hand" (p. 106).

Missing: Causes and Action Guidelines

Except for people blessed with rich funds of knowledge stored in memory, information related to the *why* and *how* questions is the type of coverage most helpful in meaning construction and most coveted by media audiences. Regrettably, it is far less pervasive than factual information (Graber, 1988). Overall, as shown in Table 5.1, only half (53 percent) of the real-life stories explained *why* the situation was occurring. In the hypothetical stories, the score was 37 percent. In some news categories in the real-life stories, such as news about law enforcement, only one-third (32 percent) of the stories provided reasons.

The *how* question fared even more poorly. It is answered by information about the steps involved in a developing event, or steps audience members might take for follow-up action or to gain additional information. On an average, only one-third of the stories supplied this type of information. The conclusion to be drawn from these content analysis data is obvious. The very kind of information most helpful for extracting desired meanings from news stories, is in shortest supply. At the same time, there is an overabundance of factual information in many news categories that overwhelms processing capacities and, therefore, does more harm than good when ease and effectiveness of learning are the main objectives.

The meaningfulness of stories is enhanced when they are placed into appropriate contexts, such as comparisons with related events or appraisals of the story's significance for various groups. Our content analysis findings, though more positive than for the *why* and *how* question, still indicate that many routine stories lack essential contexts. An average of 65 percent of the real-life as well as the directors' stories put them into meaningful perspectives. When they did not, the directors sometimes suggested that a context was not needed because most audience members could supply it from past experience—an often debatable assumption. For some types of stories for which contextual information is especially important, it was exceptionally sparse. For instance, only 45 percent of the actual reports about America's relations with its Western European allies put these stories into perspective and only 47 percent of stories about economic conditions supplied helpful context.

Dramatization—Help or Hindrance?

In line with Reuven Frank's admonition—which reflects his concern with capturing and holding audience attention—we found that all news stories contained several dramatic elements. As Table 5.2 indicates, most common were close-ups of people, showing facial features and body language (present in 93 percent of real life and 100 percent of directors' stories), and emphasis on conflictual or highly contrasting elements in the situation (72 percent for real-life and 69 percent for directors' stories). An average of 39 percent of the real-life and 75 percent of the directors' stories also showed emotional scenes. Drama was also created by depicting emotional interactions among people (41 percent real-life, 53 percent directors) and by presenting situations with which average people could readily identify (33 percent real-life, 24 percent directors). Newspeople obviously went to great lengths to obtain dramatic visuals, whenever possible, even when bland footage would have been readily available and would have supported the story as well or better.

Research supports the common-sense belief that dramatic elements in stories arouse and hold attention and facilitate long-term recall (Robinson and Levy,

Table 5.2
Dramatic Elements in Stories

Source	Conflict	Emotion	Interaction	Identifict'n	Close-ups	N
T.V.	72%	39%	41%	33%	93%	209
Lab	69%	75%	53%	24%	100%	75

T.V. = stories videotaped from broadcasts; Lab = stories suggested by news directors.

1986; Sperry, 1981). The Kennedy assassination, the astronauts' moon walk, the Challenger disaster, and Hurricane Andrew are examples of the kind of dramatic event that will linger in memory. If large numbers of routine news stories also include dramatic elements, why do they fail to produce comparable learning? The answer is that dramatic elements in routine news do enhance learning, though the effect is less pronounced because the drama generally is less gripping and not reinforced by repeated lengthy exposures. Moreover, human beings are "cognitive misers" (Conover and Feldman, 1984; Fiske and Linville, 1980). They do not expend their relatively scarce memory capabilities for stories that seem comparatively trivial to them and from which they do not expect to derive substantial uses and gratifications.

Even when dramatic framing produces learning, it is often undetected because scholars usually look for recitations of factual details, rather than reports about generalized impressions, beliefs and feelings. In fact, media critics who are disappointed by viewers' poor grasp of readily measurable facts point out that dramatic, personalized presentations may detract attention from the facts and figures by which critics judge political knowledge. They would be appalled by the suggestions of several directors who, eager for dramatic impact, wanted to frame a story about a teachers' strike in terms of youngsters loitering in the streets, rather than the teacher demands that led to the strike. Yet, can one really argue that the focus on teacher demands is necessarily more important than a focus on the context of the situation—the plight of the community during the strike?

Though dramatization may at times distract attention from important story elements, critics should not derogate it because it often increases levels of public information by attracting viewers who might otherwise ignore newscasts entirely or gain nothing from them. Dramatic framing also increases the emotional involvement of viewers and stimulates them to care and, occasionally, to become politically active. The "infotainment" format, which covers dull factual information with a dramatic frosting, may thus be a blessing in disguise. As one director put it, dramatization enriches otherwise shallow stories and spurs audiences to extract more meaning from them. "If you increase the density, what people can take out of it is more dense . . . people will make conclusions and be thoughtful." Another director commented: "If you try to make a story a tiny bit more educational, and a tiny bit more exciting to watch . . . there might be some success in actually getting the message across."

Moreover, content analysis of highly dramatic news stories has shown that they can successfully carry a substantial amount of factual information. When Dan Nimmo and James Combs (1985) examined stories about the Jonestown People's Temple massacre, the volcanic eruption of Mount St. Helens, the threatened nuclear disaster at Three Mile Island, the Iran hostage crisis, the Tylenol poisoning cases and the crash of American Airlines flight 191 in Chicago, they found that 49 percent of the reports contained in the stories were predominantly factual and explanatory. In terms of airtime, 62 percent of the coverage was factual and explanatory. Obviously, drama and information transmission, including political information, are not necessarily incompatible. This holds true even for routine news stories like the ones we analyzed and that our news directors proposed.

PROBLEMS IN NEWS PRESENTATION TECHNIQUES

Several structural aspects of television news presentation, which I have explored elsewhere, also mitigate against learning (Graber, 1990). For example, most television stories (76 percent) are quite short, taking less than three minutes. Almost one-third of the stories, although densely packed with verbal and visual data, are covered in less than one minute. One to three minutes are hardly sufficient to provide adequate information about most political happenings, including essential facts, contexts and guides for interpretation. Pictures, which carry important information-rich messages that make stories more meaningful, are flashed on the screen in extremely rapid succession. Most visual themes (76 percent) are on the screen for twenty seconds or less. The heavy dose of data presented so briefly makes adequate processing difficult, especially since viewers must also process the accompanying verbal text and sounds that often are not compatible with the visuals (Findahl and Hoijer, 1981).

There are few pauses within a newscast to serve as stopping points for assimilating processed information. Story follows story or advertisement in rapid succession, forcing the audience to make multiple switches between unrelated topics. Fragmented story snippets make it difficult to gain a good overview of political developments (Bennett, 1988; Entman, 1989). There is too much distracting advertising. Advertising in newscasts unintentionally serves the same purpose as deliberate distractors in psychological experiments. It interrupts concentration on the news and destroys attention (Chaffee and Schleuder, 1986).

One would not expect a college student, who took no notes, to learn from an audiovisual lecture that crammed information from fifteen to eighteen disparate courses into one nonstop thirty-minute lecture, interrupted only by sales pitches for assorted consumer goods or by sports scores and weather forecasts. How can one expect a news broadcast to be a successful learning experience? Just as the traditional lecture format used in college classrooms makes learning difficult, though not impossible, for many students, so the current formats of television news presentations create major learning hurdles. The surprise is not that people fail to benefit from the massive amounts of information to which average Americans are exposed; the real surprise is that they learn as much as they do, considering the difficulties.

KNOWLEDGE NEEDS—MORE IS LESS

The ideal citizen of a democracy, if we are to believe democratic theorists, would be a news junkie. Most real-life Americans are not. When offered a choice between serious political discussions and entertainment, most Americans opt for entertainment, although they proclaim otherwise. During the 1988 presidential primaries, 69 percent of the respondents to a national poll reported that they had paid prolonged attention to a story about a small child that had been trapped in an abandoned well. But only 15 percent claimed to have paid close attention to the Democratic race and only 13 percent said that they had followed the Republican campaign (Buchanan, 1991). Attention spans for political news items are short, even when they appear in the print press. USA Today has capitalized on the preference for brief snatches of news to attract the largest newspaper audience in American history.

As hungry as the people of Eastern Europe were for political information after the unravelling of Communist control, they reached the saturation point very quickly, judging by complaints about boring political news voiced at the CNN World News Contributors conference in Atlanta, Georgia, in February 1992 (Schwartz, 1992). Algirdas Kauspedas, the director of Lithuanian television, complained that governments and opposition parties had flooded the media with stories explaining the many new laws and rules. The result had been a nonstop diet of important but dull news and discussions. Eastern European audiences complained about too much political information and too little entertainment fare. Even in war-torn Yugoslavia, Croatian television audiences were bored with the flood of political information and asked for more entertainment and less news about their war with Serbia, according to Anton Vrdoljak, the director general of Croatian Radio and Television. Oversupply of political information is also a problem in the United States, particularly during American elections. A presidential campaign stretching out well over a year can hardly hope to generate and sustain a lot of excitement by the time Election Day finally arrives.

Part of the problem of attracting audiences to political news lies in the difficulty of making such news relevant to audience members. While most Americans feel a sense of obligation to keep politically informed, and a sense of guilt when reminded about their sparse knowledge of facts and figures, most do not consider such information genuinely vital to them in their personal lives. The political world seems remote, confusing and mostly dull. If it were framed to match peoples' known schemata for politics more closely—for instance by drawing parallels between familiar and unfamiliar events—that might not be the case.

The other part of the problem is that much of the news does not only *seem* irrelevant to most citizens' concerns; it *is* irrelevant. Also it often is intolerably repetitious. Journalists assume that people are interested in the minutiae of so-called Beltway information or in the day-to-day horse race news of political campaigns. In fact, people are not interested in such matters most of the time and probably need not be. By using their own well-honed abilities to judge the trustworthiness, intelligence and general competence of political leaders, and by relying upon trusted cue-givers such as party labels, civic leaders, media pundits and like-minded friends and co-workers, people can arrive at reasonable policy preferences without an extensive information base. Given that most Americans lack the time and inclination to expose themselves to massive amounts of political information, it becomes crucial to ascertain what they really need to know.

Does news content supply average citizens with the information they need to function effectively? The question of what constitutes an adequate knowledge base for effective citizenship resolves into many subissues. About what issues do people need to be informed? Does everyone need to be informed about everything, or can and ought there be some specialization in our complex age? How specific does knowledge have to be to make it usable for citizenship tasks? Is it enough, for example, to know that people are starving in Somalia before advocating aid or must average citizens also be fully informed about the politics of that troubled country? Is it enough to know that some relief supplies have gone astray or must one know precise dollar amounts and hijacking details?

The answers to such difficult questions hinge on the all-important determination of the purposes for acquiring political knowledge. For people who only vote in national elections, it may be quite sufficient to concentrate on indicators of candidate trustworthiness and job competence. To provide such information effectively, presidential job profiles must be developed and tested. Neither journalists nor social scientists have yet tackled that task, which involves determining what information is most important in judging the merits of presidential candidates. Without such profiles, journalists are guessing about what information may be relevant, possibly wasting time on unhelpful data while overlooking crucial information. For example, exploration of a candidate's childhood traumas may be far more useful in predicting success as president than prying into marital crises in adulthood. Assessing a candidate's political skills in winning friends and mollifying enemies may be a better predictor of ability to govern than a long record of service in various bureaucracies.

If issue coverage is indeed relevant for voting and other civic activities, it should focus on major issues likely to confront the candidates, rather than broad discussions of matters that are outside the political reach of the office that the candidate seeks. Moreover, issues need to be put into context so that audiences can gauge their significance. For example, the strength of legislative or pressure group opposition to the candidates' proposals needs to be assessed. Given problems of sustaining attention over prolonged time spans, information needs to be rehearsed by the media at the appropriate times. For example, it makes little sense to taper off election information in the week immediately before choices have to be made, as is common in presidential campaigns.

How will journalists know what should be covered? Past and future social science research on factors that shape the course of politics could be extremely helpful. The initial preparation of political journalists and subsequent training programs should be designed to expose them to the best available research and provide them with more expertise in political analysis. Political expertise must be coupled with far better understanding of human information processing in general, and familiarity with the norms of political culture shared by members of the audiences for which journalists are preparing newscasts. Journalists need to be concerned with the learning produced by their stories, not only with attracting audiences. This requires knowing the schema patterns into which the stories will be integrated when they are encased in particular frames.

WHAT IS TO BE DONE?

What are the remedies for failures in news transmission? My remarks will be confined to matters that seem within the realm of the possible. That means that they take into consideration that political news is very complex, and that reporters face severe technical, economic, and time and skill constraints. "The mass media dance to other tunes than those of democratic communication alone" (Gurevitch and Blumler, 1990, p. 283).

As discussed already, more research is needed about what ought to be news, judged from a citizenship perspective. Though there may be controversy about the findings, that seems preferable to the present guesswork approach. A more realistic understanding of democratic requirements is likely to produce citizens who are better qualified to meet today's political challenges. By spending less time on scanning to find what they want, and more on reading what is genuinely relevant, readers would probably extract more substantive information. Given the complexity of politics, one should expect most citizens to focus on a limited number of political concerns that are of special interest to them, rather than striving for the impossible goal of being well-informed generalists. They could then target their learning and their political activities to fewer concerns and improve the quality of their performance. Broader public interests would not suffer because "collective wisdom results from collective deliberations based on a division of labor" (Page and Shapiro, 1992, p. 388).

Much more experimental research on news framing formats is also needed, to allow reporters to tailor stories adequately to suit the cognitive frameworks of their audiences. As the authors of *The Changing American Voter* noted: "In general, the data on levels of conceptualization do support the hypothesis that the way in which citizens conceptualize the political realm is dependent on the political content to which they are exposed" (Nie, Verba, and Petrocik, 1976, pp. 121–122). Of course, there is no absolute way of structuring stories to meet the needs of all audiences at all times. Just as is done in advertising, research on news framing must be continuous. It must consider matters such as the idiosyncracies of particular audiences, the political context at the time and the focus of audience interest and attention.

Stories must be made more attractive to audiences. Current technologies should help because they make it possible to customize stories and to let audiences choose what they really want to hear and see. For example, there might be various versions of a story, from a highly detailed to a brief headline version. A menu could allow the user to scan available topics and select some for brief scrutiny and others for fuller exploration.

It will require a good deal of imagination to make routine, yet important political stories more dramatic and visually exciting without diminishing their political focus. As one news director described the challenge, to be successful, one must "continually condense this stuff into something that is so dense that it maintains interest or that is at least short enough so that the viewer knows this may be a boring story, but it can't last more than thirty seconds." A comparison of framing suggested by the news directors for similar stories shows that no story was irredeemably dull in the hands of a skilled professional. This suggests that exciting casting that is dramatic as well as rich in information is possible, even when the story is routine. This finding is also supported by our analysis of the real-life stories. In Dan Hallin's words, news is and must be "both journalism and show business, a key political institution as well as a seller of detergent and breakfast cereal" (Hallin, 1986, p. 11).

Political scientists Ben Page and Robert Shapiro (1992) contend, on the basis of studying trends in the American public's policy preference over a fifty-year span, that "the public, as a collectivity, has the capacity to govern. . . . Collective responses make sense. . . . They draw fine distinctions among different policies; and . . . they form meaningful patterns consistent with a set of underlying beliefs and values" (pp. 383–384). If performance is as good as they say, despite the major flaws in news framing (which they acknowledge), what would be the consequences of improved news framing? A cautiously optimistic answer seems appropriate. As human beings and technologies mature, the English poet Robert Browning may be right that "the best is yet to be."

NOTE

1. Three coders participated in the content analyses and 10 percent of the findings were double coded. Reliability ratings averaged 87 percent, excluding simple identifications where reliability was nearly perfect. None of the reliability scores dropped below 75 percent.

REFERENCES

Bennett, W. L. (1988). *News: The politics of illusion*. New York: Longman.
Buchanan, B. (1991). *Electing a president: The Markle Commission research on Campaign '88*. Austin: University of Texas Press.
Carpini, M. D., & Keeter, S. (1991). Stability and change in the U.S. public's knowledge of politics. *Public Opinion Quarterly, 55*, 583–612.
Chaffee, S. H., & Schleuder, J. (1986). Measurement and effects of attention to media news. *Human Communication Research, 13*, 76–107.
Conover, P. J., & Feldman, S. (1984). How people organize the political world: A schematic model. *American Journal of Political Science, 28*, 95–126.
Entman, R. M. (1989). *Democracy without citizens: Media and the decay of American politics*. New York: Oxford University Press.
Epstein, E. J. (1973). *News from nowhere*. New York: Vintage.
Findahl, O., & Hoijer, B. (1981). Media content and human comprehension. In K. E. Rosengren (Ed.), *Advances in content analysis* (pp. 111–132). Beverly Hills, CA: Sage.
Fiske, S. T., & Linville, P. (1980, December). What does the schema concept buy us? *Personality and Social Psychology Bulletin, 6*, 543–547.
Gamson, W. A. (1992). *Talking politics*. Cambridge, England and New York: Cambridge University Press.
Gamson, W. A., & Modigliano, A. (1989). Media discourse and public opinion: A constructionist approach. *American Journal of Sociology, 95*, 1–37.
Graber, D. A. (1988). *Processing the news: How people tame the information tide* (2nd ed.). New York: Longman.
Graber, D. A. (1990). Seeing is remembering: How visuals contribute to learning from television news. *Journal of Communication, 40*, 134–155.
Gurevitch, M., & Blumler, J. G. (1990). Political communication systems and democratic values. In J. Lichtenberg (Ed.), *Democracy and the mass media* (pp. 269–289). Cambridge, England and New York: Cambridge University Press.
Hallin, D. C. (1986). We keep America on top of the world. In T. Gitlin (Ed.), *Watching television* (pp. 9–41). New York: Pantheon.
Iyengar, S. (1991). *Is anyone responsible?: How television frames political issues*. Chicago: University of Chicago Press.
Lodge, M., Stroh, P., & Wahlke, J. (1990). Black box models of candidate evaluation. *Political Behaviour, 12*, 5–27.
Neuman, W. R., Just, M. P., & Crigler, A. N. (1992). *Common knowledge: News and the construction of political meaning*. Chicago: University of Chicago Press.
Nie, N. H., Verba, S., & Petrocik, J. R. (1976). *The changing American voter*. Cambridge, MA: Harvard University Press.

Nimmo, D., & Combs, J. E. (1985). *Nightly horrors: Crisis coverage by television network news.* Knoxville: University of Tennessee Press.

Page, B. I., & Shapiro, R. Y. (1992). *The rational public: Fifty years of trends in American policy preferences.* Chicago: University of Chicago Press.

Popkin, S. L. (1991). *The reasoning voter: Communication and persuasion in presidential elections.* Chicago: University of Chicago Press.

Robinson, J., & Levy, M. (1986). *The main source: Learning from television news.* Beverly Hills, CA: Sage.

Rosenberg, S. W. (1988). *Reason, ideology and politics.* Princeton, NJ: Princeton University Press.

Schwartz, J. (1992, February 3). Freedom to enjoy boring television. *New York Times.*

Sperry, S. L. (1981). Television news as narrative. In R. P. Adler (Ed.), *Understanding television* (pp. 295–312). New York: Praeger.

van Dijk, T. (1988). *News as discourse.* Hillsdale, NJ: Lawrence Erlbaum Associates.

proach would allow a genuine documentary against documentary comparison; the different channel locations in different national systems would be part of the comparison.

It would, then, be possible to mount a comparison between several national systems, based on interviews with thirty or so series producers in each of seven chosen genres. We would then only need several national studies of about 200 interviews each to fill in the research design.

There have, of course, been American studies of television producers, but, from the viewpoint of this argument, the previous studies are rather narrowly based. Studies such as Muriel Cantor's *The Hollywood Television Producer* (1971) or Todd Gitlin's *Inside Prime Time* (1983) focus upon Hollywood, and on prime-time producers; the studies consequently include producers of only two or three programming genres. Some other studies have deliberately adopted an even narrower focus by including a handful of individual producers. A new trend may well be established by Robert J. Thompson, whose *Adventures in Prime Time* (1990) focuses on a sole TV producer, Stephen J. Cannell, in a manner reminiscent of the large literature on movie auteur-directors.

To match the criteria suggested here, an American study of producers would need to focus not only on Hollywood, but on New York producers, because even on conventional television certain genres such as news and daily soap drama are concentrated in New York. The American study would also need to include sports and other genres that appear outside weekday evenings on conventional television. My suggestion is not that such a study should attempt to include every single television genre; but it should include a wide selection of genres, broadly representative of the total output of national television.

FACTUAL PROGRAMMING AND EDINFOTAINMENT

Factual programming, made-in-Britain factual programming, takes up well over half of all television screen time in Britain. Four categories each take up around 15 percent of British screen time: documentaries (and features), news (and current affairs), sports and what I call "edinfotainment."

The British "public service" tradition is evident on all four national terrestrial channels. This tradition says that broadcasting shall include education and information as well as entertainment. Several implications follow. There is a lot of factual programming, with entertainment also provided but still somewhat regarded as the sugar and fat within a more balanced diet. Programming should be predominantly made in the United Kingdom. The factual programming is seen as virtuous, because it is British, and doubly virtuous because it's overall much cheaper to make. Factual programming is especially strong on BBC2 and C4.

The greatest autonomy and agenda-setting power is probably exercised by the series producers and channel heads of these two latter channels. BBC2 and C4 each aim for only about a 10 percent share of the total TV audience. The two big channels, BBC1 and ITV, have together about a 75 percent share and are largely ratings driven. (The remaining 5 percent goes to satellite and cable channels.)

But a channel that only wants to obtain a 10 percent share is clearly not in the business of maximizing ratings. It is left to the producers and executives to decide what programming to run. In practice these channels run a majority of factual programming, partly because their budgets are smaller and factual programming is cheaper. Thus factual programming in general is strongly producer-driven, whereas entertainment is somewhat more ratings-driven.

The U.K. system gives some emphasis to market forces and the strong demand for entertainment. In midevening usually at least two terrestrial channels are showing material that has an audience maximization goal. But at least one and perhaps two channels are showing programming with an educational/informational goal or element.

This is a system in which not only is the operational goal mixed, but the precise goal-mix itself is unclear. Is the goal 60 percent entertainment and 40 percent education/information, or what? Nobody says and nobody knows, least of all the producer. The precise mix of goals is kept deliberately unclear. Prestige clearly plays a major role in such a system, but prestige itself is unclear and unmeasurable. Prestige depends upon opinion within the industry, within the genre, across genres and at the top. Prestige also depends upon what decision makers, politicians and the rest of the media think; in practice the opinion of the press is important for prestige within the industry.

Documentary is one example of a genre that is educational/informational and is prestigious. We interviewed thirty-nine documentary producers. Documentary, in my definition, includes general documentary series, which run on all four channels; three more specialized documentary areas—natural history, science and arts and music—each have several continuing series. These documentary producers live in a private world of film making. They have had precocious early success at getting their hands on the sizable sums of money involved in professional film making. They see themselves as involved in a reality-based art form. A documentary producer-director typically makes between one and two programming hours per year. Personal commitment, involvement and autonomy all reach high levels. There is also a strongly ideological element in many cases—for example a commitment to green environmentalism, and hostility to big business.

The private world of news (and news background) is quite different. These news producers see themselves not as film makers but as journalists; news producers have long ago taken vows of political impartiality. They are used to working within large-scale organizations, in a hierarchy, and alongside a ceaseless flow of scripted material. They are used to working at speed, and increasingly under "live" conditions. Within British television this is an elite area, in terms of entry and ultimate career destination.

The private world of sports producers is different again. Their prestige is much lower than that of either the documentary or the news producers. Outsiders to the genre regard them (somewhat unfairly) as merely relaying spectacles staged by others.

EDINFOTAINMENT PRODUCERS

In the United States there is infotainment, but in Britain the public service tradition leads to something that is more complex (or more muddled). ''Edinfotainment'' is my unlovely term to describe a large miscellaneous batch of material, which attempts to be educational and informative and entertaining, all within one thirty-minute program. Much of this programming seeks to spice some kind of educational intent with a bit of British humor and eccentricity. Examples of major areas, each of which has a batch of separate programs, are travel, gardening, cooking and ''Youth.'' Remember this is all on regular terrestrial channels, not on specialized cable channels.

Some of the edinfotainment programs have become eccentric and unique successes. An example is ''The Antiques Roadshow''; ordinary citizens present their family antiques and have the quality and financial value assessed on camera by professional experts. ''The Antiques Roadshow'' seems to combine greed, aesthetic appreciation and voyeuristic appeals, among others; both antique objects and their owners are beautifully filmed. The program has a regular audience rating of around 20 percent. A more recent success is the ''Clothes Show,'' also with multiple appeals, multiple goals and much praise.

But, for every such unique edinfotainment success, there is a score of less successful short series that ran this year and may not run next year. British television seems to place an extraordinary premium each year upon finding some ''innovative'' way to make a gardening, travel, food or youth program. All the obvious gardening ideas have been done already: gardens ancient and modern, famous people and their gardens, restaurants and gardens, literature and gardens and so on. Consequently we end up with something like ''The Victorian Kitchen Garden'' as a TV series. Or a new series called ''DIG,'' aimed at young first-time gardeners.

Perhaps because edinfotainment is not seen as audience maximizing, the usual strategy is not a head-on assault launched against the ratings leader of the genre. More usually new programs seek to be original, different and innovative. ''We'll do something they've ignored'' is a common note.

Much U.K. programming is mixed (or muddled) on several dimensions. Producers of this type of programming work within a private world marked by multiple uncertainties. They are uncertain about both the mix of goals and the mix of genres. They are often uncertain as to the future of the series and uncertain about their own future careers. In some cases they labor under an obvious mismatch between what they thought was the intended audience and time slot and the actual time slot in which the program is scheduled. For example a program aimed at young people may have a predominantly elderly audience.

Prestige is the biggest uncertainty. All of these producers know that they are operating under a mixed goal, and not solely a ratings goal. A producer with the highest rated program in the genre can still find the program under threat on the grounds of inadequate "quality" or "originality." Yet what exactly constitutes a high-quality gardening, cooking or travel program is never specified.

A critic can say that one result of this confusion is many programs that are neither very educational nor very informative, nor very entertaining, but that do reflect the values and prejudices of certain affluent areas of north and west London. Hence we get innumerable programs on postmodern architecture, post–nouvelle cuisine, do-it-yourself hints for your country cottage and vacation advice for people who've already been to Thailand and Kenya.

A less critical judge might say that British television offers a wide variety of factual programming to a range of niche markets on nationally available channels at convenient times. My basic point, however, is that these genre areas do have a distinctive culture and producer anxieties, and that these probably differ from what you would find in a life-style cable channel and among its program suppliers.

NONFACTUAL PROGRAM PRODUCERS

In the nonfactual entertainment areas we have talked to producers of various kinds of fiction, comedy, game, people and talk shows. Game shows and people shows are attractive to British television organizations because they are cheap to make, yet popular with audiences. Predictably they carry low prestige. The producers are well aware of this and see themselves as discriminated against for the sin of being popular.

The comedy and fiction genres share some characteristics. These are the areas with the highest ratings; they are also the most expensive programming areas per hour of output; and these are the areas which have to compete head-on with American, and increasingly Australian, imports obtained at low prices.

The British in general and the BBC in particular always congratulate themselves on being good at both comedy and TV fiction. These areas are high not only in audiences and cost, but also in prestige. British comedy and fiction producers see themselves as engaged in quality entertainment. Individual writers are honored; comedy is seen as the creation of one or two writers who should not be overworked, and the Hollywood TV practice of team writing has still not been adopted.

These producers—like the genres in which they work—are still closely linked to live performance. Many fiction producers have been previously involved in BBC national radio and in theatre, often as directors of theatres outside London. TV writers and performers continue to work in live theatre. Some shows do the studio taping on Sunday, which allows a star to continue through the week in a live theatre show.

British fiction is in some respects similar to U.S. TV drama in having at least four subtypes of output. In Britain these include soaps, continuing series, miniseries (called serials) and made-for-TV-movies (called single screenplays). However the British soaps differ in only doing two or three episodes per week and in having moderately high production values.

The prestige gradient is extremely steep within the British fiction genre. British soaps air two or three times a week at 7:00 or 7:30 P.M. In terms of cost-per-audience hour, made-for-TV-movies or single screenplays cost about twenty times as much as soaps. Prestige correlates with high cost and low audiences.

WORK SCHEDULES AND GENRE-SPECIFIC PRIVATE WORLDS

A British continuing fiction series normally requires eleven or twelve days of filming (or taping) for one fifty-minute episode. An annual run of thirteen episodes finds the series in production—working six days a week—for about six months each year. The British producer thus seems to get both more filming time per episode and more time not in production each year, compared with the Hollywood pattern.

Most British producers seem to spend up to half their year in production, which can mean working seven days a week for many weeks in succession. In the remaining weeks and months there is still plenty to keep them busy—such as working on scripts for next season, selecting writers, actors, directors and reporters. Increasingly British producers are likely to be part of small independent production companies.

Producers typically work a long day and then take other work home with them—not only scripts, outlines and bids, but also videos of the work of supplicant reporters, actors and directors. Producers typically admit that, after having watched the output of their own genre, they don't get enough time to watch television.

The unstandardized schedule, the chaotic proliferation of short series and the small back-up staff available to most producers all seem to lock producers into their own genre to the exclusion of most other things apart from food, sleep, the trade press and the newspaper TV columns.

HOW U.K. PRODUCERS RELATE TO U.S. TELEVISION

To discover how producers in different European countries relate to U.S. television would constitute, in itself, an interesting comparative project. Attitudes seem to be complex, ambiguous and contradictory. There is deference toward Hollywood as an entertainment capital, but also disdain for similar reasons.

Among British producers the attitudes toward U.S. television vary, as in so much else, according to genre, because the work experience varies so sharply by genre.

- *Fiction* is the genre that meets U.S. competition head-on. U.S. TV fiction series no longer score very high in the U.K. ratings. Among fiction imports the highest ratings positions are normally occupied by Australian soaps, followed by U.S. movies. Very few imported U.S. series of any genre get into the weekly top fifty programs.
- *Comedy* is another area of U.S. imports; they appear especially on the small audience Channel Four. This is probably the U.K. genre where the U.S. impact is largest, but domestic U.K. comedies on the major channels get much higher ratings.
- *Documentary* makers see their field as highly international. U.K. documentary makers look to PBS or Arts and Entertainment in the United States to provide perhaps one-third of funding for some series.
- *Game shows* are an area in which the U.S. tradition is extremely strong. Most U.K. game shows have used U.S. formats, sometimes heavily modified. But a strong intra-Europe trade in game show formats developed in the 1980s.
- *Chat show* producers search hungrily for familiar names whose faces have seldom been seen on British TV. A major source of supply is Hollywood stars, or former stars, plugging their latest goods. These shows, however, are better at being cheap than at being popular. In order to entice guests they must be bland, but bland interviews with fading movie stars are not big audience pullers.

Typically U.K. producers are well informed about current U.S. trends in their own genre, but they have fairly little interest in the broad U.S. domestic range of output.

THE U.S. SYSTEM—GENRE SEGREGATION

If they were asked to look at and comment on the U.S. system, what might U.K. producers say? One fundamental contrast with Britain is the *high level of genre segregation in the U.S. system*. Although U.S. independent stations run contrasting programming against the network genres, the major networks still segregate genres by time of day, while cable segregates genres by channel. This leads to a survival of the fittest contest within each genre. British producers fear that something more like the U.S. pattern is coming soon. Such fears have been expressed for forty years and usually prove only partly true.

A common British criticism is that U.S. TV series start with a successful pilot program, which is then remade over and over again. In my opinion a key difference is the position of the performing talent. A U.S. system of head-to-head competition, with long series runs aimed at a syndication gold mine, places successful performers (and their agents) in a very strong bargaining position. From a U.K. viewpoint, the U.S. system tends to generate surplus cash, which goes via agents to the talent. U.K. talent is only paid a small fraction of what U.S. performers receive. From a U.S. perspective the British system grossly underpays the talent, but uses more days of filming, or rehearsing and taping—typically 50 percent more and in some cases twice as much filming time as U.S. equivalent programming.

From a European viewpoint the U.S. interface of regulated networks and local affiliates has resulted in a strangely rigid demarcation of the evening hours, not least the massive quantities of early evening news, both local and national. Another oddity is the segregation of the low-cost soap drama outside prime time. In the U.K. a truly British compromise finds soaps, which run either twice or three times a week, in the early evening (with a daytime repeat). The soaps easily outrate all other programming types.

Another oddity: while game shows are in steep decline in the U.S., Europe is using more game shows but reformatting them in various directions, including a mixture of the game show and the old-fashioned variety show.

GENRE-BASED CROSS-NATIONAL COMPARISONS

This chapter has argued that program genre, or program type, has much to offer as a basis for comparison in cross-national studies of national television systems. A British study of producers in seven different national TV genres has been discussed. This study was based on unstructured interviews with producers and included the producers of most of the high-prestige and highly rated programs currently on British television. Unstructured interviews generate large quantities of rich material, but it would also be possible to adopt a more structured and quantified research emphasis.

The approach discussed here can be applied beyond television. Indeed the British study of TV producers was part of a larger study that also included interviews with editorial executives on London-based national newspapers. These editorial executives included the foreign editors, sports editors, political editors, features editors and picture editors of national newspapers. This approach could be used in cross-national research.

The genre basis for comparison has much to offer from the viewpoint of bringing together several different research perspectives. A study of producers, classified by genre, can encompass not only the tradition of the "constraints on the producers." This type of study can incorporate work on the content of programming. It can also include audience data and how such data are generated and used in large television organizations. In British television, as in other national systems, the producers are supplied with detailed weekly audience data—which some largely ignore and others use in order to refine the program's appeal.

A specific television genre will tend to be somewhat differently defined within each national television system. The different modes of scheduling, budgeting, writing, directing—and indeed the different producer roles—within fiction, comedy, news or sports enable the researcher to reach into the core of each national system, while at the same time discovering what is distinctive, and what is held in common, between national systems.

This proposed type of study has another potential advantage. Such a cross-national study can reach across the rather fragmented world of communication scholarship. It offers a way of combining hard data studies with, for example, qualitative studies of particular genres and particular directors, producers and auteurs.

NOTE

The study described in this report was funded by a generous grant from the Economic and Social Research Council, London.

REFERENCES

Blumler, J. G., Nossiter, T. J., & Brynin, M. (1986). *Research on the range and quality of broadcasting services* (Report of the Peacock Committee on financing the BBC). London: Her Majesty's Stationery Office.

Cantor, M. G. (1971). *The Hollywood television producer*. New York: Basic Books.

Gitlin, T. (1983). *Inside prime time*. New York: Pantheon.

Newcombe, H., & Alley, R. S. (1983). *The producer's medium: Conversations with the creators of American TV*. New York: Oxford University Press.

Thompson, R. J. (1990). *Adventures in prime time: The television programs of Stephen J. Cannell*. New York: Praeger.

Tunstall, J. (1993). *Television producers*. London and New York: Routledge.

Obstacles to Internal Communication among Subsidiary and Headquarters Executives in Western Europe

Maud Tixier

Based on research conducted over a two-year period (1989–91) in fifteen countries (the European Economic Community, Switzerland, Sweden and Austria) on executives transferred from one European country to another, this chapter describes in what ways their preferred communication styles diverge or converge and what impact this situation has on the development or use of new technologies. To the extent that communication is a management function, it is useful to examine those areas in which the management styles of the various countries differ or converge. The influence of American managerial culture, which varies according to individual European countries, is also evaluated.

Among the obstacles or filters of communication to be studied are those that depend on language and national culture, as well as those that can be imputed to corporate communication. The relevance of European experience to other multicultural groups (among them the United States) is also dealt with. Finally, by selecting three countries with extensive communication infrastructures (Germany, France and Great Britain), to which Italy, Spain, the Netherlands and Switzerland may be added, it is possible to study the potential impact of these cultural differences on the tools and technologies used for communication in these countries.

To simplify a complex subject, our operational definition of culture will be, as it is often stated in English, "the way we do things around here." The only aspects of national cultures and communication styles to be considered are those having an impact on internal communication and the way in which executives work in companies. It is assumed that English is accepted as the international language of business and that a minimal knowledge of the language can be taken for granted among European managers working in an international environment.

NATIONAL CULTURES

Differences in the conception of time have long been pointed out by researchers such as G. Hofstede and E. T. Hall. They underline the monochronic attitude of the Germans (also shared by the Americans, the English, the Dutch, the Danish, the Swedish, etc.) who do only one thing at a time, in contrast to the Latins who are polychronic and capable of performing several actions at the same time. For that reason the Germans have gained a reputation for being slow, although they themselves view monochronia as a source of concentration and efficiency. This may account for the German propensity to anticipate and plan everything and to respect schedules, deadlines and programs. Lack of punctuality and lack of respect for deadlines irritate them. The French feel less constrained by their appointment books and their programs, which can always be revised because they are not ends in themselves.

Countries having a linear and sequential approach toward time will also have a tendency to strong rationality, which represses spontaneity and displays of emotion, while in certain other countries, business relationships are very personalized and based on trust. In Portugal, for example, and this is especially true in the north of the country, the customer is always a friend. If not, he is not a customer. In Greece and Italy problems are smoothed over as soon as a rapport of friendship and trust is established. When a situation is frozen or slow to resolve itself, business tends to function on trust accorded to individuals, on the right connections and on long-standing relationships.

While in certain countries, most often Latin, trust is assumed to exist from the beginning of a relationship, in other countries trust is a reward that can only be gained with time. This is the situation in Germany, where even trust is granted in accordance with rational rather than emotional criteria. It is established little by little over the course of long periods of cooperation. This is why the Germans like continuity in their exchanges. For the same reason they reproach the French for long hours spent over business dinners. Like the Germans, the Swedish spend little time being sociable when they are in a professional situation. Social niceties are absent from business luncheons, during which they talk to solve a problem. Conversely, when Austrians meet to drink together, they think that it is impolite to discuss business.

The inclination toward discipline and rigor is contrasted with a greater propensity for flexibility and imagination. The countries that value discipline, order and organization are Germany, Switzerland, Sweden, Flemish-speaking Belgium and Austria. The more flexible countries—those that are less attached to procedures—are of course the Latin countries, but also the Anglo-Saxon countries of Europe (Great Britain and Ireland). The English are well known for their distrust of laws and for their art of compromise in negotiations.

Among the structuring factors of national cultures, the impact of which is visible in management, we will consider the following five interconnected elements: religion, upbringing, and attitudes toward work, money and success. In Denmark, for example (90 to 95 percent Lutheran), religion has had a strong impact, and attitudes toward guilt and responsibility have influenced all social intercourse. The further north one goes, the more one is expected to pay for one's acts. There is correspondingly less spontaneity and correspondingly more self-censure. Instincts are repressed and limits are internalized by the system of upbringing. Nevertheless, the Danes have neither the formalism nor the Calvinism of certain Germans. Their brand of Protestantism is less rigid and less sectarian. However, despite an appearance of liberalism in social matters, Denmark, like its neighbors, is basically a puritanical country.

In the Netherlands the influence of religion remains substantial and success is closely related to Calvinist culture. Even today a majority of high-level executives in banks are Calvinist. Financial affairs are important and a person who earns money is highly regarded. The Protestant ethic remains strong and hard work is the surest road to professional success. Religious divisions in the Netherlands (36 percent Roman Catholic, 20 percent Lutheran, 8 percent Calvinist and 32 percent without any religious affiliation) cut across many areas of social and economic life and produce noticeable compartmentalization in teaching, politics, the media, the trade unions and even leisure activities. If these compartments, or "columns" as they are called in Dutch, are weakening today, references to Calvinism remain frequent. More than a religion, it is a form of culture and a philosophy of life that has influenced the attitudes of other Protestants and even Catholics toward money, family, duty and work.

In Switzerland there is a clear distinction between Calvinists and Lutherans. The Calvinists put many screens between what they feel and what they express, and these filters kill spontaneity. Nevertheless, they are valued for their rigor, reliability and sense of responsibility. They inspire trust. The Lutherans, on the other hand, are more spontaneous, more open and less centered on the personality.

In other countries like the Republic of Ireland or Portugal, Catholicism has a strong impact on personal life. However, the 18- to 25-year-old generation living in Cork or Dublin has adopted a more liberal system of values than the previous generation or the rural population. Catholicism has given the Irish solid values of charity and mutual aid. They remain financially disinterested. It is not well thought of to earn too much money or to seek money as a priority objective. In strong contrast to Ireland or even France, certain countries like Germany or Belgium are more materialistic and give high priority to improving standards of living. Moreover, these countries, which enjoy a high purchasing power, like to display their wealth.

On the contrary, in a country like Sweden, it is not appropriate to show that one is better, richer or more gifted than one's neighbor. For this reason, in Swedish eyes, the general behavior of the Germans and the Americans represents what they have been taught above all to avoid. In Sweden, in public, one's wealth or successes are not discussed. In Denmark, too, education is much more egalitarian and, therefore, less elitist than in France. Young people are encouraged less to read and write at the earliest age, but they are quickly confronted with practical problems. Such a social system has tended to erode the dynamism and effectiveness of individuals.

COMMUNICATION STYLES

These main national characteristics lead us to consider European styles of communication, first of all the ability to manipulate one's own native language. This aptitude varies according to natural environmental factors, but it is also a function of family and religious upbringing, education and sometimes pure necessity. In Europe it is generally agreed that the French are the "finest talkers," but they are reproached for it. French executives are often given credit for a certain skill in public relations and a facility for manipulating ideas. They take great pleasure in talking, arguing and exchanging points of view. The Italians also appreciate eloquence, lively wit, quick intelligence and a certain panache. Like the French, they are often accused of being superficial.

In certain European countries, for example Portugal, Luxembourg, Belgium and Sweden, temperaments are clearly less extroverted, causing people to weigh their words, to distrust flowery language and to refrain from idle chatter. The Swedish are naturally reserved, quiet, aloof, controlled and withdrawn. They like introspection and self-analysis. Others, like the Swiss and the Belgians, maintain a low profile and are not given to making a spectacle of themselves. They are simply uncomfortable with oral expression. Among the Francophones, Belgian and Swiss executives differ sharply from French executives, who display a natural tendency for verbal brilliance and intellectual agility.

Education plays an important role, too. In Denmark, emotive expression is weak because the culture generally represses it. In fact, in general terms, the Danish system does not encourage oral expression. In Switzerland children are taught not to be conspicuous or to seek to impress others. In Sweden the natural reserve of individuals is accentuated by childhood upbringing and education.

The British constitute a special case. By their upbringing they are characteristically aloof, calm, controlled and reserved. Although it is not part of British culture to discuss one's own merits and achievements, they do have a gift for communicating well. They are good listeners, make easy contact and have a legendary sense of humor. Furthermore they know how to follow arguments, a skill they acquire in learning logic, even as young schoolchildren. The Irish present a similar paradox. They combine a certain unforced reserve and discretion with charm, personality and great simplicity in human relationships. They are even-tempered and like talking, cultivating friendships and telling jokes.

These differences are to be seen not only in executives, but also in chief executive officers (CEOs), whose role as spokespersons is more or less important in different countries. The difference between France and Belgium is a case in point. In France power is quite personalized and the names of company presidents are known to the public. They speak out on behalf of their companies on numerous occasions. In Belgium, on the contrary, it is difficult even to elect a "manager of the year" because it is not a Belgian tradition for a company president to appear on radio or television to defend his ideas or to present his views on the economy.

Many consequences flow from such differences in the interpersonal communication styles of various European executives. The first concerns a preference for either oral or written communication. Among those favoring written communication are the Germans, the Dutch and the Portuguese. German head offices, for example, often criticize their French subsidiaries for high telephone bills because written forms of communication are more natural in German companies. The Dutch appreciate the reassurance of written confirmations because they dispel doubt. They like the official weight conferred on meetings, appointments and agreements by summaries, notes and memos.

It is seems natural that the Spanish prefer oral forms of communication. The Spanish language is better suited to oral expression than written expression. Few Spaniards express themselves poorly, but Spanish is a difficult language to write well. This is why the Spanish prefer to conduct business by talking. Letters to customers confirm previous conversations and are always written in reference to what has been discussed orally. The Greeks also have an oral culture and find it equally difficult to follow regulations and procedures demanding written communication.

On the other hand, it is somewhat surprising that the Danish and the Swedish are peoples of oral culture. In Denmark, and in Scandinavian countries in general, a verbal agreement has as much value as if it were written, which is not the case in many Latin countries. In fact, even in court oral agreements are valid if they have been witnessed, and it is what has been expressed orally that is judged.

The second consequence of these differences in modes of communication concerns the length of written communication, which may be related to linguistic factors. The question of length may be related to language. Compared to English, for example, it is difficult to be brief in French. Culture can be another factor. Letters in German-speaking Switzerland are always shorter than in French-speaking Switzerland. Education may also play a role. The Swedish are taught to be brief in essays while the French are taught to expand on a subject. Brevity in written communication can be related to temperament. The Greeks think that the more they write, the better their chances are of creating a favorable impression. A different approach to logic can also be a factor. The Germans are critical of the French for synthesizing information too much and for being too concise.

Another dimension of the various forms of communication in Europe resides in the notion of implicit and explicit communication, which, as we have just seen, can change the length and the approach of a document. If the French and the Germans diverge on this point, it is because the Germans like a simple, unequivocal, clear and limpid mode of expression while the French prefer a mode of expression that is more subtle and suggestive. Germans need concrete and factual information that leaves no room for ambiguity or interpretation. They expect to be furnished with an exhaustive summary of all the information necessary for them to make a decision. This working method leads them to produce reports that the French consider far too long and to adopt a didactic tone, which the French resent. According to researchers, the British, the Spanish, the Italians and the Irish have modes of implicit communication, while the Scandinavians, the Dutch, the Germans and the Belgians have modes of explicit communication.

One consequence of differing modes of communication revolves around clarity. In light of what has already been described, it is not unexpected that German executives find their French colleagues imprecise. All things being equal, French executives feel a similar vagueness in British and Swedish executives, but for different reasons. This impression comes from the fact that the British and Swedish allow more room for individual initiative. Thus the French have the perception that the British are not straightforward. Similarly, they find that Swedish executives lack precision in their manner of delegating authority because they give their subordinates a great deal of freedom. The precision and clarity that French managers generally demand leaves less room for initiative, which explains why they consider the Swedish management style a little vague.

Clarity also depends on preferences for certain types of logic. Countries that prefer inductive logic include Great Britain, Denmark and the Netherlands. On the other hand, deductive logic is the basis of new forms of rhetoric in Germany, Italy, Spain, Belgium, Portugal and France. Another characteristic linked to different forms of communication in Europe is formality, which is manifested through the use of titles, first names and the formal form of the pronoun "you" when linguistically possible. Among those European countries whose communication is formal are Italy, Portugal, Germany and Austria. Among the less formal are Ireland, Luxembourg, Switzerland and the Scandinavian countries.

The Germans have a strong need for recognition, consideration and respect. The symbols of power count a great deal for them. Titles, the size of an office or a company car and the location of parking places are important symbols. At the workplace, the formal "you" form is used. Rarely are individuals called by their first names, and titles are routinely used. Formality is *de rigueur* in professional relationships even if all Germans call themselves "colleague" whatever their level in the hierarchy. The same formality is found in Austria and while behaviors are friendly, they are nevertheless distant. The Austrians insist even more on the use of titles, and they invariably use the formal "you" form in the workplace.

The Italians mark hierarchical distances by using the formal "you" form and by not using first names. The senior members of the company feel the need to be protected by their titles, which are often somewhat inflated. *Dottore, ingegnere, avvocato, commendatore* or *professore* rarely represent a university degree, but reflect social status and recognition among Italian executives. These titles are supposed to flatter these executives more for their general knowledge and culture than for their job competence. As for the Portuguese, they rarely use the informal "you" form, unlike the Spanish. Everywhere the title of doctor implies status and respect.

In the Netherlands the situation is ambiguous because while colleagues call one another by their first names and relationships are friendly, the culture is not any less formal. Titles are always written before names. Relationships are less formal in Swedish companies because they are supposed to be egalitarian, which is recognized in the use of the informal "you" form. This practice was imposed twenty years ago by government decree, but it is now being called into question by the Swedish bourgeoisie. The barriers set up by secretaries are easily overcome. The CEO of Electrolux answers his own phone, and many people have the number of his direct line. Generally, the Swedes are not attached to titles. In Ireland communication is particularly informal since the use of the first name is almost immediate. In general, relationships are more informal than in Britain and titles are infrequently used.

The last relevant dimension of communication is the tone of interpersonal communication in different European countries. In this area the Spanish and the Nordics can easily be contrasted. The Nordics are very humanist in their culture. They have a great respect for human beings and avoid criticizing colleagues. For this reason, even the term "evaluation" is handled carefully because it can imply a personal attack. Conversely, the Spanish, like the Italians—particularly the Romans and Neapolitans—can be noisy and scathing in their criticism of others. They can appear rough, aggressive, violent and bellicose. In other respects, the same forms of humor are shared by the British, the Irish, the Danish and to a lesser extent the Dutch.

Communication can also be seen as a management tool. Austrians, for example, tend to value the qualities of human resource management more than their German neighbors. For the Austrians, natural leadership is valued more than authority. The situation is different in Sweden, Denmark and the Netherlands. In a country of informality and egalitarian traditions like the Netherlands, human resources must be managed well because hierarchical differences are slight and it is difficult to dismiss employees. The ability to lead employees by communicating and by using qualities such as charisma, force of conviction and persuasion are, therefore, valued in executives. In Denmark, an aptitude for cooperation, delegation of authority and supervision of employee decisions requires a solid personality. In Sweden the same qualities are crucial for executives because they must adapt to the complex labor conditions of their country.

The Europeans have thus built national reputations on which employment recruiters rely. The British have a good reputation for internal communication and management of human resources; they are much sought after for personnel positions. In multicultural teams, British executives are often the leaders who coordinate group efforts or who provide a link between the group and the surrounding environment. The Irish also have a reputation for getting along well with others and for being adaptable to other cultures and other modes of thought. Significantly, they succeed well in multiracial environments, for example with Moslems and Africans.

The Austrians also have a good reputation in the area of human relations management. Because they communicate a great deal, Austrian executives are excellent salespeople and do well in situations where customer contact is required. On the other hand, German executives have the opposite reputation because interpersonal relations are not as well managed in Germany. The personality and the popularity of a leader leave them cold. They are not impressed by charisma because they themselves are generally not good communicators.

MANAGEMENT STYLES

Let us now turn to management styles in Europe. Their variety can indeed constitute a communication problem between head offices and subsidiaries. The first relevant managerial dimension in communication is the degree to which employees participate in the management of a company. Hierarchical distance can affect not only the degree of formality in a company but the whole system of internal communication. In this area, the countries of northern Europe are distinguished from those of southern Europe, in which hierarchical distances are greater because authority is more centralized and management more autocratic.

The Greeks, for example, have a deep respect for hierarchy. Management in traditional Greek family businesses is conservative and paternalistic, and power is delegated only to a small degree. The Belgians also give much importance to organization charts. In Italy the big, older companies are the most traditional; among them are the banks and insurance companies, in which management is particularly bureaucratic and centralized. In Spain there is employee involvement and participation in the management of a company. This type of monarchical company management is characterized by a very large salary scale, a big distance separating managerial staff from employees, and little weight given during training to motivation and initiative. Portuguese managers are little inclined to teamwork. Their culture inclines them to hoarding information, secrets and power and to respecting distances and hierarchy.

At the other end of the spectrum are the northern European countries, such as Germany, Sweden, Denmark and the Netherlands. The German model is often cited when co-management or co-determination are involved. The management style is democratic and participatory. Not only are employees consulted, but decision making is frequently collective, based on the model of "industrial democracy." Collegiality prevails at every level, and a decision from the top obtained without consensus is not considered legitimate.

Swedish management style is decentralized and democratic. Company organization charts have a generally horizontal structure. There are three times fewer hierarchical levels than in France, and therefore the distances between individuals are smaller. Information is not withheld, because the duty to inform is a basic accepted fact and is prescribed by Swedish law, which stipulates that all important decisions be discussed with employee representatives and negotiated with the unions. All parties affected by a decision must be consulted and all ramifications of a decision must be openly debated before it is finalized. By expressing themselves, employees imply that they understand and support company goals. They have a participatory role to the extent that they adopt the goals of a company. A company head is in direct contact with his employees and remains very available for dialogue.

In Denmark, managerial values are also based on a democratic and egalitarian system. Organization charts are very flat and hierarchical distances between individuals are not very great. Thus, the management style is cooperative and participatory. Orders can be questioned and counterproposals made. Consequently, a Danish employee may sometimes find it difficult to accept decisions from above, or to exercise authority over subordinates. In Danish culture the notion of responsibility is so internalized that Danish managers react very poorly if they are not trusted. By the same token, they do not seek to control too closely the activities of the staff, to whom they grant the same trust they demand for themselves.

An approach midway between these two is found in Great Britain, which has adopted a consultative, bottom-up style of decision making. Consulting subordinates is at the discretion of the department head, who is entirely responsible for the ultimate decision, but most problems are resolved by negotiation. Finally, there are peculiarities in certain countries such as Ireland, Austria and Switzerland. In Ireland the prevailing management style is more presidential than consensual and, therefore, not very participatory. Middle management opinions are taken into account, but in the end it is the company head who makes the final decision and imposes it.

Austria is a special case. Being state-owned, the largest companies have a bureaucratic and hierarchical style, which, in Germany, would be clearly more participatory. The whole public sector is autocratic while in the private sector different forms of management are encountered depending on the size and activities of the companies involved. Managers generally have little initiative, and autonomy in decision making is not viewed with favor.

Switzerland is an exception in northern Europe to the extent that traditionally Swiss managers run companies in an authoritarian manner based on a model inherited from the army. Even today Swiss managerial culture is imbued with military-style management in which notions of hierarchy and order are still valid. Today this management model is changing. Crédit Suisse, for example, in 1991 put in place a less hierarchical system with a flatter organization.

Generally speaking, the more traditional institutions such as banks and insurance companies and medium-sized firms are the most autocratic in their approach, while consulting firms and service companies generally have a more consensual decision-making system and participatory management styles. The tendency everywhere in Europe is toward dialogue, involvement and sharing. The most exceptional situation is in Luxembourg. There, all kinds of management styles mix harmoniously, depending on the nationality of the company. The Luxembourg style itself is difficult to define. In medium-sized companies it is generally autocratic and contrasts strongly with the German co-management style found in the big industrial companies such as Arbed or the banks. After the steel industry crisis, Arbed went from 29,000 employees to 9,000 without a single layoff or losing a day to strikes. This approach, later called the "Luxembourg model," has been the basis for very advanced labor policies and legislation in other countries.

Another important dimension in managerial communication is the degree of innovation by company managements in a given country. While participation has an impact on internal communication, innovation has an impact on external communication. Innovation can take various forms. For example it is possible to be inventive, creative and technically sophisticated like the French, or technically innovative and recognized for design like the Swedish. Others like the Portuguese demonstrate their creativity and flexibility in the manner in which they commit themselves to a project. Because of their cultural heritage, Austrians adapt and adjust well to situations and people. Likewise, the Greeks, who are naturally positive and optimistic, enjoy the opportunity to be creative and are willing entrepreneurs. The Greeks are quick, shrewd and overflowing with imagination and resources; they have a reputation for being flexible and adapting to situations quickly.

But the prize in Europe for inventiveness, creativity and business aptitude certainly goes to the Italians. Their remarkable adaptability and talent for compromise have even given them the reputation of chameleons. The Italians appreciate people who have ideas and who innovate, because they themselves are without any particular prejudices and are open to everything new. They are naturally curious and inventive and have a very sophisticated business sense. This entrepreneurship, Italian-style, has been exported and is the hallmark of Italian success abroad, the Benetton phenomenon being an example.

A third managerial dimension that has an impact on communication is attitude toward risk, which is related both to qualities of interpersonal relationships—trust, for example—and to preference for written or oral communication. Among Europeans averse to risk are the Swiss, whose caution is legendary, and the Germans, whose attachment to rules and details denotes a strong control of uncertainty and the desire to attenuate the unpredictable. Belgians, especially those of Flemish origin, do not like risk either. It is interesting

to note that the typical Belgian manager is not an entrepreneur, probably because he is afraid of complications or failure. This major difference separates
these Europeans from the Italians, the Greeks and the Austrians, who like to
innovate, but who paradoxically have a timid attitude toward risk. Among Europeans, the managers most at ease with risk and uncertainty are the British.

The value placed on performance in different European countries has a
strong impact on the style and content of corporate presentations. Among Europeans the Germans, the Swedish, the Danish and the British are focused on
performance, objectives and final results. The Swiss, notably the German
speakers, tend to reward the efforts of each employee at intermediate steps of
a project. The Swedish value goals that are not necessarily financial. The Danish, who in this respect are closer to American managerial values, have always
been much quicker to dismiss unproductive personnel. As for the British they
value operational skills, productivity and knowledge about managing profit centers. In these preferences they are close to traditional American management
styles. Other countries have not yet integrated performance into their value
system. In Greece executives are little concerned with decision making per se
and are rarely results oriented. Similarly in Portugal, setting goals and sticking
to them appears to present difficulties. Often long meetings are held without an
agenda and the tendency to dissipate effort is strong. Finally other countries,
such as Italy and Ireland, have recently incorporated the importance of objectives into their value systems.

Yet another dimension concerns the respective roles of the individual and
the group. According to Hofstede's well-known scales of measurement, certain
Europeans are more individualistic than others. This is the case for the French,
the English, the Italians and the Belgians. Others, like the Greeks, the Dutch,
the Swedish and the Germans, are more closely connected to the family or to
other social groups. The Greeks, for example, are individualists only in appearance. They have little tolerance for nonconformist behavior and are very dependent on the group. The Dutch like to gather together in large groups, which
makes them gregarious and noisy in French eyes. The Germans above all are
motivated by the group. They have a great respect for the community interest.
They favor collective success more than individual success and display solidarity among themselves against foreign competitors.

In sum, the managerial characteristics of different European countries stem
from their culture, but also from individual resources connected to their geographical situation. Production is dominant in Germany and Belgium, and technology is important in Germany, Denmark, Sweden, France and Ireland. The
ability to sell and to negotiate is prevalent among the English, the Danish, the
Dutch, the Greeks and the Austrians. Marketing is particularly developed in
Italy, Denmark, the Netherlands and France. The management of human resources, as we have seen, is better among the English, the Danish, the Dutch,
the Swedish and the Austrians. Other countries have developed specific skills
in the fields of finance, accounting or insurance (Great Britain, Luxembourg,

Ireland and Switzerland), and still others (in particular Great Britain, which, in this respect, is very similar to the United States) have produced very skilled lawyers who are much in demand in Italy, Portugal and Greece.

TECHNOLOGIES, CULTURES AND COMMUNICATION

In this last section, culture and communication are linked to one of the main themes of this book: technologies. Does culture influence the choice of available technologies of communication and do such choices affect modes of communication in different European countries?

Research has produced a number of relevant observations. Here are a few of them. In Italy, face-to-face communication is so much an integral part of conducting business that, even in technology-conscious Milan, financiers have difficulty becoming accustomed to telematics. In the Nordic countries it is the old debate over nature versus culture that explains an initial skepticism about technologies. Northern Europeans often demonstrate much distrust for new forms of technology, but use them extensively nevertheless. They are very advanced in all forms of robotics technology, while the French have the opposite attitude. Although they are fascinated by modernity, they use technology in a restrained fashion and sometimes are reluctant to spend the money to install it.

In Portugal, a strong attraction to computer equipment, parabolic antennas and satellites is immediately apparent. Similarly in Spain, observers note that high technology, telecommunications and computer equipment are widely used in public relations. Against all expectations, the economic split between northern and southern Europe does not seem to apply.

While superficial observation may suggest that culture can have an impact on choices, research indicates that it is more often supply that dictates demand. In monopoly situations in particular, the demand for technologies in European countries is, in general, strongly influenced by the supply of products and services. In each country, the supply of leading technologies depends on several factors: the deliberate policies of governments, the acceptance of large temporary financial deficits, the economic and technological leads of the country, the adaptation of strategies to the general public, the presence of particular situations such as pricing structures, government regulations, monopolies in telecommunications and so on.

Consequently, the supply of state-of-the-art technology varies from country to country. Great Britain is very advanced in the high-technology fields of computers, office and telephone equipment, mobile telephones, fax machines and image processing equipment. Demand for new technologies is high in the areas of mobile radiotelephones (unlike France and Germany), in satellite radio message services and multi-image processing. Among Europeans, the British make extensive use of corporate magazines, corporate videos, video news releases and videoconferences in their communication.

The Germans have a lead in computer, telephone and satellite equipment and display a capacity to adapt rapidly to new technologies, for example in electronic communication (telematics and internal message services), in videoconferencing and multi-image processing. However, when they communicate, the Germans use many corporate magazines, few corporate videos and relatively few videoconferences. The French are advanced in computer technology and telephones, but much less so in radiotelephones. Their national glory is to have succeeded in imposing Minitel nationwide. They use many press releases and notice boards; their frequency of use of corporate videos is about average. On the other hand, they use little videoconferencing and few corporate magazines.

This comparison of the three European countries with the largest communication budgets (France, Germany and Great Britain) shows not only the differences but also the parallels that exist between the technological advancement of a country, its capacity to adopt new technologies and the degree to which it makes use of existing technologies.

Remaining to be studied in greater depth are the links between technology and culture, first of all by distinguishing between those cultures favoring technological advances and those less predisposed to do so. Is it possible to claim that the cultural traits of rigor and rationalism incline the Germans naturally toward high technology, just as much as the Cartesianism and creativity of the French? Or that, unlike the Swiss, the Dutch and the Germans, the liking for risk has led the British to develop their videotex? Or that a French preference for centralized decisions has allowed the Minitel to come into existence, or that the French also like desktop publishing, which satisfies their desire for creativity? Or again, that the weight of written communication in Germany has hindered the development of office equipment?

In sum, two challenges emerge from this interaction between culture and technology. The first is an increased search for information in real time, which imposes new rhythms on users. As we have seen, the capacity of individuals to adapt to change and different conceptions of time varies from culture to culture. It may be observed that the most reactive and flexible countries are technologically the least developed. It could be argued that those countries with the least linear conception of time are likely to have a greater capacity to adapt to work in real time, but different levels of economic development would make it difficult to verify such a hypothesis. The second challenge is that electronic communication is blurring the lines that exist between professional life and private life. Those cultures that are comfortable with real time are also those that adapt more easily to flexible working hours. The Nordics, the Germans, the Dutch and even the Anglo-Saxons, who go home relatively early, will suffer more from this development. The interactivity and immediacy of the machine will place new demands on managers. Just how the different cultures of Europe will cope with these and other challenges outlined in this chapter will continue to be a fertile area of research well into the next century. In many respects, the analysis of the trends and behaviors emerging from the European experience may be of value to other regions of the world as they seek to come to terms with the implications of profound technological change.

REFERENCES

Annandale-Massa, D., & Bertrand, H. (1990). *La gestion des ressources humaines dans les banques européennes: Quelles stratégies?* Paris: Economica.

APEC. (1989a). *Le marché des cadres dans l'Europe de 1992.* Paris: APEC.

APEC. (1989b). *Panel Europe: L'emploi des cadres en Europe, résultats 1989 et tendances 1990, 2nd and subsequent annual editions.* Paris: APEC.

Aru, A., & Tasso, F. (1989). *Organizzazione e risorse umane.* Milan: Gruppo editoriale Jackson.

Avenel, M. (1990). *Des managers et des cadres prêts pour l'Europe de 1993.* Paris: EME.

Benayoun, J., et al. (1990). *Les ressources humaines en Europe, Excel (guide européen du recrutement et des formations d'exellence).* Paris: HCE/HCA.

Benito Alas, C. (1987). *Como ser elegido en una seleccion de personal* (2nd ed.). Madrid: Iberico Europea de Ediciones.

Besseyre des Horts, C. H. (1989, June). *Le management des ressources humaines en Europe: L'ère de la diversité.* Paris: Liaisons Sociales.

Bollinger, D., & Hofstede, G. (1987). *Les différences culturelles dans le management.* Paris: Les Editions d'Organisation.

Bournois, F. (1991). *La gestion des cadres en Europe.* Paris: Eyrolles.

British Chamber of Commerce. (1990). *Europe: Trade & Investment Services 1990.* London: Caversham Press.

Cacace, N. (1990). *Professione Europa: I nuovi mestieri del mercato unico.* Milan: Franco Angeli Libri.

Camilleri, C., & Cohen, E. (1989). *Chocs des cultures: Concepts et enjeux pratiques de l'interculturel.* Paris: Harmattan.

Cazal, D., Quicandon, F., & Peretti, J. M. (1992). *L'Europe des ressources humaines.* Paris: Liaisons Sociales.

Cherns, A. (1982). Culture and values: The reciprocal influence between applied social science and its cultural and historical context. In N. Nicholson & T. D. Wall (Eds.), *The theory and practice of organizational psychology.* London: Academic Press.

Commission des Communautés Européenes. (1989, August). *L'emploi en Europe.* Brussels: ECC.

Comoy, P. (1990, February). Etre euromanager, c'est une affaire de culture. *Revue Européenne des Ressources Humaines, 1,* 3. Paris: Egor.

Evans, P. (1989). Organizational development in the transnational enterprise. In R. Woodman & W. Pasmore (Eds.), *Research in organizational change and development.* Vol. 3. New York: Jai Press.

Evans, P., Doz Y., & Laurent, A. (Eds.). (1990). *Human resource management in international firms: Change, globalization, innovation.* London: Macmillan.

Evans, P., Lank, E., & Been-Farquhar, A. (1989, September). Managing human resources in the international firm: Lessons from practice. In P. Evans, Y. Doz, & A. Laurent (Eds.), *Human resource management in international firms: Change, globalization, innovation.* London: Macmillan.

Fondation Europe et Société. (1990, May). Libre circulation des salariés: Conséquences individuelles et collectives. *Les Cahiers de la Fondation*. Paris: Fondation Europe et Société.

Forse, M. (1990, January). Convergences et diversités des sociétés européennes occidentales. *Revue de l'O.F.C.E, 30*.

Frey, H. (1989). *Handbuch personal-beschaffung*. Munich: Kompaktwissen.

Friedrich, H. (1989). *Lebenslauf und bewerbung*. Munich: Falken-Verlag.

Gandillot, T., & Kamm, T. (1990). *Mille jours pour réussir l'Europe*. Paris: JC Lattès.

Gauthey, F., Ratiu, I., Rodgers, I., & Xardel, D. (1988). *Leaders sans frontières*. Paris: McGraw-Hill.

Gauthey, F., & Xardel, D. (1990). *Management interculturel*. Paris: Economica.

Gruère, J. P., & Morel, P. (1990, October). *Cadres français et communications interculturelles*. Paris: Eyrolles.

Gudykunst, W. B., Ting-Toomey, S., & Chua, E. (1988). *Culture and interpersonal communication*. London: Sage.

Hall, E. T., & Hall, M. (1984). *Les différences cachées: Comment communiquer avec les Allemands*. Paris: Editions Stern.

Hall, E. T., & Hall, M. (1990). *Understanding cultural differences: Keys to success in West Germany, France and the United States*. New York: Intercultural Press.

Handy, C., Gordon, C., Gow, I., & Randlesome, C. (1988). *The Handy report: Making managers*. London: Pitman.

Herriot, P. (1989). *Recruitment in the 90s*. London: Institute of Personnel Management.

Hofstede, G. (1984). *Culture's consequences*. London: Sage.

Hofstede, G. (1987, September–October). Relativité culturelle des pratiques et théories de l'organisation. *Revue Française de Gestion*, pp. 10–21. Paris.

Institut de Gestion Sociale. (1990). *L'Europe sociale de 1993*. Paris: Institut de Gestion Sociale.

d'Iribarne, P. (1989). *La logique de l'honneur*. Paris: Seuil.

Jones, R. (1990, September). Integrating selection in a merged company. *Personnel Management*. London.

JPB. (1989, August). Syntonie: L'art de se mettre sur la même longueur d'onde. *La synergie franco-allemande*. Paris: JPB.

JPB. (1989, November). Enquête sur les relations maisons-mères/filiales franco-allemandes. *La synergie franco-allemande*. Paris: JPB.

Korn, L. (1989). *The success profile*. New York: Simon and Schuster.

KPMG. (1990). *La gestion des ressources humaines en Europe*. Paris: KPMG.

Ladmiral, J. R., & Lipiansky, E. M. (1989). *La communication interculturelle*. Paris: Armand Colin.

Lloyd, I. (1990, July). Recrutement européen: Les points essentiels. *Revue Européenne des Ressources Humaines, 2, 7*. Paris: Egor.

Payer, L. (1989). *Medicine and culture*. London: Penguin.

Peretti, J. M., Cazal, D., & Quicandon, F. (1990). *Vers le management international des ressources humaines*. Paris: Editions Liaisons.

Price Waterhouse. (1990). *The Price Waterhouse Cranfield Project*. Lyon: Observatoire International de Gestion des Ressources Humaines.

Raban, A. J. (1988). *Working in the European Communities*. Cambridge, England: CRAC.

Schnapper, D., & Mendras, H. (1990). *Six manières d'être européen*. Paris: Gallimard.

STRATHOM. (1990, April). L'Europe sociale: Quelles implications pour l'entreprise? Le marché du travail européen: Nouveau contexte et conséquences opérationnelles. Paris: Institut d'Etudes Politiques.

Taddei, D., et al. (1991). *Les enjeux de l'Europe sociale*. Paris: La Découverte.

Taillieu, T., & Mooren, H. (1990). International career orientations of young European graduates: A survey of opinions and aspirations. Tilburg: Tilburg University.

Thurley, K., & Wirdenhuis, H. (1991). *Vers un management multiculturel en Europe*. Paris: Les Editions d'Organisation.

Tixier, M. (1989). *Votre CV en Anglais* (2nd ed.). Paris: Longman France.

Tixier, M. (1992). *Travailler en Europe: Mobilité, recrutement, culture*. Paris: Editions Liaisons.

Torrington, D., & Hall, L. (1987). *Personnel Management: A new approach*. London: Prentice-Hall International.

Vidal, Y. (1991). *Cadres sans frontières: Gestion internationale des ressources humaines*. Paris: Editions ESF.

Whitehead Mann, Ltd. (1989, November). *Research report: The European manager* (presented by Chris Friend Research and Ian Butcher). London: Whitehead Mann.

Part III

POLICY AND SOCIAL OUTCOMES

New Directions in Communication Research from a Japanese Perspective

Youichi Ito

INTRODUCTION

What I have been doing through my research activities in the past is to check the validity of Western social theories based on Japanese or East Asian experiences and to create social theories based on Japanese or East Asian concepts and experiences. My academic interest tends to be provoked when widely accepted Western theories were found to contradict Japanese or East Asian experiences and when some social phenomena were found to be better explained by Japanese or East Asian concepts and ideas. I have been consistent in this sense but not necessarily consistent in subject matters I cover. I may cover mass media effects, political communication, social and cultural impact of communication technologies, international communication, or development communication, but what I am doing is always the same.

This chapter covers the following three areas: (1) mass media effects, (2) international information flows and (3) development and communication. I would like to discuss what kind of problems I see in Western social theories in view of Japanese or East Asian experiences and what kind of Japanese or East Asian ideas may contribute to the solution of those problems.

MASS MEDIA EFFECTS

Joho kohdo Model

As described in my article in *Communication Yearbook 10* (Ito, 1987), what I called the "environmentalist approach" has had particularly strong influence on Japanese communication research. This approach has a root in Walter Lipp-mann's *Public Opinion* (Lippmann, 1922). Lippmann's original ideas were suc-ceeded and developed in many Western communication studies such as Lang and Lang (1960, 1968), Katz (1980), Katz, Dayan, and Motyl (1981), and so on, but they also achieved unique development in the Japanese social and cultural settings.

According to this approach, individuals adapt to their information environ-ment, which is dominated by the mass media. The information environment dominated by the mass media was described by such terms as "pseudo environ-ment" (Fujitake, 1968) or "the world of copies" (Shimizu, 1951). Combined with the "mass society theories" (for example, Mills, 1956) and the Marxist view of mass communications, this approach played in Japan a role similar to the "bullet theories" or "hypodermic theories" in the United States.

Under the influence of a more conservative intellectual movement, called the "information society fad," in the late 1960s and early 1970s (Ito, 1981, 1991), however, some scholars began to emphasize strong autonomy of individuals in their "information environment" (Kitamura, 1970; Kato, 1972; Nakano, 1980). According to those scholars, individuals are not simply and blindly re-ceiving information from an information environment dominated by the mass media. They claimed that individuals were not only selective in receiving infor-mation but were also extracting meaning out of their information environment. According to them, the individual extracts information not only from obvious information flows but even from physical entities such as industrial products. It is true that if we see the sky in the west and predict that it will rain tomor-row, we are extracting information from the sky in the west.

In May 1990, I was invited to a conference held in the suburbs of Warsaw, Poland. I tackled the question "Why were the mass media in many socialist countries powerless in maintaining the socialist regime?" Many conventional theories on mass media effects, especially "powerful media theories," could not explain the collapse of socialist regimes. If the mass media controlled or manipulated by the government had powerful effects, socialist regimes should not have collapsed. Then how can the collapse of socialist regimes be ex-plained?

The *joho kohdo,* or information behavior approach, was helpful to answer this question. According to the information behavior model, people receive information not only from the mass media but also from all kinds of non–mass media channels. People extract information from library research, the color of the sky or the quality of foreign products. Let us compare information we receive from television and the information we extract from our library research or from the quality of foreign products. Mass media experts have traditionally overestimated information we receive from television and underestimated infor-mation that we directly extract from our environment and experiences. The relationship between information *transmitted* from mass media and information *extracted* from direct environment and experiences is shown in Figure 8.1.

Figure 8.1
Joho Kohdo **Model**

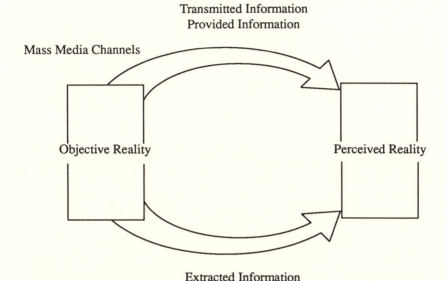

Transmitted Information
Provided Information

Mass Media Channels

Objective Reality   Perceived Reality

Extracted Information

A major reason why mass communication experts have traditionally ignored information flows through non–mass media channels is because the amount of information flows through mass media channels overwhelms the amount of information flows through non–mass media channels. To what extent, however, is the amount of information important in the light of effect?

The relationship between effect, credibility and quantity can be expressed by the following formula: $Effect = Credibility \times Quantity$.

If information *transmitted* from the mass media is congruent with information *extracted* from one's direct environment and experiences, the mass media can maintain credibility. If, however, transmitted information and extracted information are always incongruent, the mass media lose credibility. In other words, people use information extracted from their direct environment as litmus paper to test the credibility of the mass media. The mass media with low credibility does not have much influence, as is obvious from the formula above. The mass media's inability to stop the collapse of socialist regimes can be explained in this way.

Tripolar Model

This section deals with another model on mass media effects developed in Japan. Many academic studies conducted after World War II confirm that the Japanese press has heavy responsibility for the political process in Japan in the 1930s. Even Japanese journalists and executives of newspaper companies admit

Figure 8.2
Political Process in Japan in the 1930s

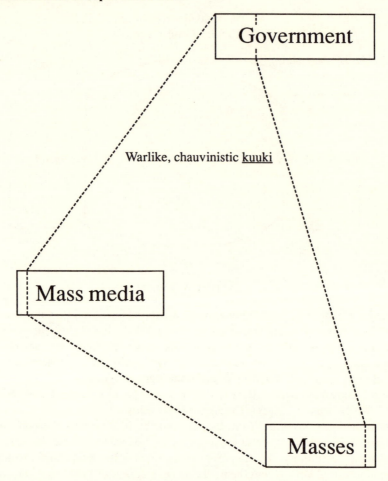

this fact. For example, Seiryu Hata, chief editor of the *Asahi Shimbun,* wrote in 1987 that "the responsibility of Japanese newspapers for the last war is the second heaviest after the government" ("Senso to shimbun," 1987). How did this happen?

In 1904 a war broke out between Japan and Russia, and Japanese newspapers had unique experiences immediately before and during that war. At that time, the Japanese press was divided between proponents and opponents of the war. The newspapers carrying chauvinistic articles increased circulation and those carrying antiwar articles suffered decrease of circulation. As a result, many newspapers changed their positions from antiwar to prowar, and some journalists left or were forced to leave their companies. Some newspaper companies that stuck to antiwar positions drastically lost circulation and went bankrupt after the war. Ruiko Kuroiwa, a famous journalist and a top executive of a newspaper that changed its position from antiwar to prowar, made the famous remark that ''newspapers should be chauvinistic during the war time and anti-government during the peace time.''

Japanese journalists and newspaper company executives remembered this experience when the Manchurian Incident erupted in 1931. Major Japanese newspapers at that time carried extremely chauvinistic articles to increase circulation. Circulations certainly increased, and the public was excited and pleased. A chauvinistic *kuuki* (a Japanese-Chinese-Korean concept to mean air, atmosphere or climate of opinion)[1] was created. This *kuuki,* however, made it extremely difficult for the civilian government at that time to control arbitrary military actions outside Japan by the Japanese military. Furthermore, based on the chauvinistic *kuuki* in the mass media and among the public, the Japanese government was gradually taken over by genuine chauvinists, that is, military generals. Japanese newspapers realized the danger in the late 1930s and tried to change the *kuuki,* but it was too late. They were oppressed by the militaristic government and could not change the chauvinistic *kuuki* that they themselves created. Figure 8.2 shows the political process in Japan in the 1930s.

A problem with Figure 8.2 is that we do not have public opinion data regarding the size of the public that was responsible for the creation and maintenance of the chauvinistic *kuuki* in the 1930s. It is also technically difficult to collect and content analyze major Japanese newspapers from the 1930s. It is, therefore, difficult to prove the existence of the political process that I have just mentioned in a scientifically rigorous way.

Figures 8.3 and 8.4 indicate how the *kuuki* developed in the case of the amendment of the Consumption Tax Law in 1989 and the withdrawal of the United Nations Peace Cooperation Bill in 1990. In this tripolar model, the mass media are considered to be effective only when they are a part of the majority *kuuki* consisting of government policies, public attitudes and the mass media themselves. Each of the three boxes represents 100 percent. The dividing line in these boxes was drawn based on the data obtained from public opinion surveys, content analyses of the mass media or questionnaire surveys of Parliament members. (For further discussion see Ito, in press a.)

These case studies, based on what I call a ''tripolar model'' of social consensus formation, indicate that it is too simplistic to claim that the government always dominates and manipulates the mass media or that the mass media always have powerful effects. Mass media effects differ from one case to another. The mass media have effects only when they stand on the majority side or the mainstream in the tripolar relationship among the mass media, the government and the masses and when they create and support the *kuuki* that functions as a social pressure on minorities to comply.

In cases in which the government and the masses agree with each other and

Figure 8.3
Anti-consumption Tax *Kuuki*

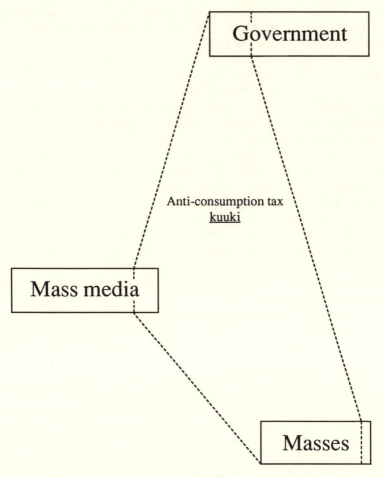

the mass media are isolated, the mass media do not have any effect on social consensus formation. Not only that, but under such circumstances, the mass media are likely to change in the long run under the pressure of the *kuuki* created and supported the government and the public. Such cases will be further studied in my future research. Changes in the mass media can never be predicted by conventional bipolar models of mass media effects. It can be predicted only by multipolar models, such as the tripolar model discussed here.

INTERNATIONAL INFORMATION FLOWS

Unbalanced flows of information among nations cause political and cultural problems. During the 1960s and 1970s, when the demands for drastic change

Figure 8.4
Anti–United Nations Cooperation Bill *Kuuki*

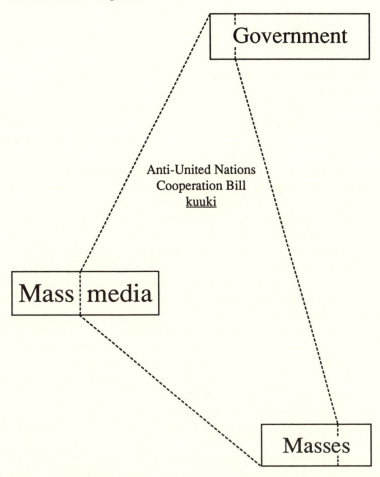

of the existing world information order (the "New World Information Order," or NWIO) were stressed, empirical studies were conducted on the causes of unbalanced flows. These studies revealed that the factors determining the direction and volume of international information flows differed from one medium to another. The factors accounting for the international flows of news, for example, are different from those accounting for the flows of television programs.

Furthermore, it was revealed that there were "static factors" and "dynamic factors." Static factors include geographical distance, common language, cultural similarity and so on; dynamic factors include military, political and economic strength and the degree of influence on other countries.

In a recent article (Ito, 1990b), I described why and how Japan changed from an information importer to an information exporter during the twenty years between 1965 and 1985. The pattern of news flows from and to Japan in the 1960s was similar to that of many Third World countries at present. The pattern, however, gradually changed in the 1970s, and in a survey conducted in the early 1980s, there were only three countries in the world where mass media coverage about Japan was less than Japanese mass media coverage about them: the United States, the Soviet Union and China. Japanese experiences indicate that there is high correlation between the pattern of news flows and the country's economic strength and political influence.

Similar arguments are possible regarding the international flows of popular culture. In a survey conducted in the early 1970s, the import and export of television programs in Japan were balanced. In a survey conducted in the early 1980s, however, the amount of export doubled whereas the amount of import remained about the same as in the early 1970s. The export amount of television programs and other popular cultural products seems to be highly correlated with the scale of the industry. If the scale of the industry is large, it can produce high-quality popular cultural products at a low cost, and those products can be highly competitive in the international market.

The scale of industry also affects international flows of investment. The Japanese electronics industry began to invest heavily in Hollywood in 1989. The total amount of investment exceeded $10 billion, which is about the same as Japan's financial contribution to the Persian Gulf War in 1990, South Korea's annual defense budget or about half of the financial aid that G-7 countries are planning to provide Russia. As a result, two of the seven major film companies in Hollywood (Columbia Pictures and Universal Pictures) were completely purchased by Japanese electronics companies (Sony and Matsushita), and two others (Time Warner and Walt Disney Productions) accepted heavy Japanese investment (by Toshiba, Ito Chu and others).

According to a recent newspaper article, five Japanese electronics companies—Sony, Matsushita, Pioneer, Toshiba and Sanyo—reached an agreement to cooperate in the production of laser disc software programs for high definition television. According to this agreement, American film companies in which these companies invested are to produce those software programs. Under this arrangement, Japanese electronics companies are to profit from selling high definition television sets and American film companies are to profit from providing software programs for Japanese high definition television sets. Since the United States does not have immediate plans to develop their own high definition television, this arrangement is mutually beneficial, but this kind of arrangement will threaten Europeans who are now developing their own high definition television technology.

Ten years ago, nobody anticipated that the Japanese electronics industry would dominate Hollywood and use American film companies to sell their new generation of television sets. Jeremy Tunstall, the author of *The Media Are American* (1977), now says that he is writing a book entitled *The Media Are No Longer American*.

What I want to emphasize based on Japanese experiences regarding this subject is that everything changes and everything is only relative. This world can be better described as the "world competitive system" than as the "world capitalist system." Where there is competition, anything can happen. Until the midnineteenth century, Japan was a small, poor, agricultural, feudalistic and peripheral country. By the 1930s, however, it emerged as an imperialistic military power, colonizing Taiwan, Korea and Manchuria. Then, as a result of World War II, it lost everything; it reemerged as a major economic power in the 1970s. Living in a country such as this, we cannot believe any social theory that tends to regard the world order as static. In our view, the world order is extremely changeable. The periphery may become the center through effort and the center may drop to the periphery due to lack of effort. Information-importing countries may become information-exporting countries and information-exporting countries may become information-importing countries. Discussions about "cultural imperialism," "media imperialism" or the "New World Information Order" should take this fluidity and changeability into consideration.

There are, however, a few areas where competition does not function effectively. Language and international political influence based on language is an example. As I have discussed elsewhere (Ito, 1992, p. 29), the number of people studying the Japanese language outside Japan is steadily increasing. However, since the absolute number of non-Japanese who can handle the Japanese language is so small compared with major Western languages, it is unlikely that Japan can affect the "world language order" as it has the world military or economic order. From the Japanese perspective, therefore, the world language order seems far more stable and less changeable than the world military or economic order.

Countries like the United Kingdom, the United States and France profit a great deal from the fact that their languages are used in many foreign countries. First, they have a stronger influence on international organizations, including the United Nations. Countries like the United States, the United Kingdom and France dominate and effectively control international organizations partly because they can conduct those operations by their mother tongues. Despite their countries' economic strength, Japanese and German political leaders and diplomats cannot function as effectively as their American, British and French counterparts in the arena of international politics.

A second advantage lies in the international propaganda competition. The annual budget of the Japanese Kyodo News Agency in 1992 was about $306 million, which was only a little less than that of Associated Press ($329 million in 1991). Although Kyodo's annual budget was only a little more than one-tenth of that of Reuters (about $2.820 billion in 1991), it was estimated to be more than twice that of Agence France Press (AFP). Yet Kyodo is little more than a national news agency, whereas AFP is a major *international* news agency.

The major reason for Kyodo's inability to compete with British, American and French international news agencies, despite its scale and financial strength, is language. In order for Kyodo to sell news reports in foreign markets, the reports must be translated into English, French and many other languages. This means higher cost and, more important, delayed distribution. Delayed distribution is fatal in the news agency business. In the case of major international news agencies, more than 20 percent of their total revenue comes from sales to foreign mass media.[2] Sales to foreign mass media account for only a small percentage of Kyodo's revenue. Kyodo does distribute news in English (mostly on Japan) to foreign mass media, but this service loses money for the agency. Kyodo says that it does not provide its English-language service for profit, but "for the country."[3]

As mentioned before, it is true that the coverage of Japan has drastically increased during the past several decades. However, most of those news flows still continue to be handled and dominated by British, American and French news agencies. It is likely that news about Japan distributed in the world is affected by British, American, and French biases. The world language order is far more stable and unchangeable than other kinds of world orders. The dependency theory, therefore, may be more applicable to international politics based on language hegemony than on the changeable fields of military, economic or technological influence.

STUDIES ON DEVELOPMENT AND COMMUNICATION

Many experts on development and communication have pointed out that there is growing disappointment with Western orthodox theories on development and communication, because the gap between advanced industrial countries and Third World countries has not shrunk. On the contrary, the gap seems to be widening in many areas despite numerous "development communication programs" in Third World countries.

This is one of the reasons why the "dependency theory" claiming that Third World countries were made and are still being kept underdeveloped by "imperialistic" industrial powers tends to be popular among Third World countries. According to this theory, the world consists of "exploiters" and "exploitees," and Third World countries cannot catch up with advanced countries without changing this world system.

In my view, the dependency theory is applicable to the situation under which a country has the power to determine and intervene in another country's economic policies. Even without this power, less developed countries can grow— if they have the will and ability—faster than developed countries, and eventually catch up. This is what Japan did between the midnineteenth century and the 1920s, and again between 1945 and 1960.

During the past several centuries, Japanese leaders as well as the masses have believed that the world system is like *sengoku ranse* (the age of warring provinces), and international rankings of nations are like the *banzuke hyo* (ranking list) of *sumo* wrestlers. Low-ranking *sumo* wrestlers can move up in the *banzuke hyo* through their efforts, and high-ranking wrestlers would have to step down if they did not make enough efforts to maintain their positions. This is still the basic belief widely shared by Japanese leaders as well as the masses.

Because of their own experiences in the past, Japanese experts tend to be more sympathetic to orthodox Western theories than to the dependency theory. Japanese experts, however, believe that the orthodox Western theories are not sufficient. Orthodox Western theories tell, for example, how to develop but do not tell how to catch up. It is obvious that developing countries have developed if compared with the past. They cannot catch up with advanced industrial countries, however, because industrial countries are also developing as rapidly as or more rapidly than developing countries. In my view, to develop or grow and to catch up are different matters, and this is the point lacking in orthodox Western theories on development and communication.

In a recent article (Ito, in press b), I attempt to answer the question, using many studies on Japanese modernization, "If Japan could quickly and successfully catch up with Western powers, why couldn't culturally and historically similar countries like China or Korea?" Of course, there are many ideas and theories trying to answer this question, but the three factors that I thought most relevant to communication were: (1) the worldview of a "hierarchy of competing human groups" held by not only the leading elite but also the general masses in Japan even before this century; (2) the existence of educated and informed masses (the literacy rate in Japan in the early nineteenth century was about the same as in major Western countries and much higher than any non-Western countries, and only Japan in the non-Western world had precursors of newspapers, similar to *Flugblat* in Europe, before the nineteenth century); and (3) Japan's state and corporate collectivism.

The second question asked in this article is, "If the 'Japanese model of development and communication' is to be applied to existing Third World countries, what are major obstacles and limitations?"

Most less developed countries (LDCs) are aware of the importance of the second condition, that is informed and educated masses, and some of them are doing very well in educating the masses and increasing the information supply. Most Third World countries, however, are not fully aware how competitive advanced industrial societies are and how strong are the competitive consciousness and ranking consciousness among leaders and the masses in advanced industrial countries.

Remember, for example, President Bush's television campaign message in the presidential election in 1992, that "the United States must be a military superpower, economic superpower and export superpower, and we must win in all international competitions." Like it or not, that campaign message well describes the nature of the present world system, which I call the "world competitive system." This world system has not changed during the past several centuries. In the midnineteenth century, Japanese leaders as well as the masses quickly understood the nature of the system, because Japan, unlike China and Korea, had been divided into many feudal territories competing with each other since the late twelfth century. Due to different historical backgrounds and social and political systems, people in most Third World countries, especially the masses, are not fully aware of the competitive nature of the world, and remain out of international competition.

Collectivism, if it functions as expected, helps achieve collective goals. It is important to note that most advanced industrial countries use collectivism in some form or another to achieve collective goals. It is too simplistic to claim that the United States is an individualistic country so there is no collectivism. Let us remember late President Kennedy's famous exhortation, "Ask not what the country can do for you but ask what you can do for your country." Even in the United States, collectivism exists at the national level and in many organizations, including the military.

In modern times, however, people can no longer be mobilized by cohesion or physical force to achieve collective interests. Also, people's loyalty to the collectivity cannot be automatic. In order for collectivism to function as expected, leaders of the group must have legitimacy and high ethical standards. A problem in many Third World countries is that leaders are neither legitimate nor ethical.

Legitimacy is given by democratic procedures in modern times, but democracy did not exist in non-Western traditions. Japan was no exception. In East Asian, Confucian traditions, however, the ethical standards of leaders have been kept relatively high compared with other parts of the world, which has made collectivism function relatively effectively even in modern times despite the delay in democratization. Probably the two most important rules that leaders must observe to make collectivism function as expected are: (1) achieved collective interests must be distributed fairly and reasonably to individual members of the collectivity, and (2) if somebody has to sacrifice his or her private interest for the sake of the collective interest, leaders must do so first.

For example, it was almost a rule in traditional Japan that the sons of commander in chiefs were the first to die in a war; they were sent to the most dangerous front where nobody wanted to go. General Nogi, the supreme commander in chief of the Japanese Army during the Russo-Japanese War in 1904–5, had two sons and lost both of them in that war. Mao Tse-tung lost his son in the Korean War.

Also in East Asian traditions, group leaders had to accept the utmost responsibility for failures. In feudal Japan this was often shown in the form of ceremonial suicide known as *seppuku*. Although Japanese no longer respect Hideki Tojo, who was equated with Hitler and Mussolini in the West, he did resign as prime minister one year before the end of the war with apologies, and he shot himself in the chest soon after the war (but failed to kill himself). Let us compare this record with the behavior of Saddam Hussein in Iraq. He started the war, and agitated the public to sacrifice for the cause of the collectivity; hundreds of thousands of soldiers died in the war, but his son was not enlisted; and he still remains in power. He is not the only exception—there have been many unethical leaders of this kind in Third World countries, such as Marcos in the Philippines, Bogasa in Central Africa, Amin in Uganda, Ceausescu in Rumania, and so on. These leaders demand dedication and sacrifice from the masses, but they themselves think and behave individualistically. Under these leaders collectivism never functions as expected.

In order to give workers a feeling of "togetherness," the average salary of company executives in Japan is kept much lower than in Western countries. According to a survey conducted by Towers & Pelin, an American management consulting firm, the average salary of American company presidents was the highest in the world in 1991, at approximately $835,600, whereas that of Japanese company presidents was the tenth highest, at approximately $415,680 ("Shacho no nenshu," 1992).

The P-E International, a British research company, compared the purchasing power of company presidents in twenty-one countries. According to this survey, the purchasing power of American company presidents was the highest in the world, at $259,600, whereas that of Japanese company presidents was the twelfth, at $116,600 ("Shacho no kohbairyoku," 1992).

These statistics indicate that the difference between the average salary of Japanese company executives and that of average workers is much smaller in Japan than in the West, because Japan's average national income is now about the same as or slightly higher than that of the United States. The *Philadelphia Inquirer* reported on January 4, 1992, that the ratio between the average salary of top executives and that of workers was 16 to 1 in Japan whereas the ratio in the United States was 160 to 1. At the onset of financial difficulties, the first thing Japanese companies do is to stop dividends for stockholders, the second is to cut salaries of executives and layoff is the last resort—but the order is the opposite in many other countries. These Japanese practices seem to be effective in making modern collectivism function as expected and in increasing international competitiveness.

Business leaders in Third World countries are not fully aware of these differences. Just as political leaders in Third World countries demand collectivistic dedication from the masses but they themselves think and behave individualistically, business leaders also demand Japanese-style dedication from their workers but they themselves think and behave individualistically. If they want to adopt individualism they must pay the cost for individualism, and if they want to adopt collectivism they must pay the cost for collectivism. The systems practiced in many Third World countries are not based on individualism or collectivism. They are a combination of individualism and collectivism mixed in the way leaders want.

The mass media can contribute to development through: (1) the creation and reinforcement of "competitive consciousness" among the masses through dissemination of information regarding international rankings; (2) provision of accurate information congruent with the "extracted information" that the masses have; and (3) surveillance and criticism of national and business leaders' behavior to make healthy collectivism or individualism function as expected.

SUMMARY AND CONCLUSIONS

In the area of mass media effects, two new models based on Japanese research, that is, the *joho kohdo* (information behavior) model and the tripolar model of social consensus formation, have been discussed. In the *joho kohdo* model, the credibility of the mass media is considered to play a decisive role in determining the degree of effects, and the credibility of mass media is considered to be determined by what extent mass media contents are congruent with information and knowledge that people *extract* from their direct experiences and conscious "research" activities. In this model, "extracted information" (gained from direct experiences and conscious "research activities") is considered to be used as litmus paper to check the credibility of mass media contents.

In the tripolar model of social consensus, the mass media are considered to have effects on social consensus formation only when they belong to the majority or "mainstream" formed by the three major components of social consensus, that is, the mass media themselves, the government and the public, and when they contribute to the creation and maintenance of *kuuki* (social pressure for compliance). This model resembles somewhat the "spiral of silence theory" of Elisabeth Noelle-Neumann. The difference, however, is that in the spiral of silence theory only the mass media are considered to form social pressure for compliance, while this model assumes that, depending on the subject matter, the government and the public actively participate in the formation of *kuuki*. In many defense and foreign policy issues, the Japanese mass media have been under the pressure of *kuuki* formed by conservative government policies and public opinion poll results. In some other issues, the mass media together with the public (or the government, depending on the issue) formed *kuuki* and functioned as a strong social pressure on the third component. Actually, however, the mass media, the public and even the government can be divided between proponents and opponents, and when we consider these divisions within each component, the model becomes more complex.

Regardless of whether they are pro-Marxist or anti-Marxist, many theorists on international information flows have assumed that the directions of international information flows are "as regular as the trade wind" (Schramm, 1964) and that the world economic and political order behind it is stable and unchangeable. Japan, since the midnineteenth century, however, has changed its position in the world economic and political order several times, and information flows from and into Japan have also drastically changed accordingly. From the Japanese perspective, therefore, the world order as well as the direction of international information flows are very changeable.

Then what makes the world order and the direction of international information flows so changeable? It is nothing but international competition. In the areas where competition functions effectively, the dependency theory, theories on cultural imperialism or media imperialism are not valid. There are, however, a few areas where competition does not function effectively. Language and international political influence based on language is an example. Unbalanced international information flows caused by the English (and, to a lesser extent, French) language hegemony may continue for some further centuries, but those based on economic and military reasons are more changeable than most theorists have so far assumed.

Research on international information flows is somewhat related to the study of development and communication. Because there existed competition among many feudal territories in Japan, as in Western Europe, in the seventeenth and eighteenth centuries, Japanese leaders as well as the masses came to hold a worldview of a hierarchy of competing human groups. Also, competition for many centuries brought Japan relatively high per capita income (for a non-Western country at that time) and well-educated masses. Furthermore, intergroup competition for many centuries fostered ethics (especially for leaders), rules and know-how regarding intergroup competition and collectivism. These three factors, that is, (1) a worldview of a hierarchy of competing human groups, (2) the well-educated and informed masses and (3) ethics, rules and know-how for intergroup competition and collectivism, constitute a "Japanese model of development and communication."

Since the Japanese model is based on unique Japanese history and experiences, this cannot be automatically applied to all Third World countries. It is wrong to assume that simply because Japan is a non-Western country, the Japanese model should fit better in any non-Western country than the Western model. If the Japanese model is applicable to a country, however, the mass media can contribute to development by disseminating the worldview of the hierarchy of competing nations and making people more competition-conscious, by educating and informing the masses and by disseminating and forcing ethics, rules and know-how for intergroup competition and collectivism. Some countries, South Korea for example, are apparently practicing these policies, therefore the Japanese model has some validity in some countries.

NOTES

1. Yamamoto (1977) first used this concept to explain the political process in Japan in the 1930s. *Kuuki* in Japanese is similar and related to *qi feng* in Chinese and *kong ki* in Korean.

2. Revenues from overseas services in 1976 were about 80 percent at Reuters and 25 percent at United Press International (UPI) and AP (Tunstall, 1981, p. 260).

3. From a personal interview with Takenori Nishiyama, Director of Economic News Department, Kyodo News Agency.

REFERENCES

DeFleur, M. S., & Ball-Rokeach, S. (1975). *Theories of mass communication* (3rd ed.). New York: David McKay.

Edelstein, A. S., Ito, Y., & Kepplinger, H. M. (1989). *Communication & culture: A comparative approach*. White Plains, NY: Longman.

Eisenstein, E. L. (1983). *The printing revolution in early modern Europe*. London: Cambridge University Press.

Fujitake, A. (1968). *Gendai masu komyunikeishon no riron* [Contemporary mass communication theories]. Tokyo: Nihon Hoso Shuppan Kyokai.

Ito, Y. (1987). Mass communication research in Japan: History and present state. In M. L. McLaughlin (Ed.), *Communication Yearbook/10* (pp. 49–85). Beverly Hills, CA: Sage.

Ito, Y. (1990a). Mass communication theories from a Japanese perspective. *Media, Culture and Society, 12*(4), 423–464.

Ito, Y. (1990b). The trade winds change: Japan's shift from an information importer to an information exporter, 1965–1985. In J. A. Anderson (Ed.), *Communication Yearbook/13* (pp. 430–465). Newbury Park, CA: Sage.

Ito, Y. (1991). *Johoka* as a driving force of social change. *Keio Communication Review, 12*, 33–58.

Ito, Y. (1992). What makes a language international? *Media Development, 39*(1), 28–31.

Ito, Y. (in press a). From bipolar models of mass media influence to a tri-polar model of social consensus formation. In W. B. Gudykunst (Ed.), *Communication in Japan and the United States*. Albany: The State University of New York Press.

Ito, Y. (in press b). Theories on development and communication from a Japanese perspective. In Andrew A. Moemeka (Ed.), *Communicating for development: A multi-media perspective*. Albany: The State University of New York Press.

Kato, H. (1972). *Joho kohdoh* [Information behavior]. Tokyo: Kohdan-sha.

Katz, E. (1980). Media events: The sense of occasion. *Studies in Visual Communication, 6*, 84–89.

Katz, E., Dayan, D., & Motyl P. (1981). In defense of media events. In R. W. Haigh, G. Gerbner, & R. B. Byrne (Eds.), *Communications in the twenty-first century* (pp. 43–59). New York: John Wiley.

Kitamura, H. (1970). *Joho kohdoh ron* [Information behavior]. Tokyo: Seibundo Shinkoh-sha.

Lang, K., & Lang, G. E. (1960). The unique perspective of television and its effect: A pilot study. In W. Schramm (Ed.), *Mass communications* (pp. 544–560). Urbana: University of Illinois Press.

Lang, K., & Lang, G. E. (1968). *Politics and television*. Chicago, IL: Quadrangle Books.

Lippmann, W. (1922). *Public opinion*. New York: Harcourt, Brace.

McLuhan, M. (1962). *The Gutenberg galaxy: The making of typographic man*. Toronto: University of Toronto Press.

Mills, C. W. (1956). *The power elite*. New York: Oxford University Press.

Nakano, O. (1980). *Gendaijin no joho kohdoh* [Information behavior of modern man]. Tokyo: Nihon Hoso Shuppan Kyokai.

Schramm, W. (1964). *Mass media and national development*. Stanford, CA: Stanford University Press.

Schramm, W. (1965). How communication works. In W. Schramm (Ed.), *The process and effects of mass communication* (pp. 3–26). Urbana: University of Illinois Press. (Originally published in 1954.)

Senso to shimbun [War and newspapers]. (1987, August 29). *Asahi Shimbun,* p. 4.

Shacho no kohbairyoku: Nihon wa sekai 12i [Purchasing power of company presidents: Japan is 12th]. (1992, September 11). *Sankei Shimbun,* evening ed., p. 3.

Shacho no nenshu [Annual revenue of company presidents]. (1992, September 5). *Sankei shimbun,* evening ed., p. 1.

Shimizu, I. (1951). *Shakai shinrigaku* [Social psychology]. Tokyo: Iwanami Shoten.

Tsujimura, A. (1976). Yoron to seiji rikigaku [Public opinion and political dynamics]. In Nihonjin Kenkyu Kai (Ed.), *Nihonjin kenkyu, no. 4: Yoron towa nanika* (pp. 173–238). Tokyo: Shiseido.

Tsujimura, A. (1981). *Sengo nihon no taishu shinri* [Social psychology in postwar Japan]. Tokyo: Tokyo Daigaku Shuppankai.

Tunstall, J. (1977). *The media are American.* London: Constable.

Tunstall, J. (1981). Worldwide news agencies: Private wholesalers of public information. In J. Richtstad, & M. Anderson (Eds.), *Crisis in international news: Policies and prospects* (pp. 258–267). New York: Columbia University Press.

Yamamoto, S. (1977). *'Kuuki' no kenkyu* (A study of 'kuuki'). Tokyo: Bungei Shunju-she.

Communication Research on Children and Public Policy

Ellen Wartella

In this chapter I wish to make one argument: Both the historical record and current events demonstrate that communication research and scholarship *can* make a difference in children's media, but that they usually do not. For this situation to change requires no less than a redirection of research and scholarship and a fundamental change in how we envision them, requiring us to put aside our "paradigm debates" and focus instead on the public nature of our enterprise.

To advance this argument, I would like to treat briefly several current issues in children's media and to survey the history of the interplay between communication research and children's media policy and public debate. Consider these three issues: the Children's Television Act of 1990; the case of Whittle Communication's Channel One daily in-school news program; and the 1992 battle over funding for public television.

The passage of the Children's Television Act in 1990 was a milestone: It was the first federal law regarding children and television to gain congressional approval and presidential acquiescence in the history of television; indeed it was the first federal law regarding children and media in this century. While some critics of children's television feel it has little power actually to change the problems of children's television, it does establish a precedent for treating children as a unique audience with special needs who therefore deserve special services. Among its provisions, this law now requires that broadcasters must serve the "educational and information needs of children through programming" and that they may be held accountable for their actions with regard to children when they come up for license review every five years; it limits the amount of advertising time during children's programs to 10.5 minutes per hour on weekends and 12 minutes per hour on weekdays; and it establishes a National Endowment for Children's Educational Television, through which new programming ventures can be funded.

Since passage of the 1990 act, there has been movement on the various proposals within it: local broadcasters seem to be interested in child audiences (for example, the National Association of Broadcasters [NAB] has held at least one national conference on children's television); and *TV Guide* now regularly identifies programming for children that parents might want to know about. Advertising time standards are now in place, although the extent to which they are being enforced is still at issue. The National Endowment for Children's Educational Television has been established as of October 1991, and the first board meeting of the endowment was held in September 1992.

In spring 1989, Whittle Communications began broadcasting its ten-minute news show, "Channel One," to school districts across the nation and providing those districts with the hardware—a satellite dish, VCRs and television monitors—to show the program to all students in a school. Now in over 8,000 districts, "Channel One" is an attempt to combat the deficiencies of American high school students' cultural literacy—their knowledge of current events, political issues, geography and so forth—with a daily student-oriented news program aired in school. The controversy focuses on the two minutes of advertisements for things like jeans, candy bars and Coke that are inserted in each program and that help make the service profitable for Whittle. However, recent research commissioned by Whittle (Johnstone and Brzezinski, 1992) suggests that relatively little learning about the news is actually going on. Nonetheless, this past spring, Chris Whittle announced his plans for the Edison Project, a national network of private schools that will exploit communications technologies such as television and computers to provide exceptional education for school-aged children.

During April and May 1992, conservatives in Congress (and in the public arena) debated a Senate appropriations bill to fund public television. Although funding did pass, the political opposition to the Public Broadcasting Service (PBS) left its future in question and raised new charges against the idea of public stewardship of television. Reiterating the arguments made in the early 1980s regarding the need to deregulate broadcasting, conservative critics of the "liberal tilt" of PBS argued that a federally funded public broadcasting system is no longer necessary or "even worthwhile because cable networks have arisen that offer the same kinds of programs" (*New York Times,* April 1992). Even the highly acclaimed "Sesame Street," one of the few preschool programs available on over-the-air broadcast television, was criticized: the Heritage Foundation's Bradley Resident Scholar, Laurence Jarvik, was quoted in the *Times* as saying " 'Sesame Street' is just another kids' show. No better than 'Underdog' or 'The Flintstones.' What did the taxpayers get for their investment in 'Sesame Street'? A generation of kids who spray graffiti on the walls of New York City. If 'Sesame Street' was so effective, why do we have such a literacy problem?'' He went on to argue (falsely) that the Children's Television Workshop (CTW) should not be taking public money for "Sesame Street" when it makes millions of dollars through its licensing agreements. (The fact is that CTW is well off, with an existing endowment of more than $50 million; however, CTW has not taken any money from the Corporation for Public Broadcasting since 1982, and funds "Sesame Street" with its own money, amounting to more than $90 million in the past ten years.)

These are but a few of the current public issues that cry out for reasoned discussion and informed communication scholarship. Yet too often communication research is not mentioned in the discussion, is irrelevant, or uninformative or all three.

These public issues underscore the intense public interest in, attention to and concern about the role of communication in modern life. The issues focus on the effects of television on viewers, and in particular, on children viewers. This chapter will examine the question: How has communication research on children and media informed these discussions or influenced policy making? By communication research I mean a very wide range of research study, including policy research, historical study, traditional audience effects research and interpretive analyses of various media products.

These are questions about the ability of communication researchers and our research to have a visible public face in the current controversies about the communications media.

As James Carey (1989) has noted, communication and the various types of cultural expression are a site for "social conflict over the real" (p. 87). And so in one sense many of these debates might be regarded as skirmishes in the larger political battles of the conservative right to control the political and cultural agenda of this country; they need to be responded to nonetheless in ways that have both moral power and persuasive appeal. In this sense, the ability of communication researchers to mount appealing arguments in the public arena of debates about media is certainly one way of assessing the state of our discipline beyond the paradigm debates of the past decade.

As I have argued elsewhere (Wartella and Reeves, 1985), the public controversies about the effects of media on children, and in particular the ability of the major mass media of film, radio and television to provide for the educational benefits of children, have been part of the recurring controversies about children and media throughout this century. Scrutiny of the vast literature on children and media in the United States through the century demonstrates that it has been the *public agenda* of concern about media effects on youth that in turn has set the *research agenda* for communication scholars and others who have heavily studied the role of media in children's lives and how children learn and are influenced by media portrayals (Wartella and Reeves, 1985). I believe that by reexamining the current public controversies about children and television—by examining the influence of communication research on public discussions and the development of programming for children—we can come to some tentative conclusions about the influence of communication research in public life.

Furthermore, such an assessment might provide us with prescriptions for future communication research, which as this book suggests will go beyond the current paradigm debates and research agendas to have an impact in the public arena.

While this is not the place for an extended critique of the state of the field of communication study, it could be useful at least to consider the ways in which the body of communication research in the broadest sense of various traditions and methods has enlightened public debates about children and media issues. For this purpose let me consider the three issues outlined earlier. In doing so, I hope to illustrate my point about our field and its public responsibilities.

COMMUNICATION RESEARCH AND PUBLIC DEBATES
ABOUT CHILDREN AND TV

By one yardstick, 1990 was a banner year for those concerned about children's television and for the influence of communication research in the policy arena. With the 1990 act, two of the most visible public controversies about children's television of at least the past twenty-five years were attended to legislatively; the need for more educational programming for children, and concern over the proliferation of advertising to children (see Kunkel, 1991). These two topics have received considerable research attention since the 1970s (Wartella and Reeves, 1985).

The 1990 law was the last version of a series of congressional bills regarding television broadcasters' responsibilities to children, bills that had been introduced into Congress nearly every year between 1981 and 1989. The new law has not, however, ended the controversy about the appropriate regulation of television for children. For instance, in June 1992, legislation was proposed in Congress under the "Ready to Learn" act that would use public television and cable to become involved in providing educational programming to preschool children as part of an intensive national effort in preschool education and health. Promoted and encouraged by Ernest Boyer of the Carnegie Council on Education, Ready to Learn hopes to utilize television in the service of national preschool preparedness in a manner that extends "Sesame Street" beyond its current confines.

Furthermore, as Kunkel (1991) has noted, the 1990 Children's Television Act will not ameliorate all of the perceived problems of children's television. For instance, it does not address at all the issue of television violence (the number one topic to occupy public discussions about television since its inception). Neither will the law in and of itself resolve the two major issues of educational programming and advertising limits. According to Kunkel (1991), there are considerable battles yet to be fought in the policy arena. For instance, the Federal Communications Commission (FCC), in implementing the law, has held that thirty- and sixty-second informational "drop ins" could qualify as educational programming, not just full-length children's programs as children's advocates would prefer.

Nonetheless, as Kunkel (1991) notes, "the most meaningful change accomplished by the Act is that the law now says that children's television matters; it is an essential part of the public interest that broadcasters are licensed to serve" (p. 199). Furthermore, a case can be made that the past twenty years of research on children and television has been influential in bringing about this law. A specific example is the effect that Edward Palmer's 1988 book *Television and America's Children: A Crisis of Neglect* had on the policy debates. It served as a catalyst for the establishment of the National Endowment for Children's Educational Television. The book led to Senate hearings conducted by Senator Daniel Inouye in the summer of 1989 and the inclusion of this proposal in the 1990 law. It should be pointed out that this was not the first time such an endowment had been proposed; Eli Rubinstein, a co-editor of the first surgeon general's study of television and social behavior in 1972, had made just such a proposal in the mid-1970s (see Rubinstein and Brown, 1985).

Moreover, throughout the congressional hearings (and throughout the 1990s in the various hearings over different children and television bills) communication research was central and pertinent to the arguments marshalled for passing such bills. In particular, advocates for better children's television were able to point to research on the paucity of educational programming on commercial television, the ability of television to educate children when produced with an educational goal and with a well-formed curriculum, and the enormous amount of time children spend with television. All of these studies formed a persuasive argument to suggest the failure of the "free marketplace" of deregulated television to accommodate the needs of child audiences with high-quality, educational and informational programs.

This has not always been the case: in the late 1970s and early 1980s, communication researchers and advocates for better children's television were spectacularly unsuccessful in bringing about either Federal Trade Commission (FTC) advertising policy or FCC programming policy (see McGregor, 1986). The reasons for this are multiple. First, in the early 1980s the Reagan presidency brought an antiregulatory environment to Washington; specifically, both the FTC and FCC set about actively dismantling regulatory apparatus. Second, Entman (in press) argues that unlike other areas of federal regulatory policy, which rely on empirical evidence for shaping policy initiatives, the First Amendment area has been devoid of empirical research in policy making. Clearly, the political winds were favorable in 1990 as they had not been a decade earlier (Kunkel, 1991).

I think scrutiny of the record regarding the 1990 law would demonstrate that communication research was helpful in the political process of negotiating this bill. The research was germane to the public issues about educational potential and advertising limits, and it was used by advocates in the policy arena—that is, it made it into the policy discussions.

Whittle's "Channel One," however, may be a counterexample. When Whittle announced plans for this news program in 1989, a hue and cry developed over the advisability of using classrooms and the captive audience of teenagers found there for advertising messages. A number of school districts around the country publicly announced they would not accept Whittle's offer, for to do so would lead to the commercialization of children in schools.

The outcry against commercialization of the nation's classrooms was largely from education faculty; communication researchers were most prominent by their absence from the debate. Nowhere in the public discussions have communication scholars, or others, come forth to place this issue in the larger context of media commercialization of youth and the lack of a reasonable treatment of television issues in American public schools.

The mass media have been commercializing youth at least since the 1920s, when they helped to identify and promote the youth culture of America's college students, the flappers. Since then ever younger age groups of youth have been the target of media programming and advertising campaigns: the teenagers of the 1950s with their teen pictures and rock music were succeeded by elementary school children, who became the market for 1960s and 1970s "kidvid" on American television. During the past decade, the merging of television programming with toy production to develop an overall strategy to market toys to preschool children has left no age group of youth uncommercialized or excluded as a segment of the mass audience (Wartella and Mazzarella, 1990). As any parent of a preschooler can attest, the interrelatedness of television programs featuring a character based on a toy line, such as "Teenage Mutant Ninja Turtles," the toys themselves and the proliferation of products with the character's logo, reaches children still in diapers.

Now marketers have found a new venue for commercialization of youth: the schools. When looked at against the history of commercialization of youth through the mass media, it seems obvious that keeping Whittle out of the schools will not resolve the problems of overcommercialization of young children. That does not mean the line could not or should not be drawn here. For moral or ideological reasons, we could well decide that schools are out of bounds, or that young children are out of bounds as an audience for marketers' messages. But this is a moral argument. The only useful communication research that might be brought to bear on the argument is descriptive research on what commercialization exists and historical evidence of its proliferation.

Whether we do or do not allow Whittle into the schools, it is clear to me that the educational establishment has been neglectful in treating television seriously. For instance, schools might consider utilizing "Channel One" to educate their students about commercialization, to critique the media presentations and to make their students more media literate. It will be interesting to see how the proposed Edison Project, Whittle's foray into for-profit schooling, will utilize television. The educational community has by and large framed television as an out-of-school nuisance and a threat to its domain.

To use television as a positive force in children's education would require that educators take a more serious look at television and not dismiss it quite so easily as a bad influence on children, an influence working at odds with the public school system. It would require that more than the controversy about the effects of TV violence on children's social behavior make its way into the textbooks and coursework of students training to become teachers.[1] Education elites would need to change their views of television; they would need to recognize that not all television is bad, that some programming can be beneficial and informative and even morally uplifting (as viewers of the public television series "The Civil War" and "Eyes on the Prize" might agree). To change educators' and others' views, communication researchers need to consider this larger context of the role of television in children's lives, as well as the role of television as a cultural forum and popular art form. In short, we need to reshape the discourse about children and television into a larger set of considerations. Here, we as communication scholars must help reshape the public's understanding of the television and children issue. As a community, communication researchers have failed at this task.

Lastly, consider the battle over the funding of public television, the major purveyor of educational television today. As Willard Rowland and Michael Tracey (1990) have argued, public broadcasting throughout the major industrialized democracies has been under assault for at least the past decade. The growth of cable and satellite television, fiscal and political problems, as well as the complicity of public broadcasters, who define their mission in marketplace terms rather than as a public cultural forum, are forces all working to dismantle public broadcasting. As Aufderheide (1991) has argued, public television should provide the "public space" for cultural and political discussions. This is the promise of ITVS, the federally funded independent television service, which is supposed to channel money to independent producers and multicultural and minority programs. However, there are plenty of examples of public television actively shying away from broadcasting such minority programming for fear of fanning the fires of conservative attack on the grounds of being too liberal. The 1991 controversy over "Tongues Untied," the PBS program on homosexuality, is such an example.

What intrigues me most in this debate is the assault on even the educational benefits of public television. Even the seemingly unassailable "Sesame Street" was assailed. Conservative critics of public broadcasting challenged the well-documented evidence that "Sesame Street" does teach viewers its educational curriculum (Palmer, 1988). There is a considerable body of research on the effectiveness of different programming forms and formats for increasing children's attention to and understanding of television content (Huston and Wright, 1983).

And, more important, the success of "Sesame Street" has set a model for the production of children's educational television. This model involves the use of communication research—on how children of different ages attend to and make sense of programming elements—in the actual production of such shows. It is now standard policy for children's educational television to include what is called formative research (research that is the basis of production decisions) in their production. Moreover, indeed whether and how communication research is used in the production of children's television often helps to distinguish the quality of the programming—and whether or not the programming has educational potential.

There is ample evidence that public television has been the main source of educational programming for children available on over-the-air broadcast television (Wartella et al., 1990). Although cable television does have considerably more educational programming for children than does commercial television, not only is cable not available to all American children (fewer than two-thirds of American homes have cable), but it is unclear what sort of commitment cable television has to the production of new educational programs for children. Any perusal of this year's new programs, and there is a lot of children's programming on cable, suggests that the vast majority of such programs are comparable to the commercial networks. That is, they are produced to deliver the child audience to advertisers and therefore the most important criterion of production is whether or not they attract the children's attention. Indeed, Nickelodeon makes it a point to advertise itself as the kid's channel that's fun for kids (implying it is not one that's educationally good for you).

Indeed, the recurring public controversies over first film, then radio and television programming for children, demonstrate that the commercial media systems of this century have never lived up to their educational promises for children. While public concern about children's use of media echoes wider concerns about the adoption of new technologies into American society, such concern also rests on the fact that commercial media have been unwilling to support educational programming (Wartella, 1990). This is the case even when commercial media interests publicly promote the educational benefits of new technologies. Why? Because such programming is viewed as "uncommercial," unable to attract large enough audiences (there are about 15 million children in a nation of 250 million) to bring in the advertising dollars and profit margins wanted in the industry. I should point out that even when successful educational programs are produced that do attract large numbers of child audiences, such as "Sesame Street," such programs are viewed as unviable for the commercial system—they are too expensive.

How should we assess the impact of communication research in this public arena? It's a mixed response. As far as I have seen, the communication policy arguments about the need for a public space for public broadcasting have not yet entered the wider policy debates about public television. Neither has the historical research demonstrating a failure of the industry to live up to its professed social responsibility to children been used effectively in marshalling arguments for the need of a public broadcasting space. What public discourse there *has* been has been monopolized by a marketplace metaphor and in the service of the political right, which held sway in Washington during the Reagan-Bush years.

More successful has been the use of research on child audiences in the actual production of educational programs for children. Here, studies of how to produce programs for children of different ages that they both like to watch and can learn from have enjoyed some success. Communication researchers and developmental psychologists studying children and television often serve as advisers to such programs. However, without motivation to air such programs, the latter success is illusory.

This leads me to my concern for how communication research can be more effective in the public arena: How can we improve the public face of communication?

THE PUBLIC FACE OF COMMUNICATION

As the argument thus far suggests, I think as communication researchers we can and should direct our research and scholarship to addressing the public debates about media in contemporary life. To my mind, one's theoretical or methodological perspective matters far less than the quality of the argument one brings to bear on questions that the public has with full force let us know it believes are important. Further, no one perspective or method has a corner on truth; the debates of the past dozen years should at least have convinced us that each perspective can bring something of interest to enlighten our understanding of a problem area. It is by the quality of the research and its interpretation that we assess the worth of a piece of scholarship. While its political worth may depend on its ideological commitment, its worth as scholarship does not.

I want to argue that irrespective of the theoretical perspective, the methodological tools and the particular paradigmatic commitments of the researcher, the important issue for the future research agenda is to address the public arena. Elsewhere I have argued that communication researchers lack a clear vision about who we are, which is manifested in a fractured set of subfields whose practitioners not only know little about each other but seem more intent on the internal debates of our field than on our public responsibility as scholars of an increasingly important topic. We have little visible presence as public intellectuals. We offer an inchoate curriculum for communication study on the undergraduate level that perpetuates generations of college graduates (including communication majors) who know little about communication scholarship, including what is covered by the term "communication study" (Wartella, 1990).

The nature of communication scholarship, its politics and its impact, is predicated upon how we approach our research and how we relay it in the public arena. Mostly, my fear is that our scholarship never even makes it to the public arena (a lot of bad research in *any* paradigm our field embraces should not, of course). We do have a body of knowledge after eight decades of study of mass communication that I believe we are too timid in sharing. We are, moreover, often ignorant of how to act as public intellectuals and advocates for a particular point of view. Is this a manifestation of what the American academy has been criticized for—an overwhelming commitment to the study of narrow academic subspecialties, thus forsaking the kind of scholarship that makes for public intellectuals (as Jacoby argued in 1987)? Is communication study plagued with the problems besetting other disciplines in the academy?

Clearly, to the extent that the popular media take up intellectual questions about communication, they will seek out scholars to comment and contribute to the public dialogue. If communication faculty are to be those public scholars commenting on communication, then we need not just to promote our research in all of the usual ways—by insuring that it is well written and well situated within public definitions of concerns, and that it is presented in a public forum beyond our academic journals, such as in op-ed pieces, letters to the editor, articles for the elite intellectual magazines and, most important, in book form; we also need to insure that we craft our work to have a pragmatic commitment. One public we cannot ignore is our own students, communications and journalism majors who can and do emerge from university with no real sense of what communication research is, does, knows or what it can contribute to the world. The ruptures between speech communication and mass communication, between journalism education and media studies, must be addressed. Moreover, undergraduate education throughout communication needs to integrate better theory, research and practice. And once we take up that pragmatic commitment we need to think about which public we are addressing in our research: the public at large, those media audiences we often study, public policy makers at the federal and state levels, communication practitioners or other cultural elites who write and talk about communication?

Furthermore, to approach communication scholarship today without an understanding of the political commitments inherent in a line of research, in the kind of issues that are taken up for study, and in the potential uses of that research, is incredibly naive. We can no longer claim timidity as public scholars.

The message seems pretty clear to me. Communication scholarship (like all scholarship) needs to be addressing public issues. How we maneuver through the public agenda, select problems and frame research about them in terms of our theoretical understanding is up to each individual scholar. I do not believe that one type of scholar or theoretical position is inherently more attuned to public issues or is more political than another; indeed, just calling oneself a "critical" communications scholar does not insure that one's work will have the political outcome intended, and calling oneself a "communication scientist" or "television researcher" does not imply that one's research is apolitical.

The politics of research is not easily read off with reference to question, theory or method.

Rather, we need to understand self-consciously what research questions we take up in our work, how we situate them within the national public and intellectual debates, and how we attempt to convey our work to that segment of the "public arena" we believe we are addressing.

The recent history of public controversies about children and television issues suggest that there is ample opportunity for communication research to have a visible influence in shaping public debates, but this happens far too rarely. My suggestion, then, for going beyond agendas is to renew our commitment to public scholarship and to reinvigorate the public face of our field.

NOTE

1. In my examination of a dozen experimental psychology and introductory psychology texts, I found that typically fewer than a dozen of the 400 to 500 pages of each text were devoted to questions about media and children. What mention there was tended to be dominated by the violence controversy, with occasional reference to "Sesame Street." Missing, then, were any references to the power of television to influence racial, ethnic and gender attitudes; the range of social and affective development, including identity formation; and the relationship of television to academic achievement.

REFERENCES

Aufderheide, P. (1991). Public television and the public sphere. *Critical Studies in Mass Communication, 8,* 168–183.

Carey, J. W. (1989). *Communication as culture: Essays on media and society.* Boston: Unwin Hyman.

Entman, R. (in press). Enhancing American democracy through the press: Putting the first amendment in its place. *University of Chicago Legal Forum.*

Huston, A. C., & Wright, J. (1983). Children's processing of television: The informative function of formal features. In J. Bryant & D. Anderson (Eds.), *Children's understanding of television* (pp. 33–54). New York: Academic Press.

Jacoby, R. (1987). *The last intellectuals: American culture in the age of academe.* New York: Academic Press.

Johnstone, J., & Brzezinski, E. (1992, April). Taking the measure of Channel One: The first year. Ann Arbor, MI: Institute for Social Research.

Kunkel, D. (1991). Crafting media policy: The genesis and implications of the Children's Television Act of 1990. *American Behavioral Scientist, 35*(2), 181–202.

McGregor, M. (1986). Reassessing the Children's Television Task Force. *Journalism Quarterly, 63*(3), 168–183.

Palmer, E. (1988). *Television and America's children: A crisis of neglect.* New York: Basic Books.

Rowland, W. D., & Tracey, M. (1990). Worldwide challenges to public service broadcasting. *Journal of Communication, 40*(2), 8–27.

Rubinstein, E., & Brown, J. D. (Eds.). (1985). *The media, social science and social policy.* Norwood, NJ: Ablex.

Wartella, E. (1990, November). *The public face of communication.* Sage Anniversary Lecture, Stanford University, Stanford, California.

Wartella, E., Heintz, K. E., Aidman, A., & Mazzarella, S. (1990). Television and beyond: Children's video media in one community. *Communication Research, 17*(1), 45–64.

Wartella E., & Mazzarella, S. (1990). An historical comparison of children's use of time with media: 1920's to 1980's. In R. Butsch (Ed.), *For fun and profit* (pp. 173–194). Philadelphia: Temple University Press.

Wartella, E., & Reeves, B. (1985). Historical trends in research on children and the media: 1900–1960. *Journal of Communication, 35*(2), 118–133.

Will Traditional Media Research Paradigms Be Obsolete in the Era of Intelligent Communication Networks?

Jennings Bryant

Joseph Dionne once noted: "The Industrial Revolution changed the way we work in two centuries. The Information Revolution has done as much in two decades" (Dionne, 1987, p. 1). Indeed, the most recent era has seen many remarkable changes that have affected not only our work but practically every dimension of our lives. As far as the mediated communication landscape is concerned, even more dramatic changes appear to be just around the corner, and the rate of change seems to be accelerating. As a recent *Business Week* cover story reported, "While many folks are still fretting over whether to trust automated teller machines, a new wave of technology is building that has the potential to alter fundamentally the ways in which we entertain ourselves, educate our children, and get our work done" ("Your Digital Future," 1992, p. 56).

Perhaps the most significant of those changes is the fusion of many of our traditional media forms and functions into integrated intelligent communication networks. For the first time, we will be able to receive all of the media services to which we have become accustomed, along with many new ones, over a single electronic information utility. This universal communication and information utility sometimes is conceived of as an information pipe, and analogies are drawn to network infrastructures that provide electricity, gas and water. No one knows precisely what form this advanced communication network will take or what the ownership, control or operational patterns will be; moreover, new developments in wireless communication, such as Personal Communication Networks (PCNs), may ultimately yield hybrid wire-wireless network systems. Nonetheless, it seems highly likely that by the year 2010 to 2015 most mediated communication in modern societies will take place via some form of intelligent networks. Indeed, a significant portion of our current mediated communication, most notably telephony, already takes place via rudimentary intelligent networks; and many experts see the information utility of the future as a high-tech extension of the public switched telephone network. What will be new and different from the current telephone network will be the ready availability of mediated communication services that require expansive bandwidth, for example, interactive full-motion video, three-dimensional simulations, virtual reality and other complex messaging systems.

The federal government of the United States has focused a great deal of attention recently on intelligent networks, especially as U.S. planners and policy makers realize that in many ways they are behind other countries in designing and implementing advanced communication systems. This heightened attention is illustrated by three recent government reports on the topic. Two were prepared under the auspices of the Office of Technology Assessment of the United States Congress. They are *Critical Connections: Communication for the Future* (U.S. Congress, 1990), and *Rural America at the Crossroads: Networking for the Future* (U.S. Congress, 1991). The third was a product of the National Telecommunications and Information Administration of the United States Department of Commerce, and is entitled *The NTIA Infrastructure Report: Telecommunications in the Age of Information* (U.S. Department of Commerce, 1991).

As might be anticipated, the focus of these three reports has been technical and public policy oriented. The orientation of the present report will be slightly different. First, we will consider the features of advanced intelligent networks that will encourage and enable certain types of communication behavior and discourage and (de)limit others. Next we will turn to aspects of communication processes and behaviors that might be expected to be altered as a function of intelligent network capabilities and functions. Since it can be anticipated that using these new forms of mediated communication will have some social, psychological and cultural impacts on users, we will also consider methods and procedures that would appear to be ideally suited to examining media uses and effects in this new media environment. Of additional interest will be the question of whether extant communication models and theories, as well as the old faithful research protocols, will be adequate or even appropriate to describe, predict and explain communication behavior and its consequences in the new media environment.

This might be an appropriate time to answer a question that might be on the minds of some readers: Why should we be interested in creating theories of the uses and effects of advanced intelligent networks long before such entities become readily available? After all, we have a great need for veridical theories and models of extant media systems. Constructing those should be a full-time job. True, but to plan future telecommunications systems without taking full advantage of the *predictive* potential of telecommunications theory leaves the discussion to public policy makers, who in the past have not seen the need for theory and research until it was too late to generate either to aid in policy legislation (e.g., Zillmann, 1989), and to engineers, who typically are more enamored with the technical possibilities of a system than with its human potential. Moreover, prototype intelligent networks already exist, so useful theoretical as well as applied research on intelligent networks can already be undertaken, long before the era of advanced intelligent networks becomes a full-blown reality. So, without apology, let us examine a media technology whose time has not yet come. We begin by examining intelligent networks descriptively.

INTELLIGENT NETWORKS

First, what are intelligent communication networks? Intelligent networks have been defined in many different ways, usually in terms of their technological components (e.g., Bloom and Miller, 1987) or in terms of the services they can provide (e.g., Alliance for Public Technology, 1990); but let us begin our discussion at another level, with reflections on a precursor to modern intelligent networks. In *Signals,* Pierce and Noll (1990) remind readers that:

The human operators of Alexander Graham Bell's day and later provided many "intelligent" services. If I was not at my desk, the operator could take a message or could forward the call to where I might be. If I did not wish to be disturbed, the operator could be instructed not to ring my phone unless my boss called. If I went to lunch at the corner coffee shop, the operator would know where I was and could reach me in a dire emergency. The intelligence of the human operators gave the network of the distant past considerable functionality. (Pp. 193–194)

In order to serve the widest possible customer base and still make a profit, the expensive but intelligent human operator had to be replaced with efficient but "dumb" electromechanical switches. Our present and future generations of intelligent networks are made possible by the replacement of electromechanical switches with new, computer-controlled, digital switching systems that are programmable, flexible and "intelligent" in the sense that they have advanced computer processing capabilities and are interconnected with almost unlimited information sources.

A cynical view is that "all of these 'new' intelligent services simply mimic what was possible a long time ago with human operators" (Pierce and Noll, 1990, p. 194). Actually, that is not quite true. The amount of information and intelligence available via modern communication networks never would have been possible with all the human operators who could possibly squeeze into a telephone company's central office or a cable television company's control room, and certainly they could not send voice, video, text and data over the same line. Even more important, the expensive human intelligence of such a primitive service network never could have kept the costs down so that the sophisticated telecommunications services would be available and affordable to the vast majority of the citizens of the information age.

To understand fully intelligent networks, we should consider (1) their technical dimensions, (2) the sorts of mediated services they can provide and (3) the basic elements of the (tele)communication process that are altered in intelligent network operations.

Technical Features of Intelligent Networks

Considered at a relatively low level of technical sophistication, three key elements of the communication infrastructure are particularly important for intelligent networks to function to their potential. The first is *switching* capability. At the simplest level, switching machines in the network determine the best possible path needed to transmit voice, data or video messages from one party to another. Conventional packet-switching is limited in the sort of information it can cost-effectively transfer, but technological developments leading to fast packet-switching permit voice, data and video images to be switched in an integrated fashion at extremely rapid speeds, so that intelligent networks become feasible. By the late 1990s, when optical switches become readily available, the speed and fidelity with which symbols and images are switched in the form of information will become awesome (Greenfield, 1986).

Also essential to the intelligent network are adequate *transmission* technologies. Fortunately, technological advances in this area have kept pace with those in switching. The key to removing transmission barricades is the widespread availability of broadband (high-capacity) systems. With rapid developments in fiber optics, which are a superb medium for transmission, the technological limitations of broadband transmission appear to be solved. Fiber allows many signals to travel swiftly over long distances with little transmission loss. With the rapidly developing capabilities of light wave transmission and wave division multiplexing, tremendous transmission capability is readily available. "Given these advances, it is clear that any constraints on the deployment of fiber technology will be economic, not technological" (U.S. Congress, 1990, p. 155).

A final key in the development of intelligent network capabilities is *digitalization*. Digitalization is the process of transforming analog messages (e.g., a photograph, a spoken word) into signals with discrete pulses that can be transmitted, processed and stored electronically. As Pierce and Noll (1990) report, "the future of communication is clear. Everything will be put into a cheap, reliable digital form as soon as possible" (p. 155). One of the motivations for digitalization is that when audio, video, and text messages are in digital form, they can be combined and integrated at will. As Brand (1987) described:

With digitalization all of the media become translatable into each other—computer bits migrate merrily—and they escape from their traditional means of transmission. A movie, phone call, letter, or magazine article may be sent digitally via phone line, coaxial cable, fiberoptic cable, microwave, satellite, the broadcast air, or a physical storage medium such as tape or disk. If that's not revolution enough, with digitalization the content becomes totally plastic—any message sound or image may be edited from anything into anything else. (P. 19)

With these technological advances in switching, broadband transmission and digitalization, there has been a trend toward the convergence of services, integrating voice, video and data into a *broadband integrated services digital network* (B-ISDN). Geeslin (1989) has succinctly described the potential of networks with these technical features:

The capabilities of the intelligent network of the future are defined by distributed intelligence, centralized database control, increased bandwidth, high speed, large capacity circuits, and flexible service configurability. This enhanced network provides access, transport, and intelligence. It is the highway over which a host of residence, business, scientific, educational, and public interest services could be offered, resulting not only in the promotion of commerce but also in a better way of life for all citizens. (P. 16)

One way to consider the human aspects of network operations is to recognize that each technical feature of the network may either unleash or constrain some human communication potential. Common technical capabilities of network design that would seem to have the potential to alter communication behavior include: the speed and volume of information transmission *(capacity)*, the degree of ease with which technicians or consumers can modify the system *(flexibility)*, the extent to which the network offers a wide range of applications *(versatility)*, the degree to which the network can exchange information automatically on demand *(interoperability)*, the speed with which messages can be exchanged *(timeliness)*, the degree to which the network maintains message quality *(fidelity)*, its ability to safeguard messages *(security)*, the degree to which the network withstands and can be restored after natural or human crises *(survivability)*, the range of the network's service area *(reach)*, the ease with which the network can be accessed *(openness)*, the number of customers served in an area *(penetration)*, and the level of consumption of network services *(usage)*. For purposes of the present discussion, we will assume an advanced network that rates high on all of these technical indexes, recognizing that any shortfalls in technical capabilities will restrict human usage.

The potential of such an intelligent network to provide all sorts of true multimedia, interactive communication is limited only by the human imagination. In fact, its potential for radically altering the quality of life in this era is remarkable. As Dillman and Beck (1990) have noted: ''Modern highway systems' success comes in part from the development of balloon tires that allowed vehicles, from freight trucks to motorcycles, to use roads simultaneously. Developing a system in which television signals, computer signals and voice communication can simultaneously flow through the same conduit is as critical to our era as balloon tires were to the earlier era'' (p. 36).

Service Features of Intelligent Networks

Whereas much of the work on technical features of intelligent networks has been conducted at the federal level or in R & D labs in the private sector, in the United States a great deal of the systematic consideration of the services that advanced communication networks can and should provide has taken place at the state or municipal level. In several states, the primary focus of telecommunications planning has been in the service of economic development. In other states, concerns with telecommunications and economic development have been balanced with foci on the role of telecommunications in promoting political involvement and social progress. Using the latter model, states as diverse socially and economically as Alabama and California have issued reports (*Founding a First-World Alabama,* 1991; *Intelligent Network Task Force Report,* 1987) calling for remarkably similar service features of intelligent networks, including:

- Conventional telephone services, including long distance access, 911 service and so on
- Access to publicly supported as well as commercial information services, including databases, historical archives and public library services
- Interactive text, print, audio and full-motion video services on demand, including a wide range of educational, informational and entertainment materials
- Provisions for serving customers not fluent in English
- Network facilities for persons with disabilities, including impediments to access common to the elderly
- Provisions for making essential network services available in public places at subsidized rates for those unable to afford customer-premise access equipment

The dominant recommendation of study groups, task forces or commissions in these states has been to advocate some sort of extended or expanded universal communication and information service, using the public switched telephone network as the operational base. Indeed, considerable attention has been given by public policy experts to the inadequacy of current formulations of the concept of universal service (e.g., Alliance for Public Technology, 1990; Dizard, 1989; Williams, 1991), but such deliberations are beyond the scope of the present report.

Operational Features of Intelligent Networks That May Affect Human Usage and Human Telecommunications Theory

Of paramount importance to us is an examination of how the operational features of advanced communication networks serve as catalysts to or limiters of the way we will communicate via the new advanced communication utility. What are the dominant communication characteristics that intelligent networks can be expected to offer users, regardless of the specific form or operational procedures of the network?

When compared with use of traditional mass media systems, several aspects of human communication are potentially altered when using advanced intelligent networks. First and foremost is *selectivity*. When individuals have 200 or more channels of video messages readily available, as do many of today's citizens of Queens, New York, plus access to an almost unlimited number of databases and the like, selectivity is practically forced upon the system user. At this point, key issues become: What features of this information utility will consumers choose to use? Will selections be "logical," predictable, or at least psychologically valid? How will selections be made? What sort of electronic program guides should system operators install to aid users in their selectivity? The overarching question, however, is: When intelligent network users really can and do have abundant information available "on demand," how will they go about choosing what they want to watch, read or hear? These are not simple issues, nor are they easy to test. Perhaps because of this, not very much scholarly or practical attention has been paid to them, although some progress has been made of late (e.g., Heeter and Greenberg, 1985; Zillmann and Bryant, 1985; Becker and Schoenbach, 1989; Salvaggio and Bryant, 1989). User selectivity may well be the dominant feature in the use of intelligent networks, and we must understand this concept and incorporate it into our theoretical and operational models if we are to design and use intelligent networks to full advantage.

Related to selectivity is the notion of *diet*—the media and/or message diet of the user of the information utility of the future. Advanced intelligent networks undoubtedly will offer users a rich smorgasbord of choices. What diet plan will users follow? Will they take advantage of the diversity of fare and choose media messages judiciously, with variability from the three basic programming groups (information, education, entertainment), or will they binge on "sweets?" In other words, will their diet be heterogeneous, balancing enrichment and information with education? Or will usage be significantly biased toward light, popular culture fare? Certainly intelligent network systems offer ample opportunity for utilizing either approach. In fact, current media systems are beginning to approach such abundant proportions. By my informal calculations, on today's "normal" thirty-plus channel cable television system, an action-adventure buff can watch approximately sixteen hours of action-adventure per day without ever turning on a VCR for time shifting. Personally, I am a mystery buff, and I am particularly fond of British mysteries by the likes of P. D. James, Arthur Conan Doyle, Agatha Christie and Dick Francis. If I choose to do so, I can indulge my predilections luxuriously: From my family room in Tuscaloosa, Alabama (hardly the media capital of the world) I can watch between ten to twelve hours of mysteries per week—from "Sherlock Holmes" to "Lovejoy" to "Petrocelli." If I allowed myself, how unidimensional I could become! The universal information utility of the future will offer such rich abundance that issues such as "diet" become crucial. Moreover, with advanced networks, diet will not only mean programming choice, it will refer to sensory modality as well. Remember that with full digitalization, message malleability soars. Not only will we be able to select what information we want, we will be able to determine through which sensory modality or modalities we want to receive information.

A third essential human element of intelligent networks will be *interactivity*. The same system that will facilitate two-way or multiway desktop videoconferencing will permit users to engage in all sorts of preprogrammed interactions— advanced versions of today's Compact Disk Interactive (CD-I) learning or entertainment systems and Digital Video Interactive (DVI) networks. Whether we will want to select the personalities or physical characteristics of our soap opera heroes, or to choose the denouement and resolution for our dramas, or to vote electronically, or to learn via interactive systems are empirical issues to which as yet we do not have satisfactory answers, but the system will have the potential for this degree of plasticity and interactivity, if we want to use it. Again, the alterations in communication behavior that will occur in the interactive media environment are largely unknown, but might be expected to result in qualitatively different sorts of media use in the era of intelligent networks.

A fourth critical dimension of the use of advanced intelligent networks is what is often referred to as system *agency*. "Agency" refers to the "degrees of control that an individual possesses in relation to a device" (Westrum, 1991, p. 217). The term can be used to refer to individual differences among network users; and we have growing evidence that personality factors, such as locus of control, and organismic factors, such as gender, substantially alter the use of traditional as well as advanced communication technologies (e.g., Bryant and Rockwell, [in press]; Morley, 1986). However, here we use "agency" to refer to the potential for system control provided to the user by the designers and developers of the intelligent network; that is, the potential built into the medium for user empowerment. In traditional mass mediated communication, the potential for a high degree of agency is extremely low. Certainly users can choose to use or not use the system, but flexibility within the system's operational parameters is very limited. In contrast, intelligent networks are designed to be personalized. They are easily customized to fit the needs and tastes of individual users. Use decisions can be made a priori (e.g., the consumer preprograms her or his daily newspaper, newstext or newsvideo to select and publish all available business news from Southeast Asia) or spontaneously (e.g., as with the typical use of today's remote control devices). The current degree of user control has led many to use of the term "Sovereign Consumer" (e.g., Bryant, 1989) to refer to modern media users, who, in contrast with media consumers of the recent past, have rather abundant media choices. But the use of the term may be premature. Perhaps this metaphor should be reserved for reference to media consumers in the era of intelligent networks. They really will have access to virtually unlimited information, education and entertainment "on demand."

These four human elements of intelligent network operations are intended to be illustrative, not exhaustive. Nonetheless, they should amply indicate just how different from current orthodoxy tomorrow's intelligent network will be in terms of unleashing human potential.

With these distinguishing features of intelligent networks in mind, we now examine traditional media research models and ask whether such theories and models of mass communication will be adequate in the era of intelligent communication networks. Of course, we cannot be exhaustive in this aspect of our inquiry either. Instead, we will choose some "classic" models as exemplar cases.

TRADITIONAL THEORIES AND MODELS

Since we have been discussing technical matters such as transmission and signaling, it seems appropriate to begin our treatment of traditional mediated communication theories by discussing one that is based on transmission and signaling. Of course, it so happens that this theory formed the taproot of the modern social scientific iteration of our discipline. It is Shannon and Weaver's (1963) so-called mathematical model of communication (see Figure 10.1). As is well known among communication scholars, Shannon and Weaver's model describes communication as a "linear one-way process" (McQuail and Windahl, 1981, p. 12). Frequently characterized as a "transmission model," the operations indicated in the mathematical model are mechanistic in nature in that it was designed to measure the accuracy of signal transmission, not the content or substance of messages, and certainly not the meanings users have for messages (see Tan, 1985). At a recent telecommunications conference, a prominent telecommunications engineer pointed out that "even engineers do not consider the Shannon and Weaver model to be practical today; it's just too simple" (Johnston, 1991). Indeed, standard engineering textbooks on network performance analysis, which have extensive sections on accuracy, do not cite or even mention Shannon and Weaver (e.g., Stuck and Arthurs, 1985). However, it is not the problem of being "dated" or overly simple that causes the mathematical model to be inadequate for application to intelligent networks.

Figure 10.1
A Mathematical Model of Communication

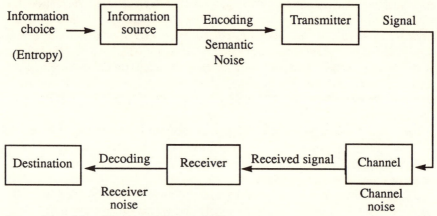

Source: Adapted from Shannon and Weaver (1963).

From the perspective of *human telecommunications theory,* the model's lack of ability to deal with meaning as the core of symbolic interaction is its fatal flaw. The other shortcomings become irrelevant, given this restriction.

The next model or set of models that we will examine is a simple exemplar of the *media effects* tradition. Of course, ''media effects'' is more than a re-search tradition, a set of models or some shared research modus operandi; it is a subculture with its own set of values, a special vocabulary and a particular *weltanschauung* (e.g., Bryant and Street, 1988). But we will consider it much more simply at this point. Looking at an archetype of this research model, we see that so-called sources send messages to so-called receivers (see Figure 10.2). The message is seen to serve as a stimulus that elicits particular re-sponses, called effects. This simple model has produced literally thousands of research studies.

Of course the model has matured with time and such extensive use, with consideration given to such elements as message features, intervening personal-ity variables, situational variables and the like (see Figure 10.3). It has also generated considerable debate, such as whether the concept of effects really is useful and valid, just how powerful media effects really are, how active media

Figure 10.2
A Primitive Stimulus-Response Model of Media Effects

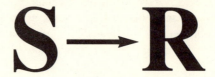

Figure 10.3
A More Elaborate Media Effects Model

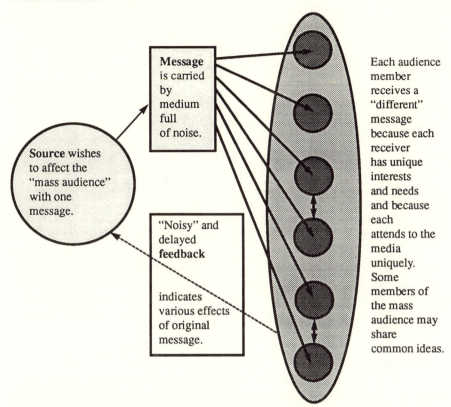

Source: Adapted from Black and Bryant (1992).

users are and how this user activity modifies or even nullifies potential media effects.

It is not these questions that cause me to cast doubt on the verisimilitude of existing media effects models for describing, predicting and explaining media behavior in the era of intelligent networks. The primary reason that current iterations of media effects models will be inadequate in the intelligent network environment is that they cannot account for the very elements of human behavior that the intelligent network can be expected to facilitate: selectivity, diet, interactivity, agency and the like.

Consider, if you will, routine functions of today's primitive computer communication networks. A common use of these networks is for computer conferencing. During a lively computer conference, eager users frequently step all over each others' messages, just as people do in informal, nonmediated group conversations. Or take the example of video teleconferences. Recently I participated in a board of directors meeting held over an interactive, full-motion vid-eoconferencing system. The sites were New York City, San Francisco, Chicago and Houston. In the video teleconferencing system we were using, the audio and video automatically switch to the transmit site when someone speaks, so that you can see who is talking. A second monitor permits users to view their own site, so that they can stay on camera, wipe crumbs off their chins, or whatever. On at least ten occasions during this board meeting, all anyone could hear or see was white noise and a blur, as audio and video switched almost constantly back and forth from coast to coast and from border to border, fol-lowing board members' lively discussions. At one point in our session we were to watch two segments of a manufacturer's video demonstrating and "pitching" a new Personal Digital Assistant. The potential for "media ef-fects," notably education and persuasion, appeared to be high, since we were required to make a policy decision regarding marketing of this product. How-ever, when we tried to view the video segments, reception of the video was interrupted repeatedly with questions or comments from viewers at the various sites, so that the impact of the excellent video was virtually nil.

Are extant media research models able to chart the sorts of interactive behav-ior that will be facilitated by intelligent networks or to predict adequately media uses and effects in these environments? No way. And remember, these are very primitive intelligent network operations that we are describing. As was stressed in the Office of Technology Assessment report *Critical Connections* (U.S. Con-gress, 1990): "The sender/receiver model is . . . much too orderly to ade-quately describe many of today's mediated communication processes. It as-sumes that communication takes place as a consistent, linear sequence of events—an assumption that is not supportable in today's technology-mediated information environment" (pp. 31–32). Only when, at the very least, we can account for selectivity, diet, interactivity and agency as basic components of the model will we have uses and effects models that will be useful in today's partly interactive media environment, much less in tomorrow's fully interactive intelligent networks.

Unfortunately, the same holds true for current uses and gratifications models, or uses and effects models, or what have you. To the best of my knowledge, no extant media model is equipped to handle the complexity of communication behaviors that will characterize the era of intelligent networks.

In fact, if we look at the sort of media effects questions that are already being asked of intelligent network communication, the questions are so differ-ent from those that have been asked in the traditional media environment that radically different models would appear to be required. For example, Cunning-ham and Porter (1992) identified a dozen different impact questions that should be relevant to intelligent networks. Most of these questions are more molar and global than any of the research questions commonly addressed in traditional media effects research.

It may be, however, that for other research questions, the most veridical and useful models for intelligent networks are not macroanalytic. Indeed, it may be that the most useful intelligent network models will be derived from theories and models of interpersonal and organizational communication. Naturally those would have to undergo modification to permit descriptive, predictive or explanatory specificity regarding the uses and effects of a unified, intelligent information utility.

Given all this uncertainty and such abundant choices, what is a scholar to do? The first step is to upgrade our research protocols and methods. The second is to expand our models and theories or to scrap them and construct others. Let me briefly address both issues. First, we will consider an exemplar case in which several steps already have been taken to make the sorts of adjustments in research methods required for assessing intelligent network uses and effects. Then we will turn to an "editorial" regarding considerations that must be made when expanding models and theories.

ALTERING OUR RESEARCH METHODS FOR INTELLIGENT NETWORK SCHOLARSHIP

Several scholars have published books describing the sorts of research methods and theories that might be appropriate for examining communication behavior in the new media environment (e.g., Rogers, 1986; Williams, Rice, and Rogers, 1988; Dervin, Grossberg, O'Keefe, and Wartella, 1989). As useful and interesting as these treatises are, it is not my intention to review or synthesize their findings. Suffice it to say that the list of new or revamped theories and methods mentioned—for example, network analysis, action theory, "social construction of technology" (SCOT) theory, technology transfer theory—is extensive and filled with promise, although perhaps it should also be noted that performance has failed to match promise. I have chosen to take another course. Permit me to leave the abstract for a time and to describe what we have done to create an infrastructure for testing media usage and effects in the new media environment. The infrastructure is the physical aspects of the Institute for Communication Research (ICR) of the College of Communication at the University of Alabama—10,000 square feet of space customized for and dedicated to communication research.

From the initial conceptualization of our institute, we planned to accommodate research into human elements of intelligent network operations. For example, in the ICR, opportunities for media usage are provided in a model home or a model office. When research participants choose to take advantage of the media fare provided in this information-rich environment, evidence of their media use is recorded unobtrusively. Moreover, all data acquisition is fully automated. Whenever a research participant turns on a television set or stereo system, switches channels, engages an interactive video disc or CD-I machine, selects a computerized information service, uses a touchscreen multimedia station or even reads a magazine, book or newspaper, records are made of that behavior via a range of automated data acquisition devices, including candid cameras, microphones and tactile sensors.

The information that the research participant selects can be chosen from the constellation of fare typically available in the Tuscaloosa market (e.g., cable channels, area radio signals, local and regional newspapers and magazines, local library and commercial on-line services), or we can control all information available in the environment, using a bank of interconnected VCRs and audio playback machines as well as our computer network.

Earlier we discussed the malleability of media messages in intelligent network operations. To a certain extent we have emulated that by incorporating digital production and postproduction facilities. These advanced message creation and editing systems permit precise manipulation and/or control over many types of media messages. The operational results are that the research participant in the model home laboratory might think he or she is choosing from what is normally available on cable, but every program provided might be one we have selected or manipulated in some way and are transmitting from our control room.

In order to simulate the intelligent network environment, we had to install a broadband backbone throughout the institute, which in most ways emulates an intelligent network, although we do not yet operate in a broadband ISDN environment. This infrastructure permits the instantaneous interchange of voice, video, text and data throughout the facility. Special software applications also permit the data from almost any automated source to be readily translated into various charts and graphs, which in turn can be superimposed and stored on a videocassette that is also recording whatever content the user has selected.

A fully automated Content Analysis Center permits on-line, real time assessment of up to twenty features of the media content that is being consumed, whether the content is video, text, audio, print or whatever. Data that result from the content analyses can also be translated into graphic profiles and superimposed upon the messages being consumed by the participant, at the same time as all data are being exported via the local area network for on-line statistical analyses.

We assume that media use in the intelligent network environment will be sufficiently complicated and cerebral that automated behavioral assessments and observations by experimenters alone will rarely provide adequate explanations of communication action, no matter how astute or well trained the experimenters may be. Therefore, we have made provision for guided interpretation by research participants. Across the hall from the simulated home and office labs are rooms designed for focus groups and in-depth interviews. During the interviews that follow a period of media use, the experimenter can show the research participant an audiovisual record of whatever media messages were watched, read or listened to. Moreover, if the experimenter desires, the research participant can view on multiple monitors time-encrypted video graphs demonstrating different aspects of her or his media use experience: One monitor can present the content that was consumed, another can display an audiovisual record of the participant's facial reactions during use and another can present graphics indicating specific message features that were noted by coders in the content analysis of the messages selected by the participant. In this way research participants can become co-experts as well as informants, if such is desirable. The interview process allows us to move more readily from information to knowledge. And, if this interpreted experience enables research participants to understand their own communication behavior better and act on their knowledge, they can use the research experience for personal empowerment.

At present we are working on interview protocols that will enable and motivate participants to contribute most meaningfully to their own interpretations of their media use and any effects such use may have had upon them. We are also pretesting several ways for presenting the graphic records of media use, of the content analyses, and of the candid camera and microphone recordings of media use.

If the situation or design calls for media usage to be more tightly controlled, either instead of or in addition to the *in situ* media use in the simulated home or office environment, a Media User Assessment Lab is located next to the home viewing environment. It features preference analyzer equipment, whereby, using a constellation of buttons or dials, the media user can report his or her voluntary responses to the messages being watched or heard. Among the many constructs that can be reported on are attitudes or opinions about the content, enjoyment of the content and many other attributes of interest. Again, the automated data acquisition can be graphically superimposed over whatever messages the participant selected and stored on videocassette. The preference analyzer system also permits fully automated administration of numerous personality inventories, batteries of dispositional assessment items and other forms of inquiry. The data can be recorded and reported by individual user or they can be integrated into an aggregate data set and reported as group norms.

If so desired, several types of physiological or neurological measures can be taken automatically, via sophisticated instrumentation. These data can be reported as charts or graphs and superimposed over the content selected by the participant, in addition to being stored for date- and time-identified statistical analyses. Each of the physiological systems permit individual records of responses to be played back to the research participant in subsequent interview sessions.

These and several other automated data acquisition systems are designed to contribute to an in-depth, fully integrated record of the way participants use and respond to media. In line with the characteristics of the intelligent network environment, *selectivity* is not hampered, *diet* can be assessed under relatively normal conditions, *interactivity* can be incorporated and assessed and the degree of *agency* of the research participant typically is not altered with reactive measures. What results is unobtrusive, yet fairly comprehensive, monitoring of media use. The automated data acquisition instrumentation, if used correctly, greatly reduces the amount of error that traditionally has stemmed from data transcription and data entry. At present we are spending considerable effort to assess reliability where such is appropriate.

When these relatively "objective" data are interpreted by the research participant in the interview sessions that follow media usage, what should result are descriptions of user behavior that feature the thickness and richness of qualitative research methods coupled with the precision made possible through quantification and subsequent statistical assessment. What we hope will result, of course, are theoretical explanations that are isomorphic both with observed behavior or at least with the meanings respondents have for their own behavior. Well, we all can dream, can't we?

With these aspirations in mind, we turn to our final topic, the need to adjust our theories and models for the era of intelligent networks.

ADJUSTING OUR THEORIES AND MODELS FOR THE ERA OF INTELLIGENT NETWORKS: AN EDITORIAL

In our discussion of traditional theories and models, I indicated some of the sorts of refinements to existing theories that would be required for valid intelligent network analysis. All that I want to add to those ruminations are some brief editorial comments. First, permit me to offer a note of explanation for the title of this chapter: "Will Traditional Media Research Paradigms Be Obsolete in the Era of Intelligent Communication Networks?" Although the term "paradigm" was used in the title, discussion of this term has been absent to this point. This has been intentional. In reading Dervin, Grossberg, O'Keefe, and Wartella's *Rethinking Communication: Paradigm Issues* (1989), I was struck by the fact that many of the contributors to this volume argued that the notion of a paradigm is not very useful to contemporary communication study. More than that, however, I was struck by the fact that the term "paradigm" has moved from being somewhat of a "god term" to being all things to all people. I chose to use the term with just such poetic license, not in its restrictive sense as used in formal logic or philosophy of science. Nonetheless, let me introduce this brief treatment of theories and models by looking at something a bit more abstract than theory, something that is almost as molar and abstract as a paradigm. I am convinced that the complexity of human telecommunications behavior in the new media environment will require theories constructed and research conducted from extremely diverse epistemological and metatheoretical perspectives. There are tremendous benefits to epistemological diversity, and I encourage all that would travail in the intelligent network environment to enter this fascinating realm, whatever their epistemological ilk. There is critical need here for those who would do scholarship from rocking chairs, for those who labor in the fields, and for those who use the laboratory as their crucible. All that I would ask is that we all remember to integrate our inquiry whenever possible.

As we think about creating theory regarding advanced communication networks, I would only encourage us not to retreat from the kind of intellectual pluralism that this diverse interdisciplinary heritage provides. Certainly we need to create our *communication* theories of intelligent communication networks, but we should continue to incorporate the thoughtful work of others with theoretical perspectives vastly different from our own.

We began our discussion with Joseph Dionne's (1987) provocative quote: "The Industrial Revolution changed the way we work in two centuries. The Information Revolution has done as much in two decades" (p. 1). If we are going to be able to understand mediated communication behavior in the not too distant future, we must recognize the limitations of our current methods and models and struggle to revamp them accordingly. The challenges that lie ahead are great, but the promises and privileges of the intelligent network should make the effort worthwhile. If we do not use all of our tools, knowledge and insights judiciously, we are apt to create just another jumbled, irrational media system. Surely we have seen enough of those.

REFERENCES

Alliance for Public Technology. (1990). *An information age agenda: The telecommunications service platform.* Washington, DC: Alliance for Public Technology.

Becker, L. B., & Schoenbach, K. (Eds.). (1989). *Audience responses to media diversification: Coping with plenty.* Hillsdale, NJ: Lawrence Erlbaum Associates.

Black, J., & Bryant, J. (1992). *Introduction to mass communication* (3rd ed.). Dubuque, IA: Wm. C. Brown.

Bloom, P., & Miller, P. (1987, June). Intelligent network/2. *Telecommunications,* p. 58.

Brand, S. (1987). *The media lab: Inventing the future at MIT.* New York: Viking.

Bryant, J. (1989). Message features and entertainment effects. In J. J. Bradac (Ed.), *Message effects in communication science* (pp. 231–262). Newbury Park, CA: Sage.

Bryant, J., & Rockwell, S. C. (in press). Remote control devices and television program selection: Experimental evidence. In J. Walker & R. Bellamy (Eds.), *The remote control in the new age of television.* New York: Praeger.

Bryant, J., & Street, R. L., Jr. (1988). From reactivity to activity and action: Evolution of a concept and a *weltanschauung* in mass and interpersonal communication. In R. P. Hawkins, S. Pingree, & J. M. Wiemann (Eds.), *Re-thinking communication research: Synthesis of divergent perspectives* (pp. 162–190). Sage Annual Reviews of Communication Research, vol. 16. Newbury Park, CA: Sage.

Cunningham, S., & Porter, A. L. (1992, January/February). Communication networks: A dozen ways they'll change our lives. *The Futurist,* 19–22.

Dervin, B., Grossberg, L., O'Keefe, B. J., & Wartella, E. (Eds.). (1989). *Rethinking communication: Paradigm issues.* Newbury Park, CA: Sage.

Dillman, D. A., & Beck, D. M. (1990, March). Information technologies and rural development in the 1990s. *The Journal of State Government,* 29–38.

Dionne, J. L. (1987). *The information revolution* (Pamphlet). New York: McGraw-Hill.

Dizard, W. P., Jr. (1989). *The coming information age: An overview of technology, economics, and politics.* New York: Longman.

Founding a first-world Alabama: Alabama's Information Age Task Force: Full Report. (1991). Birmingham: Alabama Information Age Task Force.

Founding a first-world Alabama: A summary of the Information Age Task Force Report. (1991). Birmingham: Alabama Information Age Task Force.

Geeslin, B. M. (1989, July/August). Funding the future infrastructure. *Society,* p. 16.

Greenfield, L. (1986, June 26). Optical computing. *Computerworld,* pp. 83–89.

Heeter, C., & Greenberg, B. (1985). Cable and program choice. In D. Zillmann & J. Bryant (Eds.), *Selective exposure to communication* (pp. 203–224). Hillsdale, NJ: Lawrence Erlbaum Associates.

The Intelligent Network Task Force report. (1987). Sacramento: California Intelligent Network Task Force.

Johnston, F. W. (1991, July 24). Personal communication. BellSouth Tech-KNOWLEDGEy Conference, Atlanta, GA.

McQuail, D., & Windahl, S. (1981). *Communication models for the study of mass communication.* London: Longman.

Morley, D. (1986). *Family television: Cultural power and domestic leisure.* London: Comedia.

Pierce, J. R., & Noll, A. M. (1990). *Signals: The science of telecommunications.* New York: Scientific American Library.

Rogers, E. M. (1986). *Communication technology: The new media in society.* New York: The Free Press.

Salvaggio, J. S., & Bryant, J. (Eds.). (1989). *Media use in the information age: Emerging patterns of adoption and consumer use.* Hillsdale, NJ: Lawrence Erlbaum Associates.

Shannon, C. E., & Weaver, W. (1963). *The mathematical theory of communication.* Urbana: University of Illinois Press.

Stuck, B. W., & Arthurs, E. (1985). *A computer and communications network performance analysis primer.* Englewood Cliffs, NJ: Prentice-Hall.

Tan, A. S. (1985). *Mass communication theories and research* (2nd ed.). New York: John Wiley.

U.S. Congress, Office of Technology Assessment. (1990). *Critical connections: Communication for the future.* OTA-CIT-407. Washington, DC: U.S. Government Printing Office.

U.S. Congress, Office of Technology Assessment. (1991). *Rural America at the crossroads: Networking for the future.* OTA-TCT-471. Washington, DC: U.S. Government Printing Office.

U.S. Department of Commerce, National Telecommunications and Information Administration. (1991). *The NTIA infrastructure report: Telecommunications in the age of information.* NTIA 91-26. Washington, DC: U.S. Government Printing Office.

Westrum, R. (1991). *Technologies & society: The shaping of people and things.* Belmont, CA: Wadsworth.

Williams, F. (1991). *The new telecommunications: Infrastructure for the information age.* New York: The Free Press.

Williams, F., Rice, R. E., & Rogers, E. M. (1988). *Research methods and the new media.* New York: The Free Press.

Your digital future. (1992, September 7). *Business Week,* pp. 56–64.

Zillmann, D. (1989). Pornography research and public policy. In D. Zillmann & J. Bryant (Eds.), *Pornography: Research advances & policy considerations* (pp. 387–403). Hillsdale, NJ: Lawrence Erlbaum Associates.

Zillmann, D., & Bryant, J. (Eds.). (1985). *Selective exposure to communication.* Hillsdale, NJ: Lawrence Erlbaum Associates.

Part IV

FUTURE DIRECTIONS

11

Everything That Rises Must Diverge: Notes on Communications, Technology and the Symbolic Construction of the Social

James W. Carey

My title is a play on a remarkable collection of short stories by Flannery O'Connor, *Everything That Rises Must Converge.* Her stories, in turn, provided an ironic gloss on the work of the late Jesuit paleontologist Pierre Teilhard de Chardin, who experienced five minutes in the intellectual sun thanks to publicity given by Marshall McLuhan to one of his books, *The Phenomenon of Man.* McLuhan, scavenging for support for the notion of a "global village" evolving through modern electronic communications, appropriated Teilhard's concept of a noosphere, a moment in the evolution of human knowledge in which the globe was engirdled by a dematerialized belt of human intelligence lifting us to an "omega point," outside history, where everything had risen and converged.

The spare and ironic intelligence of Flannery O'Connor was the necessary corrective to Teilhard and McLuhan's redemptive vision, to any "fatuous happiness" in abstractions. In story after story of cruelty and suffering, she gave to the forces of chaos and disorder, disintegration and death, the power they actually possess in life. In episode after episode, in the world as in ourselves, they won. She reminded us that while we may have evolved a noosphere of human understanding, we have not reached an omega point. Everything has risen but diverged.

We have our noosphere. The earth is now engirdled, thanks to satellite technology, with an organized belt of intelligence. Words and images, converted by the magic of our lingua franca, plus and minus, zero and one, circulate endlessly through space. Pop on a computer, or a television screen, appropriately wired, and such images emerge from everywhere and nowhere; pop it off and they disappear while still circulating in space. Words and images created on one continent are processed on another and returned to their original home. Human intelligence has lodged itself, extrasomatically, in the very atmosphere that surrounds and supports us. Yet, back at home, we have a surplus of disorder and disarray.

My take on the title "Everything That Rises Must Converge" was inspired by some lines in the proposal for this volume: "However, the convergence of communication forms and channels that characterizes the information age in which we live goes beyond engineering and hardware. . . . The fragmentation of society, the emergence of new communities of interest and newly articulate ethnic and linguistic groupings offer serious threats to social well-being."

At the same time, we were encouraged to "examine options within the context of convergence." This theme encapsulates certain exhausted ideas, which, to use an expression of William Pfaff (1991), are like "dead stars" in the cultural atmosphere yet remain central to the way communications is discussed and to the formulation of national policy. These are ideas that people want or need to be true merely because it would be bewildering to be without them. I have in many other places (Carey, 1989a) characterized this way of talking and thinking about communications and technology as the "rhetoric of the electrical sublime": the hope, against all odds, that the dual elixirs of communications and technology will dissolve our troubles and transport us to a new plane of economic advance, social harmony and human understanding.

The opposite is the case. Cultural fragmentation and postmodernist homogenization, to rename divergence and convergence, are not opposing views of what is happening but two constitutive trends of a single global reality (Appadurai, 1990). Divergence is not some random and unfortunate occurrence, a snake in our idyll of convergence, but a necessary consequence of the technological change we so eagerly support. We are living, engineering and hardware notwithstanding, in a period of enormous disarray in all our institutions and in much of our personal life as well. We exist in a "verge" in the sense Daniel Boorstin gave that word: a moment between two different forms of social life in which technology has dislodged all human relations and nothing stable has as yet replaced them. Media may be converging, as we are continuously told these days, but only in a minor sense: All modern media are rooted in the power of the computer to convert words and images into numbers, analog models into digital ones. Social convergence does not follow the technical convergence, however. Alas, the only social convergence about these days is found in simulated electronic cottages such as MIT's Media Lab. Out on the streets, in the cities, in our neighborhoods, things continue to fall apart.

Another, more useful though whimsical gloss on this subject, comes from the 1992 Republican National Convention in Houston. Patrick Buchanan, one-time challenger for the Republican nomination and full-time polemicist, painted a vivid picture of the Democratic convention that had been held in June of that year in New York. The delegates to the Democratic convention were, he said, liberals and radicals "dressed up as moderates and centrists in the greatest single exhibition of cross-dressing in American political history." The *New York Times,* never to be outdone, gravely interpreted Buchanan's remarks as homophobic but was disappointed that he had overlooked and thereby taken a swipe at "the largest group of cross-dressers in the United States, women."

The larger significance of Buchanan's remark is pursued, albeit indirectly, by Marjorie Garber in *Vested Interests: Cross-dressing and Cultural Anxiety* (1992). Professor Garber's book poses this question: "Why have cultural observers today been so preoccupied with cross-dressing? Why is it virtually impossible to pick up a newspaper or turn on television or go to the movies without encountering, in some guise, the question of sartorial gender-bending?"[1] She tells us that in the previous two years Phil Donahue had sixteen programs on cross-dressing and transsexualism, and Geraldo Rivera more than seven. Movies of the 1980s (*Tootsie, Yentl, Victor/Victoria*) were based on the theme; indeed transvestism and transsexuality are issues of intense popular and academic interest.

Garber claims that the distinct figure of the transvestite fills an important role in all cultural life. The cross-dresser signals a category crisis, a moment when established cultural boundaries of any kind, not only sexual, are being crossed or put in doubt. The transvestite thus stands for or "marks" any transgressive leap and creates a crisis of category itself. She means by category crisis a failure of definitional distinction, a borderline that becomes permeable and permits crossings from one distinct category to another: between black and white, noble and bourgeois, master and slave. The binary distinction male and female, fundamental to the categorical structure of all cultures, is put into question by transvestism.

Admittedly this is poststructuralism gone round the bend. However, the notion of a category crisis, a historical moment when the distinction between male and female (and with it all other binary categories) is put in question, has an independent usefulness. We may have thought at one time that people came in two types, plain and fancy, but all that has been placed in doubt, is under erasure. We no longer can take the established categories of the culture for granted, whether they are seen as constructed, biological or cultural. The prominence of cross-dressing represents a melt-down in the established categories of the culture, the categories through which we normally make sense of the world. Old binaries are displaced or radically conventionalized without new ones replacing them. This represents a displacement of fixed and given identities and subjectivities and sets in motion a restless search for new ones that can act as the countersigns of new practices, sexual and otherwise. In turn, the category crisis sets in motion the search for new metanarratives with which to tell the story of our lives. The story of progress, of the melting pot, of freedom and liberation, the American story, no longer seems capable of catching what is going on today in our lives.

We live then in a moment of divergence, when things fall apart and the center will not hold, when all that is solid melts into air. It is not only genres that are blurred, to invoke Clifford Geertz (1983), but all cultural categories are gauzy, losing their sharp-edged distinctiveness. We are experiencing a displacement and transgression of the symbolic, but it is unclear what will replace the terms on which we have navigated our sense of the world and our own nature for at least the last hundred years.

Despite those apocalyptic lines, I am not suggesting that we are living in an "imaginative proximity to revolution," to appropriate Perry Anderson's useful phrase. This is all rather normal, even predictable, just about what one would expect when existing patterns of communications and social relations are displaced, existing structures of community life dissolved under the impact of new forms of communications technology and yet another phase of capitalist expansion. It is not so different than what was experienced one hundred years ago when the modern system of communications was put into place. We are at the end of a long cycle of communications, a cycle which for lack of a better name and in order to have a stick with which to beat it, we might call the cycle of the modern. The cycle stretches from the birth of the national magazine in the 1890s through the disintegration of the network era in television, which occurred sometime in the late 1970s.

In framing this as a long cycle of some eighty to ninety years' duration, I do not wish to deny the profound changes wrought by the introduction and growth of motion pictures, radio and television, but only to characterize these changes as elaborations and intensifications of a common secular trend: the development, institutionalization and later disintegration of what Gilbert Seldes called the "great audience." The long cycle of the modern, the cycle that formed the now dissolving great audience, is, in turn, composed of shorter epicycles revolving around the introduction of motion pictures, radio and television.

In the 1890s a fundamentally new, national system of communications was put into place. Since then, this structure has been refined and improved, corrected and completed, through successive waves of invention in motion pictures, radio and television without disturbing the basic underlying pattern. Along this extended axis continuous adjustment has occurred, such as the important changes that took place when television replaced radio and film as the central medium in the national system. However, these shorter cycles have moved around a long secular trend: the formation of an ever larger and more inclusive mass audience, the deeper penetration of the media into every corner of the national system and the progressive displacement of other forms of social relations that were not mediated by technology.

In the late 1970s a structure that had persisted across time and technology started to unravel. The national, mass audience was fractured by cable television and transcended with the creation of the first effective system of international communication. The key technological ingredients in both the splintering and the transcendence were the satellite and computer. A long cycle appears now to be complete and we face a wave of technological and social change in which the scalar dynamic is tied, not to the nation, but to the globe, or least a globe divided into the three parts dictated by satellite technology.

The convergent order of the information society may appear from a safe distance as a neat geometric order with straight lines running into the future. However, on the streets this convergent order of the information society dissolves into ceaseless and disorderly flows: new people and new things flowing to new places along new routes; flows of migrants, guest workers, tourists, entrepreneurs and itinerants; new flows of capital, factories, messages, products, ideas, images and currencies. Things are flowing from new places to new places, upsetting established patterns of geography, trade and communications, imploding and exploding at the same time.

The central problem in these interactions that today occur as never before on a global scale, is the tension and contradiction between cultural homogenization and cultural fragmentation, between the order of technology and commerce and the disorder of migration, messages and settlements.

It was within a similar conjuncture, contained within a different scalar dynamic, that of the nation and the city (rather than the globe), that the modern system of communications was created.[2] In the nineteenth century Western countries were hit with two successive waves of change, separated in time but tied in logic. The first was the Industrial Revolution, which reorganized the nature of work and the structural basis of class and community and set loose a worldwide movement of migrants from low to high industry areas. The second was a change in communication and culture, which reorganized the basis on which art, information and culture were made available and the terms on which experience was worked into consciousness. These were not independent events but successive moments in the same social process. The timing, interrelationship, speed and extensiveness of these changes varied considerably from country to country, but both the direction and major implications of the changes were everywhere the same.

The industrial and cultural revolutions of the modern era were remarkably telescoped in the United States. The full tide of industrialization struck between 1840 and 1860. The communications revolution, presaged by the growth of the telegraph and the penny press in the decades before and after the Civil War, decisively began in the 1890s with the birth of the national magazine, the development of the modern mass, urban newspaper, the domination of news dissemination by the wire services and the creation of early, primitive forms of electronic communication. The latter constituted the infrastructure of a nation-wide system of signalling tied to a largely local network of telephony. By the 1920s the dominant tendencies of this revolution were clear, although they continued to work themselves out even into the 1970s.

The most explored dimension of the cultural revolution was the rise of national or mass media of communication—media that cut across structural divisions in society, drawing their audiences independent of race, ethnicity, occupation, region or social class. This was the creation of a new collectivity, a great audience, in which we were destined to live out a major part of our lives. The great audience was both a new social formation and a new body of lived experience. This was the first national audience and the first mass audience and, in principle, it was open to all. Modern communications media allowed individuals to be linked, for the first time, directly to the imagined community of the nation (at least for nations as large as the United States) without the mediating influence of regional and other local affiliations. Such national media laid the basis for a mass society, understood in its most technical and least ideological sense: the development of a form of social organization in which intermediate associations of community, occupation and class did not inhibit direct linkage of the individual and primary groups to the state and other nation-wide organizations through mass communications.

The rise of national media represented a centripetal force in social organization. Such media greatly enhanced the control of space by reducing signalling time (the gap between the time a message is sent and received as a function of distance), by laying down direct lines of access between national centers and dispersed audiences and by producing a remarkable potential for the centralization of power and authority.

However, there was a second dimension to this communication revolution, one that acted in precisely the opposite fashion, creating a centrifugal force in social organization. Specialized media of communication transformed inchoate groups into national but specialized audiences organized around ethnic, occupational, class, religious, racial and other affiliations and interests. These minority media were in many ways more crucial forms of communication because they were the foundation stones upon which the social structure was built up and they served as intermediate mechanisms linking local and partial milieus to the wider national community.

Specialized or minority media indexed the progressive differentiation of social structures. They mirrored a process whereby groups formerly dependent upon face-to-face contact were transformed into audiences, and audiences were, in turn, devolved into groups. More important, such media created entirely new groups by providing collective symbols that transcended space, time and culture. Finally, while such media addressed themselves to narrow dimensions of their audience's life, they created national communities of interest by allying themselves with national bureaucracies and selecting their audiences on a national basis. The formation of national economic and ethnic communities is one dimension of this process; the formation of national racial and sexual communities is another.

Collectively, then, the first two dimensions of the communications revolution represented centripetal and centrifugal forces, the systolic and diastolic beats of the social, creating a national mass audience while at the same time creating new groups, transforming existing groups into audiences and nationalizing the sentiments and interests of everyone in virtually every dimension of their lives. They were simultaneously moments of universalism and fragmentation, moments when a common though mass-produced culture was created, as well as moments of intense cultural differentiation and fragmentation.

In 1892 it was announced that the frontier had closed, that the society had been fully enclosed in space. The expansion of the railroad and telegraph had, first of all, connected the major cities into a national system of transportation and communication. Then, in the later years of the nineteenth century, the vacant spaces were "backed and filled," hooking "island communities" into a national society. This process everywhere met local resistance, but the "system was the solution" and communities everywhere were either integrated into it or circumvented by it and left to die.

The closing of the frontier represented larger closings and transformations. Space was enclosed in two senses: first the nation was enclosed, reaching its manifest destiny as a prelude to a leap beyond its own borders in imperial expansion. Second, space was enclosed institutionally as national networks of communication invaded the space of local institutions. That is, local institutions of politics, commerce and culture were reconfigured as end points or nodes in national structures. Local political organizations became outposts of national parties; local business became elements in chains; local newspapers, lectures, performances, concerts and educational institutions became, in a manner of speaking, stops on a national circuit. They lost their autonomy and, increasingly, their local identity.

Time was also transformed and opened as a new frontier. Time was, first of all, standardized into a national grid so that everyone was on the same clock of awareness. The telegraph organized and controlled time zones so that organization and activity could be coordinated nationally. But new "times" were also opened as commercial and other forms of activity broke into the Sabbath and then onward, via the electric light, into the nighttime. It began with the Sunday newspaper invading the Sabbath in the 1880s. Eventually, nationally produced communications would occupy every space and every time: every office, home, street, city and institution; every time, sacred and secular, seasonal and annual, daytime and nighttime; we would never be out of earshot or eyeshot of national media. This imperialism of images spread the representation of the national into all geographic times and spaces and into all cultural times and spaces as well. The system represented an imperative that every social time and space should be filled by commerce and communications. The national system, the system of the modern, was, for "advanced" nations such as the United States, enclosed in the 1890s and subsequent developments in communications—motion pictures, radio, television—from this perspective were protracted and relentless mopping up operations.

There were other, concomitant changes that must be noted. The urban milieu, which was the center of the social drama in which the national society took on its existence, was the scene of parallel change: explosive growth fueled by two forms of migration. The first was the emptying out of rural areas as migration from the farm and small town accelerated. The second was the international migrations that largely had the city as their terminus and that filled these spaces with new faces.

The city, then, was the site of conflict and accommodation as new groups struggled with one another to occupy the turf of urban areas. There were three kinds of ecology involved here. The first was a purely physical ecology as groups radiated out over the transportation system of the city and created new patterns of settlement and new forms of community life. There was a struggle for physical space. However, this struggle was transformed into a symbolic ecology as groups cast their experience in dramatic form: friends and enemies had to be named and identified, competitive groups had to be characterized and their motives represented. Third, there was a media ecology that overlaid both of these processes as newspapers, magazines and eventually radio and television stations articulated to the underlying physical and symbolic struggles. The city, at one level a purely physical world, contained an imaginative world of social relations as well. For example, each ethnic group had to define itself, which meant each had to know, understand, compete, name and struggle against other ethnic groups inhabiting contested physical and symbolic space. The media were overlaid on these baser ecologies, producing yet another imaginative world of the city, one articulated to and integrated with the national community.

The communities of the city were in every case transmuted or diasporic communities of two kinds. Some were formed out of the physical diaspora of migration, both national and international. In their native habitat people were known only as country people or rural folk or had subnational identities deriving from clans, provinces or dialects. In the cities they became hillbillies or hicks, Italians or Irish: identities and subjectivities made within the migratory process itself rather than being formed in advance of it. Other groups were formed by imaginative diaspora—cosmopolitans and the new professionals who lived in the imaginative worlds of politics, art, fashion, medicine, law and so forth. These diasporic groups were twisted and knotted into one another within urban life. They were given form by the symbolic interactions of the city and the ecology of media, who reported on and defined these groups to one another, fostered and intensified antagonisms among them, and sought forms of mutual accommodation.

The new communications technologies of the 1890s were a force of social disorganization, if we understand that term technically rather than morally as referring to a moment when established routines, institutions and identities ceased to offer enough structure to conduct social and psychological life. Disorganization was a temporary state, however; this was not a mass society aborning. Eventually new identities, new routines and new institutions established themselves and took on the illusory permanence and stability of those recently displaced. The social may have gone opaque, resisting representation at that moment, but the very opaqueness of the social motivated the intellectual and cultural work necessary to map and configure a new urban world. Out of it came the structures of ethnic, racial, occupational and class groups, the new "progressive" institutions of the economy and polity, and the new routines of love, marriage and child rearing that were the predominant features of the "modern."

The ethnic and other groups were creations of a process of symbolic interaction, and to understand these formations required a sociology of border crossings, of migration across the semipermeable membranes of social life that constituted the disorderly fronts of urban living.

Surrounding the structural changes of modern society were a variety of cultural and social movements that were both responses and assertions: progressivism, populism, the creation of ethnic groups, nativism, the Know-Nothings, women's suffrage, temperance, the Grange. There was also the creation of a new class structure organized around the plutocrats, a structure Henry Adams lamented and Charles Beard described. These movements—some modern, some antimodern, some even postmodern—expressed a restless search for new identities and for new forms of social and cultural life. Taken together these movements offered new ways of being for a new type of society. The 1890s appear to have been a moment when people actively shed their past, shed ways of being and belonging and created a society in motion that lacked a clear sense of where it was going or what it would be when it got there. These were movements organized by media, defined by media, commented upon by media, formed within media or at least as responses to new conditions of social life brought about in part by new media.[3]

The 1890s also involved kicking over the narrative structures of the past, searching for a new metanarrative within which to tell the story of the modern. This required, above all, displacing and deconstructing the story Americans had told themselves about themselves. The story of the small town as either barren or romantic is one of achievements of this period. The image of the American small town, the country town, as a seat of unrelieved bigotry, Babbittry and philistinism, a site of class conflict and exploitation, is an achieved image despite the fact that it is now an unquestioned one. The attack on the small town was a necessary part of the modern movement. The emergence of the national society depended in part on a burning of its predecessor, the agricultural society and the small town credo that justified it. Just as the emergence of the postmodern depends on the destruction of the modern in all its forms, the emergence of the modern relied upon the denigration of the phase of history that preceded it.

The struggle to create a modern society was simultaneously a displacement of an older way of life. The creation of new groups and social structures depended on a complex reconstruction of the past, a reconstruction that delegitimated an older order so as to pave the way for a new world of industry, the city, the professions and modern life-styles. Metanarratives do not simply end; they are actively attacked and destroyed within the complex actions that move the social from one phase to another.

I have described the interlinked changes—social, political, and intellectual—of the 1890s as the creation, in Benedict Anderson's (1983) useful phrase, of the "imaginary community of the nation": the formation of a national economy, a national polity and a national culture. Since the late 1970s, we have been undergoing a similar communications revolution, but one whose scalar dynamic is at the global rather than the national level, a revolution producing, in the words of the former chairman of Citicorp, "the twilight of sovereignty" (Wriston, 1992). However, it has produced similar phenomena: a category crisis or cultural meltdown in which established conceptual schemes no longer make adequate sense of the world; a frenzied attempt to build new conceptual schemes to account for changed circumstances; an attempt to deconstruct the metanarrative of the modern and build a new historical understanding through the category of the postmodern; a destruction of fixed subjective identities and the search for new forms of self-understanding and new forms of social relations; a reconstruction of the dimensions of space and time through the agency of new communications technologies; the eruption of new social movements attempting to reconstruct politics, economics and social life; a new migration that has unsettled the established social fronts of the city and, even more, the nation; and, of course, the international expansion of multinational capitalism, which is the ingredient that has kept the pot boiling.

We are living through yet another crisis of representation, another episode in our attempt to produce a knowable society and a livable community. The global village turns out to be an unstable and in many ways an unfriendly place, in which ethnic nationalisms again occupy the center of the stage. Everywhere state and nation are pitted against one another; primordia have been globalized, and identity politics is practiced on a world scale. A new informational class, represented by Walter Wriston (1992, p. xii) as a figure with the skills to write a complex software program that produces a billion dollars of revenue and can walk past any customs officer in the world with nothing of "value" to declare, has replaced an old plutocracy.

This story could be told as the tale of the satellite and computer, the key instruments of the transformation, or as the tale of postmodernism, the process and ideology through which we are living or as a story of yet another rebirth of capitalism. In closing, however, I want to take up but one aspect of the contemporary situation, the one troubling most institutions these days, namely the question of diversity.

In an early essay (Carey, 1967) I suggested that human diversity was disappearing, at least in a spatial sense. Communications, technology and economic modernization were reducing variations in conduct, culture and human institutions throughout the world. The contrasts that remained were paler and softer than those detailed in the anthropological texts. All of us were increasingly living one uniform way of life under very similar economic and political circumstances. However, I also suggested that the end of diversity was not yet at hand. As spatial diversity decreased, temporal diversity increased. As differences among people in space declined, differences among people in generational terms increased. The axis of diversity, in other words, had shifted from space to time, from differences between societies to differences between generations within societies. The sharpest evidence of this is the development of new age-segregated patterns of living and, more important, the generational styles of popular culture that bear new and discontinuous outlooks and sensibilities.

In other words, we are living in a world where under the force of communications and transportation—all the imperialisms of which we are daily reminded—it is getting rather hard to find headhunters, people who climb mountains on their knees, and others who predict the weather from the entrails of a pig. The good old days of cannibalism and ritual sacrifice of virgins may be gone forever. Moreover, the strangest tribes we face these days may not be in Borneo, where the people look familiar, but in our living rooms, where we confront the strange ways of thinking, believing and understanding current among our own children.

But that argument misses something of vital importance relative to the diversity of people in both space and time. As Clifford Geertz (1985), from whom I am rather freely drawing, has suggested, it is not that spatial differences are being eliminated but that they are being relocated from there to here. The age of large undifferentiated total societies facing off against one another is, relatively speaking, gone. The old comparisons of East versus West, primitive versus modern, developed versus underdeveloped, anthropologist versus native do not work anymore. There is no longer an East here and a West there, a primitive in Malaysia and a modern in New York. The natives, if you will forgive me, are everywhere and so are we. If someone is predicting the weather from the entrails of a pig, chances are he is living next door. If there is widow-burning going on, it is likely to occur outside of town rather than halfway around the world. The most recent cases of cannibalism I have encountered have not been in darkest Africa but in relatively enlightened Milwaukee.

The force of this change was caught by Marshall McLuhan's suggestion that the period of explosion, when the West sailed forth to convert the natives, was over. The communication and transportation system was now running in reverse, cultures were imploding, taking up residence next to one another on the television screen and in the housing subdivision. You can now sample many of the tribes of the world by taking a one-hour stroll through the neighborhoods of most cities or by grazing through cable television channels.

But if space has imploded so that what was once out there is now in here (next door, around the corner, in the next office, on channel 51), so has time. The differences in generations are still substantial and our first contact with the mysteries of the Orient may occur when our son shaves his head and takes up the sitar. But even with those differences, it remains true that the French, despite all the upheavals in the world, remain cussedly the French, whether you find them in Paris, Quebec City or Woonsocket, Rhode Island. Or to give the same matter a different spin, despite the rise of heroic atheism, it is still necessary to ask the unbeliever whether he is a Protestant atheist, a Catholic atheist or a Jewish atheist. Ancient cultural differences remain, in paler and softer tones, even if we rename them.

Finally, our capacity to reawaken the past, to reclaim all sorts of ancient traditions, customs, crafts and habits, has reached new heights in postmodern culture. The past appears more than ever to be less like a solid glacial deposit than an infinite and discontinuous set of geological layers, all of which are accessible for mining for whatever strange purpose. The "way we live now" is not only a pastiche of the cultures of the world but of the cultures of history. This pastiche quality is nicely caught in Hannah Davis's (1990) description of life in a small Moroccan agricultural town, where

symbols from different worlds overlap; a picture of the king of Morocco hangs next to a poster of the Beatles. The sounds of a religious festival outside . . . mingle with the televised cheering of soccer fans. . . . In the morning we watch a holy man curing a boy, then stop off at the fair where we see a woman doing motorcycle stunts; in the evening we watch an Indian fairy tale or a Brazilian soap opera or an Egyptian romance. (P. 13)

Davis remarks: "It is not the contrast between the elements that is striking; it is the lack of contrast, the clever and taken-for-granted integration" (p. 12). As Annabelle Sreberny-Mohammadi (1991) comments: "The transcultural mix of symbols is apparent when one young girl organizes a traditional religious feast yet defiantly appears wearing a denim skirt and earrings; thus, such symbols may be used in personal struggles to 'define, test or transform the boundaries' of local lives" (p. 133). The same description can be applied, with an inversion or two, to any street on virtually any day, in Manhattan.

If I can shift the metaphor to an aesthetic one and work toward a conclusion, we can no longer understand the world as a still life through the standing back of perspectival painting; rather it is a collage of conflicting and randomly assorted elements in which the artist is absorbed into the art. From the penthouse of the informational society this may look all rather peaceful, calm and progressive, but down in the streets, where most people have to live, it is really rather messy. We live amidst enormous cultural and social diversity, part of it the persisting traces of older ways of life, and part of it generated on new axes of differentiation, such as those of gender and sexuality. There seems to be no end to the delicacy and invidiousness with which we can describe, impute and elaborate human difference. We can no longer count the number of tribes—old and new—that array themselves before us.

As I said at the outset, the global village created by communications technology has turned out to be a rather peculiar place. It is not a place of convergence where the cultures of the world arrive at some omega point of agreement and identity. Everything has risen: Communications and transportation have uprooted human cultures and set them in motion once again. Yet nothing has converged: These cultures are in motion in their infinite variety and painful diversity. There are days when we wish for the dangerous certitude of squared-off countries pitted against one another—the United States versus the Soviet Union. However, today we encounter collage societies barely hanging together, where host and migrant cultures leak into one another. The very technology that is bringing us together physically and imaginatively is just as assuredly driving us apart.

Our temptation at moments like this is to chant mantras such as race, class and gender, another kind of talisman, a modern crucifix, to ward off postmodern vampires. Such invocations do not signal, for all the bluster, a settled analysis of a settled world but only that our inherited notions have dissolved and that we have nothing with which to replace them; we live in a world of nameless things and thingless names. We are all transvested.

We do not know how to describe this transvested society we are creating willy-nilly at a new conjuncture of a physical ecology, a symbolic ecology and a media ecology. To call this an information society of convergent media is but to express the puritanism of the deracinated. To believe that we have a purchase on a new world of diversity is a delusion of those who visit difference armed only with spiritual traveler's checks. We are as confused, though often as arrogant, as the first anthropologists encountering the first natives. And we have a critical problem. Because in the midst of these unsettling changes we stubbornly cling to the hope of forming a democratic world, we wish to retain amidst globalized diversity a public space for citizenship. But what can public space or citizenship mean when Time Warner proclaims that "the world is our audience"? Having failed to create a national public space, we now are charged with the problem of creating an international one. And, closer to home, our received notions of democracy are tested by forms of public diversity they were never created to contain.

The recovery of a public space for citizenship can only occur if we can describe the social differences being produced and reproduced in what we often naively call the information society. For public spaces are only recovered from the interstices where difference collides with difference and where both collide with the global. There is a fragile, fugitive moment between these forces where we might, with the right language and the right descriptions, and with a lot of luck, recover something of value. For only if we can describe difference in an intelligible and mutually acceptable way, only if we can humanely articulate difference to difference, can we produce a public space and a public sphere. Only then can we insert, between the global and the fragmented, a public space of citizenly discourse.

NOTES

1. I have taken some of this formulation from Anne Hollander (1992).

2. I have drawn some of the material that follows from two earlier essays (Carey, 1969, 1989b).

3. Many of the movements typical of the city spilled over into the international arena

as a wave of romantic nationalism swept over Western societies leading up to World War I. In that conflict the slogan was: Every nation deserved a state, and every ancient people—Celts, Slavs, Turks—would be restored to their rightful identity in social life. These movements, as with domestic counterparts, can hardly be understood without reference to the spread of international communication, particularly via high-speed shipping and underwater cable.

REFERENCES

Anderson, B. (1983). *Imagined communities: Reflections on the origins and spread of nationalism.* New York: Verso Books.

Appadurai, A. (1990). Disjuncture and difference in the global cultural economy. In M. Featherstone (Ed.), *Global culture: Nationalism, globalization and modernity* (pp. 295–310). Newbury Park, CA: Sage.

Carey, J. W. (1967). Harold Adams Innis and Marshall McLuhan. *Antioch Review, 27*(2), 5–37.

Carey, J. W. (1969). The communications revolution and the professional communicator. *The Sociological Review,* monograph no. 13, 23–38.

Carey, J. W. (1989a). *Communication as culture: Essays on media and society.* New York: Unwin Hyman.

Carey, J. W. (1989b). Communications and the progressives. *Critical Studies in Mass Communication, 6,* 264–282.

Davis, H. (1990). American magic in a Moroccan town. *Middle East Report, 159*(19), 4, 12–18.

Garber, M. (1992). *Vested interests: Cross-dressing and cultural anxiety.* New York: Routledge.

Geertz, C. (1983). *Local knowledge.* New York: Basic Books.

Geertz, C. (1985). *The uses of diversity.* Tanner Lectures on Human Values, University of Michigan, Ann Arbor, November 8.

Habermas, J. (1970). *Toward a rational society.* Boston: Beacon Press.

Hollander, A. (1992, August 31). Dragtime. *The New Republic,* 34–41.

Pfaff, W. (1991). Redefining world power. *Foreign Affairs, 70,* 1, 40.

Sreberny-Mohammadi, A. (1991). The global and the local in international communications. In J. Curran & M. Gurevitch (Eds.), *Mass media and society* (pp. 118–138). London: Edward Arnold.

Wriston, W. (1992). *The twilight of sovereignty: How the information revolution is transforming our world.* New York: Scribners.

12

Informing the Information Society:
The Task for Communication Science

Denis McQuail

THREE THEMES IN ONE

The full title of this book invites contributors to go beyond agendas for research and to take a fundamental look at the field. This is not easy to combine with another recommendation, which is to draw practical or policy-relevant conclusions. I have followed the first aim more closely than the second, although my concerns are ultimately practical, related to the quality of the communication environment in an information society. My choice of theme, or themes, stems from some different, but interrelated preoccupations of my own during the last few years. One of these relates to the direction being taken by mass media and communication policy under the impact of technical innovations and social changes. It is this that leads to my singling out of the term "information society" in the title as a catch-all for the outcome of significant developments in communication and society. The attempt to make sense of changes both in the means of production and delivery of communication and in organized media systems (especially in Europe) inevitably leads to wider questions about conditions and trends of present-day societies. Among these questions, the future role for public communication policy and the continued relevance or not of any strong version of a "public interest" in communication are matters high on the agenda.

A second preoccupation relates to the definition, the substance and the boundaries of a relatively new and growing field of inquiry and teaching in the field of media and communication studies. The causes of this growth may be circumstantial, but in some degree they are also likely to be a response to the changes mentioned. There is still no consensus on what the relevant field of teaching or research should consist of, nor even on what it should be called. For reasons of convenience, as much as anything, I have used the term "communication science." As the enterprise develops it will become important both for practical as well as intellectual purposes to have a more coherent idea of the location of the study of communication in relation to other fields and to have some better sense of direction than now obtains.

My choice of overall theme has also been influenced by recent experience of research into mass media performance in matters that bear on the public interest (McQuail, 1992). The main aim of this project has been to consider what communication research might have to say about the degree to which public (mass) media fulfill reasonable expectations from society on matters relevant to wider and longer-term welfare of society, as this has been variously conceived. This has entailed an effort to identify the most relevant principles of such performance, as they have been deployed in different societies, and to examine what mass media research can contribute to the process of assessment. Inevitably, the results of such a broad inquiry have been tentative and incomplete, although there is clearly an important role for research. In one way or another, the field of communication science is inextricably tied in with the future of the media themselves, and we have to attend closely to the institutional and technological developments of the latter.

This helps to tie together three subthemes: an interest in media and social change, the question of communication science and a critical approach to the media in terms of the general welfare of society. It may well be that communication is not yet a sufficiently central feature of modern society to warrant the expression "information society," but it is clear that *if* we are entering an information society, then media institutions must be considered as central and, in turn, communication science acquires an obvious logic and purpose, even if many internal and border disputes remain, as in any maturing branch of inquiry. My main aim is to reflect on this possibility and to explore some of the resulting implications and lessons.

A CRISIS OF COMMITMENT

Relevant to the discussion of these issues are certain social and cultural changes of recent years, especially the seeming decline of ideology, the reduced opposition to capitalism and the increasing recognition and even celebration of a "postmodern condition" (Harvey, 1989), which implies an absence of fixed forms, direction, values or belief. One correlate of the current zeitgeist is a weakening or delegitimation of some of the social theories that used to sustain both critical inquiry into media performance and communication policies with a social purpose. The changes referred to have claimed numerous theoretical casualties. There is now: less concern with media violence and pornography, because of the decline of any dominant consensus on relevant values; less opposition to commercialism and to media monopoly, because of the celebration of the free market and the weakening of support for socialism in the world at large; less concern with social inequality, for similar reasons. The once strong attachment to "high cultural" values is weaker, in the wake of abandoning judgments in matters of taste. The celebration of the popular and the "empowerment" of the media audience has tended to take its place. Former theories of social and cultural integration and identity have given way to more fashionable attachments to the globalization of media culture (Ferguson, 1992).

The elements of social and normative theory that sustained the old belief system were not very consistent, but they did serve to supply plenty of motivation and direction to practitioners of the early media critical tradition, whether these sought to uphold the established order (by a moral critique of the media) or to undermine the same order for ideological reasons. At least there was no shortage of normative certainty. It is hard to find the replacement in the way of a coherent theoretical or normative base for guiding the emerging field of communication science in its present expanded task of tracking and making sense of the changing communication scene. It is not credible to suppose that normative concerns have simply disappeared or can simply be dispensed with. There is plenty of evidence, for instance, that relatively new causes such as feminism, antiracism or environmentalism do still provide plenty of moral purpose and fervor. Even so, in comparison with former systems of ideas, they are narrower in their scope, more short term in goals and have less to say about the wider condition and direction of society and history. More important, perhaps, they are not centrally concerned with communication.

The present stage of development of communication science is beyond the minimal point of having a broad agenda of concerns, but it is still well short of having any clear project or coherence of purpose. There probably have been moments when such conditions did prevail, along with a sense of intellectual excitement. This was true in the early days when the media were seen as potent instruments for good or ill and when the challenge of measuring media effects was fresh. Subsequently, when the critique of dominant ideology in the media was more compelling and the results of research promising, there was a similar sense of excitement. In both respects, routinization or disenchantment has long set in and the joy of discovery is rare. For the reasons given—especially the uncertain theoretical status of the field and the normative crisis of the times— aspirations toward any larger project appear to be thwarted just when the conditions for expansion and wider recognition of communication studies are present. One aim of this chapter is to suggest that the phenomenon of the information society, if approached in an appropriate way, might supply what is missing and compensate for what has been lost.

This is not to claim that there can be a single correct or best direction and purpose for the development of the field, just that there needs to be some sense of purpose that is convincing to enough people and broad enough to encompass very different kinds of inquiry. Ultimately, we are all likely (even certain) to be proved wrong in whatever choice we make, theoretically or empirically, to judge from the past fate of enthusiasts, whether they were radical revolutionists, media determinists, behaviorists, cultural pessimists or held to some other cause. But it has undoubtedly helped to have had some unattainable goal or some conviction to be wrong about.

The goal I am proposing has already been stated in my title and may already be thought to belong to the company of failures and illusions. For instance, the idea that the mass media technologies of the twentieth century would lead to a more free, equal, informed and civilized world was canvassed from early days and now probably counts more agnostics than believers. The revolution in information technology of the last few decades has equally still to prove its once-heralded power for social good and has as many skeptics as advocates. Simple propositions about salvation through communication are usually rather mindless, capable neither of proof nor disproof, but they do open up a terrain of questions and ideas that can be intellectually and normatively challenging.

THE IDEA OF AN INFORMATION SOCIETY

A precondition for taking this discussion further is to have a more satisfactory version of the information society concept than is usually deployed. In the line of earlier typologizing, the dominant definition has been in economic and material terms, identifying information as the emerging power resource and calling those national economies information societies in which a majority of the economically active are engaged in "information work," predominantly the service sector of the economy (Rogers, 1986). Such societies are also characterized as large and rapidly expanding producers and consumers of information (Ito, 1980). The implications for society and culture are not usually explicated, so that the term information society is often empty of meaning, beyond serving to identify what Melody (1990) usefully refers to as "societies which have become dependent upon complex electronic information and communication networks and which allocate a major portion of their resources to information and communication activities" (p. 26). No doubt this historical phenomenon is itself significant, and the information work criterion provides the basis for constructing a league table of national economies.

The sociological discussion of the essence of modernism has followed somewhat similar lines, in giving primacy to the growth of complex information-based social systems. More recently, characterizations of modern society seem to have converged on ideas concerning information societies. For instance, Giddens (1990) emphasizes the separation of time and space (essentially an informational achievement), as well as increased dependence on experts, complex systems and symbolic transfers (e.g., money). Modern societies are also described as high-risk societies, exposed to great uncertainty, subject to considerable surveillance, constantly engaging in reflexivity and self-monitoring. This characterization is not identical with that of a postmodern condition, but each element presupposes enhanced informational activity, in comparison with pre-modern forms of society. A sociological version of modern society along these lines puts some flesh on the economic bones. Even so, neither of the two seems to open up any new path for inquiry into communication or to connect very obviously with the field of communication science. Communication science will have to find its own version of the information society, and in doing so renew the theoretical and normative challenge that is so essential.

What might be the key elements of an information society for purposes of study by communication research? The simple fact of abundant production, distribution and consumption of information of all kinds and by many different media does obviously matter, although how and why is less easy to say. The consequences for culture, however defined, as mediated by newly available means and systems of communication will also require special attention from communication science. It may be here that the concept of postmodernism is most to the point. The globalization of mass mediated culture and the possible convergences, clashes and weakening of existing cultures rooted in places, beliefs or settled ways of life are features of the information society. This relates to what Giddens (1990) refers to as the "disembedding of social systems" under conditions of modernity. A concept of "information culture" would probably be more useful than that of an information society, if one knew what it meant. Probably we are faced with numerous different information cultures.

With these points in mind and making some large assumptions, an information society might be defined, from the perspective of communication science, in terms of a greater incidence and salience of information transactions, more power to produce and manipulate symbolic environments and a more informed consciousness and recognition of different values and beliefs. This is not yet a definition, and it signals a direction rather than an arrival, but it has some advantages over, as well as points of difference from, the conventional economic version. The most important difference is the parity with information in the narrow, cognitive sense that should be afforded to belief, emotion and imagination. This does not imply a less rational form of culture and society (in fact just the opposite, since the condition referred to is one of greater awareness and reflexivity, as in Gidden's concept of modernism). The reigning definition does, however, tend to privilege a notion of information in the sense of "hard data" and to imply that material progress will lead to, or require, a culture in which beliefs, emotions and commitments are subordinated to rational calculation, tests of "reality" and agreed rules of evidence.

An advanced information/communication/culture/society is no less likely to be rich in imaginary worlds, alternative representations, possibilities for expression and the living out of value commitments than were premodern social forms. One main difference will be the element of diversity and freedom of choice, made available by the innovations and the productive power of new consciousness industries. These remarks do not require us to abandon the ideal of an informed society—one in which the general public is broadly and adequately knowledgeable about conditions and issues of their society and the wider world. However, this desirable state cannot be achieved without taking account of the evaluative, emotional and even ludic dimensions of information. This argument is strongly supported by a wide range of efforts made within communication science to assess progress toward a more informed society.

COMMUNICATION SCIENCE REVIEWED: THREE TYPES OF INFORMATION RESEARCH

An inspection of the record of the field of communication inquiry indicates that the notion of information has been quite variously conceived (often without the use of the word at all) and studied in quite different ways. Three different kinds of relevant inquiry can be found in mainstream communication research. First, there is the concern with information in the limited sense of reliable, factual data about the social environment, especially in the form of mass media news and knowledge gained from news. The second variant refers to media-related processes of constructing and deploying frameworks for representing reality, of giving and taking meaning concerning experience (with reference to both fiction and nonfiction). Third, there is the large territory of research into values, beliefs, commitments and social-cultural attachments, as these are communicated in mass media. At issue have been ideology, morality, cultural identity, but also aesthetics and cultural values. This threefold division of information research—broadly conceived—is not exhaustive, but it does serve to identify the main alternative traditions of inquiry.

Media and Public Information

The line of research attention is long and fairly unbroken, although marked by occasional real or apparent conceptual breakthroughs, and some digressions. The earliest research was guided by learning models largely adapted from an even earlier tradition of educational research. The main stimulus was curiosity about the new media of film and sound recording/transmission. From the 1920s onward, much, largely experimental, work was directed toward establishing the possible merits and demerits of alternative media for instructional purposes. World War II gave a strong impetus to such work and widened its concerns. Research paid more attention to general knowledge of the world (military personnel were supposed to know something of the causes and context of the war). Media effects on attitudes and opinions about the events of the war (in the interests of motivation) were also examined (e.g., Hovland, Lumsdaine, and Sheffield, 1949).

This tradition of research into communication effects on knowledge (information in context) was continued in the postwar period in more fragmented forms. One of these was the study of election campaigns, in which attention was paid to the degree and sources of learning about politicians, their policies and the political issues of the day. The focus of attention was criticized as rather narrow and short term, but in the days before campaigns were taken over by image manipulators the topic was quite central for democratic societies. Several new lines of research were also stimulated by the seemingly low yield from campaign research. These included: attention to possible bias in campaign coverage and in media news more generally; the birth of the agenda-setting research tradition; attention to audience motivations and information needs in respect to political communication; a revived interest in intermedia differences, with especial reference to television and print.

Most relevant to the present theme are lessons from such research about the possibilities for the normal mass media to communicate information about the world to the general public, especially by way of news, documentaries, public affairs programs and broadly educative content. Unfortunately, there has never been a very strong constituency for such research (but see Trenaman, 1967; Robinson and Levy, 1986; Graber, 1984). Mass media do not usually *need* to know about how effectively they communicate. It is not part of the task of most regular news media to inquire into the communicative success or failure of what is a very undirected activity, conducted according to no plan or logic, other than the demands of the market and organizational routines.

Despite this, a basis for assessing the informative effect of media news has been laid. The acquisition and comprehension of information by the public from mass media is evidently governed by a number of powerful conditions relating to source, channel, message content and receiver, which can be expressed as general probabilities concerning direction and degree of change. In respect of sources and channels, it seems to be confirmed that trust is an essential factor for credibility and is not very freely bestowed by the public, but has to be earned and reearned. It does not seem to matter a great deal which medium is involved—television, press, radio or another—aside from the questions of differential reach and of content. In respect to content, it is clear that the information offered by the media is both very selective and patterned in such a way as to limit its potential to inform more widely, or to extend public knowledge in any significant degree.

Two other points can be mentioned: one the fact that mass communication still does not work on its own, but is supported or supplemented by interpersonal communication, which in turn depends on social organization; another that we are rarely dealing with a one-way flow of information, but with a triangular interactive situation in which complex relations between sources, media and audience/public determine the conditions for ''successful'' communication. All this sounds either like a great deal of hard-won knowledge or a set of generalizations that leave all specific questions unanswered and maybe unanswerable.

Standing back for a moment from this problem, what conclusions can be drawn about the informative achievement (or potential) of mass media after half a century of near-universal media immersion? One is that levels of public knowledge are still very stratified along lines of class and education. The structural discontinuities in knowledge are still with us and are highly resistant to change. The predominant impression is of a ceiling having been reached, with regression more likely than progress. This seems to have much less to do with the media as such than with the conditions of a society. Thus, on certain points, in respect to events of great moment or interest, these barriers are broken down and the will to know, harnessed with the means to find out, can lead to powerful results. What matters most is motivation. A second general impression is that such knowledge as has been diffused in the public as a whole is often subject to boundary limitations imposed by many aspects of cultural experience and values. Conditions of life, varying relevance, tastes and preferences, values and beliefs all still strongly shape the pattern of distribution of information in society.

Social Construction of Reality Research

The theory and research that falls under this heading has deep roots in phenomenological sociology, but has had to struggle for recognition against the earlier dominant conceptions of communication as transfers of information and ideas from sender to receiver. Not infrequently, the failure to discover direct informational or attitudinal effects was attributed to the "obstinacy" or resistance of an audience that preferred to ignore incoming signals or was judged not competent enough to understand or accept the media message. Early communication models were biased against the notion of an actively participant receiver as a necessary condition of lasting effects from communication.

Although such bias was increasingly exposed and denounced, communication researchers were often reluctant to accept the full implications of the demonstrated power and preference of communication receivers to establish their own individual and also collectively shared worlds of meaning. Even so, there has been progress in recognizing not only this essential condition of human communication but also the fact that what is offered as communication (certainly by mass media) is itself also patterned by language, culture and social circumstances according to frames of understanding and meaning that are very largely outside the manipulative control of "senders." In other words, the notion of "messages" as units of more or less unambiguous information or ideas is illusory.

Much of the research that seemed an advance on early causal models of media effect, such as research into the reflection or not of reality or into the cultivation of dominant perceptions of society and of cultural messages, has sought to incorporate basic insights of meaning construction theory, but has remained limited by an unfounded confidence in propositions about the power of mass media messages. There have been alternative directions and methods of inquiry within this broad stream of work. One branch has focused on the deeper meanings embedded in the constructed or transmitted "texts" of communications, starting with semiological analyses and ending with deconstructionism, which leaves no fixed meaning. Another approach has, in various ways, chosen to pay more attention to the receivers or to the relevant "interpretative community." The more pragmatic variety of "reception" research has been largely content to establish, as far as empirically possible, the broad meanings of incoming communication as selectively perceived or preferred by receivers (the audience). In neighboring "cultural studies," reception has been treated as the creation of new meanings, often ignoring, reshaping, even totally reversing any intended meaning. In this view, the reception of communication is more likely to be a subversive game or a solipsistic indulgence than any process of "meaning creation."

The Media and Public Values

The third relevant strand that can be distinguished within communication research is even wider in its range of reference, having to do with questions of values, as distinct from facts or (cognitive) definitions of meaning. The earliest examples of research under this heading were those directed at possible harmful effects of mass media on established systems of personal values, with particular reference to children. Value research rapidly widened in scope, and the record is now thick with inquiries into the value direction of media content, with most attention being given to political and ideological bias, to racism and sexism. Also relevant is research concerning questions of belonging and identity in relation to community, locality, group or belief. Increasingly salient (and also problematic) are questions of cultural identity, autonomy and integrity in an age of globalized communication.

Information is evidently much more than facts, and communication processes are often expressions and affirmations of the values and identity of their participants. This goes beyond the notion that meaning is subjectively taken and given, since many of the values at issue are rooted in collective experience and are salient and potent because they are shared with others and rooted in systems of belief and power. They are social facts that cannot be ignored. For most of the world's inhabitants, attachment to place, to other people or to belief is a powerful force that still shapes processes of communication reception and whatever significance they may have.

Communication theorists and researchers have not really been very successful in coping with the issues raised under this third heading. This stems less from any personal insensitivity to questions of value, belief or identity or from their own cultural postmodernism than from an absence of theory and research models capable of handling the issues. The development of methods has been very uneven. With some exceptions (relating mainly to methods of content analysis), the tools for the cultural/communication analysis of complex social processes and ties are still primitive. Descriptive ethnologies of this or that event, moment or place are neither sufficient nor sufficiently reliable.

These remarks are not intended to be dismissive of several quite different lines of inquiry, each of which happens to undermine any project of establishing a more informed society. There is no need to adjudicate between the perspectives outlined or to say which is nearer the truth under certain conditions in order to accept that new ideas, relevant to the circumstances of an information culture, are being developed within this broad subfield of communication science.

The essential point, however, is not the fragility of whatever progress has been made, but the need to keep the task of cultural and value analysis high on the agenda of communication research. It would be a mistake to think of an information society as one that is notably more devoted to rationality, less moved by beliefs and values. Its body of shared knowledge will be in no less degree emotional and normative in composition, even if the relative position of science, expertise and fact increases in some notional stocktaking of the store or supply of information in society. What can be different is the degree and quality of awareness and understanding of the processes by which societies represent and understand themselves by way of communication. In summary, the chief lessons should be that *informativeness,* in the widest sense, not only depends on the effective transmission of much objective information, but also on adequate structures of provision and conditions of reception, which take account of social and cultural differences. Any action on behalf of a more informed society needs to attend to these matters at a policy level as much as to questions of technology, media and message.

IMPLICATIONS FOR THE INFORMATION SOCIETY IDEA AND THE TASK OF COMMUNICATION SCIENCE

This review of a disparate field of inquiry leads to a number of conclusions relating to issues raised earlier. One broad conclusion can be expressed in the form of additions to the characterization of an information society that is found in economics and sociology. Aside from an overabundant supply of information, it seems that members of information societies should be seen as particularly active and selective users of information resources, often playful with symbols, ideas and definitions. Information societies are not so predictable, orderly or open to control or surveillance by experts as in the sociological version referred to above. They certainly have both the means and inclination to be reflexive, self-conscious and self-monitoring—one reason for the difficulty of manipulation and prediction. Although the evidence is indirect, it does seem that citizens of modern societies have the capacity and the means (provided mainly by the mass media) to cope with a higher degree of impermanence and rootlessness (Meyrowitz, 1985). This is connected with the rise of a global media culture.

A second conclusion is the implied necessity for any social science of communication to have a broad and humanistic mandate. While this might seem like a recommendation for abandoning any disciplinary identity and all limits to topics for research, this does not necessarily follow. It is simply to assert that communication cannot be studied without recognizing its subjective, emotional, participant and evaluative dimensions and entailments. As Hall (1989) provocatively remarks, "Communication studies cannot be more 'scientific' than the practices it theorizes" (p. 49). It is also a prescription that follows from the representation of an information society just given—a society that has more self-knowledge, and hence more capacity for choice and self-control. Oddly enough, communication science, without intending to, seems to have discovered all this for itself the hard way, as it were, constantly undermining or resisting its own drives toward utilitarianism and scientism.

Third, the previous remarks suggest a normative role for communication science, which is additional rather than an alternative to those critical foci that have been a powerful impulse toward creative research in the past. This role is essentially that of advancing knowledge of communication processes in the collective life of society. It calls for attention to be paid to communication structures and to patterns of use, to cognitive as well as evaluative implications of content and to sense-making in diverse contexts. This implies a bias against abstracted individualism and against a privileged status for effects research or factual content. If the object of study is itself fundamentally value-laden, then science has itself to embody a normative dimension. This version of the field of communication research also leans against the commodification of its subject matter. Neither the contents of communication, nor the multiple webs of social relationship that make communication possible, can adequately be conceived in terms of markets, supply and demand or rational calculations of costs and benefits. To follow that path is to lose essential contact with the reality of communication and of the information society.

MEDIA POLICY IMPLICATIONS

The arguments advanced above concerning a social science of communication and its potential for normative commitment have a number of implications for communications policy, if the improvement of the quality of the information environment is adopted as a legitimate and desirable objective. It is hard to be against virtue itself, but there are powerful voices that speak against communication policy as an infringement of liberty, a distortion of the market and an impediment to the very expansion and change that appear to be indispensable to the emergence of the information society. Accordingly, a minimalist view of the role of society (via legislation, government or regulatory agency) portrays the information society as the outcome of an economic and technological revolution in which consumers get increased choice at lower cost and only essential matters to do with infrastructure, potential monopoly and social order are matters for policy. The productive benefits of new communication and information technology are valued above social wants or any potential social and cultural costs.

Within this framework, many problems in the information sphere do not have to be recognized as such or are left to the relevant social institutions to explicate and deal with in isolation from each other, if at all. Lack of political knowledge or interest in politics becomes a problem for politicians; ignorance about health is a medical problem; illiteracy and low skills are a problem for education; low standards of "media performance," if acknowledged, are matters for the profession or the industry; low standards of cultural taste barely receive consideration, since the market does not recognize the concept. This perspective relies on self-regulation by market forces and on the same forces for generating change. It supposes a system in which there are no social deficits in the sphere of culture and information, because everything is either self-financing or self-destructing. All decisions that count are made by individual consumers or suppliers, who cannot be mistaken in the logic of the market.

The alternative approach (favoring an active policy) is often assumed to be obsolescent or in decay and can be represented unsympathetically as both interventionist and arrogant, guided by elite notions of what is good (especially "serious" information and "high culture"), insensitive to and ignorant of actual popular tastes. In this version, policy can be attacked as unsuited to a free and changing society with abundant communication resources. A critique of past communication policies and their remnants does not, however, constitute an argument for economic libertarianism. It is possible that the policies that led to regulations about licensing, limitations on access, public scrutiny of press performance, stricter control of monopoly, guarantees of universal provision, subsidization of certain kinds of "quality" and diversity, were appropriate and progressive in their day, while less appropriate or even obstructive under other conditions.

The critique of some communication policies does not destroy the case for all policy, or nullify the notion of a "public interest" in communication that may need protection and support. According to a very simple logic, there would seem to be a stronger public interest, in general, in the quality of communication in what is widely called an information society. Nevertheless, the problem of specifying the public interest in communication remains, and this too is a proper object of inquiry for communication science. Aside from following the lines indicated by simple majority popular choices or some dominant ideology or belief system, the only way of establishing which communication policy aims or means might be in the public interest—in the sense of promoting the wider and longer-term welfare of society—is by way of debate and argument within some relevant political forum. The more informed this debate, the more likely it is to produce solutions (policy measures) that are appropriate, viable and acceptable in a democracy. It is by contributing to this debate that communication science can best contribute, in however small a way, to the realization of a more informed information society.

CONCLUSION

In this spirit, I would like to conclude with a diagnosis of the vulnerability of the type of information society as sketched, based on the findings of communication research and assuming that a more rather than a less informed society is preferred, whether for reasons of rationality, efficiency, democracy or just personal preferences. The main threats can be named under three headings, although all three have in the end to do with equality or its absence. First, unequal distribution of chances to realize communication potential has led to a stratification of informational welfare, which can only reinforce a more total pattern of social inequality, one that is harder to escape from by the traditional routes of self-improvement, education and mobility. There are signs of a ceiling to information growth and of the emergence of an informational underclass, which is less capable of acting and choosing politically on its own behalf. It is also denied many of the benefits of communication and is relatively excluded from the processes of reflexivity and the ability to create, which are key elements of the information society.

Second, there is a potential risk of a growth of increasingly unidimensional culture, to adapt a term from an earlier critic, Marcuse (1964). His unidimensionality was that of a very widely shared mediocre consumer culture that would dissolve class antagonisms in a mass consumerist society. What is emerging in the present information society, under conditions of ease of communication production and capitalism, is quite differentiated in its forms of expression and meanings, but it is still ranged along a single hierarchical dimension, corresponding to social class, of much more choice for the few and cultural poverty for the many. A trend in this direction can only be reinforced by the loss of other sources of diversity (e.g., national, regional or ethnic identities) as well as by the growth of media monopolies. Where cultural pluralism survives, it cuts across the hierarchy and contributes to equality.

Third, there is the threat for many of a new species of "information chaos," which will make it difficult to learn from the public information resources of society. The abundance of means and products of communication is potentially perplexing and unmanageable, and trustworthy sources are harder to identify. In the sketch of the communication environment that emerges, however shadowily, from the outcomes of research, it appears that to learn from the kind of information that is supplied publicly, or to benefit from wider cultural resources, depends on having either access to frames of reference on which one feels one can rely, or the autonomous ability to create and apply such frames. The more traditional mass media of press and broadcasting have until now usually provided at least a coherent and orderly set of (alternative) perspectives on the world. The logic of market-led abundance has shaken the foundations of this more secure communication order, and the capacity to cope with the new situation is unequally distributed.

These conclusions, although obviously personal, are consistent with a more broadly based view of communication policy as more than and different from an instrument of economic regulation, political control or social surveillance. Instead, policy is an outcome and expression of value choices and beliefs, and a crucial element in the self-reflexive and monitoring process that has been described as an essential aspect of modern information societies. An early characterization of public communication, which seems no less relevant today, portrayed it as the nerves and the conscience of society (Hardt, 1979); this conception would embrace debates about, and proposals for, the wider social role of mass media. If such a view is accepted, it will be necessary for communication policy making to survive and develop as a legitimate institutional activity, and equally important for communication science to maintain its informative and formative role in relation to policy.

REFERENCES

Ferguson, M. (1992). The mythology about globalization. *European Journal of Communication, 7,* 105–121.

Giddens, A. (1990). *The consequences of modernity.* Stanford, CA: Stanford University Press.

Graber, D. (1984). *Processing the news.* New York: Longman.

Hall, S. (1989). The orthodox consensus and the emerging synthesis. In B. Dervin, L. Grossberg, B. J. O'Keefe, & E. Wartella (Eds.), *Rethinking communication: Paradigm issues* (pp. 40–52). Newbury Park, CA: Sage.

Hardt, H. (1979). *Social theories of the press.* Beverly Hills and London: Sage.

Harvey, D. (1989). *The condition of post-modernity.* Oxford: Basil Blackwell.

Hovland, C. I., Lumsdaine, A. A., & Sheffield, F. D. (1949). *Experiments in mass communication.* Princeton: Princeton University Press.

Ito, Y. (1980). The "johoka shakai" approach to the study of communication in Japan. In G. C. Wilhoit & H. de Bock (Eds.), *Mass communication review yearbook,* vol. 2 (pp. 671–698). Beverly Hills, CA: Sage.

McQuail, D. (1992). *Media performance: Mass communication and the public interest.* Newbury Park, CA and London: Sage.

Marcuse, H. (1964). *One dimensional man.* London: Routledge, Kegan and Paul.

Melody, W. (1990). Communication policy in the global information economy. In M. Ferguson (Ed.), *Public communication: The new imperatives* (pp. 16–39). Newbury Park, CA and London: Sage.

Meyrowitz, J. (1985). *No sense of place.* New York: Oxford University Press.

Robinson, J., & Levy, M. (1986). *The main source: Learning from television news.* Beverly Hills, CA: Sage.

Rogers, E. M. (1986). *Communication technology: The new media in society.* New York: The Free Press.

Trenaman, J. (1967). *Communication and comprehension.* London: Longman.

13

Communication Research in the 1990s: New Directions and New Agendas?

David H. Weaver

This is the sixth occasion since 1979 that I've had to think seriously about communication research directions. Each time, it gets more difficult to have something new to say, let alone something that might be considered insightful by others!

But our field of communication is forever changing—more rapidly so in the past ten or fifteen years than ever before—and so is research about communication, as indicated by the explosion of new books, journals, articles and convention papers in the past few years. As an example of this growth, one book publisher has recently divided the field into sixteen different subfields, including communication alternatives, communication and law, communication and participation, communication and social space, communication and social change, communication and development, communication pedagogy, critical studies in communication, feminist studies, interpersonal communication, mass communications and journalism, mass media and telecommunication systems/effects, new media policy and social issues, organizational communication, political communication and quantitative methods in communication (Hampton Press, 1992).

Likewise, the structure of the International Communication Association (ICA) suggests fifteen possible subfields of communication, including information systems, interpersonal, mass, organizational, intercultural, political, instructional, health, philosophy, technology, popular, public relations, feminist, law and policy and social interaction (ICA, 1992, p. 15).

Even within the subfield of journalism and mass communication, there are numerous special interests or areas, as indicated by the fifteen divisions of the

Association for Education in Journalism and Mass Communication (AEJMC): advertising, communication theory and methodology, history, international, law, magazine, minorities, newspaper, management and economics, mass communication and society, public relations, qualitative studies, radio/television, secondary education and visual communication (AEJMC, 1992, pp. 80–82).

Is it any wonder that there is increasing specialization in the different areas and subareas of communication in the face of such complexity? Is it surprising that there are few general concepts and theories of communication that are relevant to the majority of us who study communication and teach about it?

A 1991 survey of 231 key communication scholars (most-cited authors, administrators and journal editors) suggests there are some core concepts and theories that cut across many of these subfields of communication, including systems theory, information processing, symbolic interactionism, cultural studies and rhetorical theory (So and Chan, 1991, p. 45). But the most frequently cited concepts and theories tend to be within the different subfields of communication, including agenda setting in mass and political communication, uncertainty reduction in interpersonal communication, diffusion theory in intercultural and mass communication and uses and gratifications in mass communication (So and Chan, 1991, p. 47), reinforcing the utility of "middle-range" approaches.

In this chapter, I'll review some past trends in journalism and mass communication research—the branch of communication research with which I'm most familiar—then highlight some of the major developments in communication practice and research in the late 1980s and finally offer some suggestions about future research approaches. In doing so, I'll try to emphasize approaches and methods, rather than subjects of study, as the title of this volume suggests by asking us to go beyond agendas (*what* is communicated) to considering new directions in research on *how* communication takes place—although I'm doubtful that we can ever fully separate the "what" from the "how" of communication or research.

PAST REVIEWS OF RESEARCH TRENDS

1979

The late Richard Gray and I presented a paper at the 1979 convention of the Association for Education in Journalism (AEJ) entitled "Journalism and Mass Communication Research in the United States: Past, Present and Future." It was my first attempt to explore the history of research about mass communication and to think seriously about what kinds of research might be most needed in the future (Weaver and Gray, 1979). One of our main conclusions was that many mass communication researchers were more concerned with media audiences, and the effects of media messages, than with journalists and the organizations that produced these messages. We suggested more research on the pro-

Table 13.1
1979 Recommendations for New Directions in Mass Communication Research

Recommendation	Would make in 1992? YES	NO
1. More research on the production of media messages and on society's effects on media		X
2. More research on the impact of new technology on journalism and on the larger society		X
3. More research on the effects of media criticism	X	
4. More on media economics and management		X
5. More on new sources of information	X	
6. New approaches to communication history		X
7. New approach to communication law		X
8. More external funding of mass communication research	X	

duction of media messages and on the effects of the larger society on the media to balance what we perceived as a preponderance of research about media effects on society.

In addition to this recommendation for more studies of the production of media messages, we also recommended more research on the impact of new technology on journalism and the larger society, the effects of media criticism, media economics and management, new sources of information and new approaches to mass media history and law (see Table 13.1). Today, thirteen years later, it would be difficult to make exactly these same recommendations, because during the 1980s there was much high-quality research on many of these subjects, especially media economics, the impact of new technologies on media audiences and new approaches to communication history and law.

Gray and I also concluded that much research about mass communication and journalism had been sporadic, disjointed and short term, and that well-developed research programs had been stimulated by the interests of funding agencies as much as, or more than, by the interests of individual scholars. Through a study of two key journals in mass communication from 1954 to 1978, we identified certain kinds of studies that were more likely to attract outside funding, including surveys, experiments and some historical research (Weaver and Gray, 1979). An unpublished follow-up study of four key mass communication journals from 1983 to 1992 found similar patterns, although content analyses were more likely to be funded in the past decade than in the previous three.[1]

Studies using quantitative methods were more likely to be funded than studies using nonquantitative methods from 1954 to 1978, but not from 1983 to 1992, where the percentages of funded and nonfunded quantitative studies did not differ significantly.

But in comparison to other fields, only about one-fourth of published research on mass communication from 1954 to 1978 acknowledged an outside funding source, compared to about one-half of the studies in political science, psychology and sociology. This remained true in the past decade as well, with 24 percent of the published studies acknowledging a funding source.

The other social sciences relied much more on government agency grants than did journalism and mass communication research, which was supported about equally by universities, the government and private sources. During the past decade, however, funded mass communication research was more likely to be supported by universities (43 percent) and less likely to be sponsored by government (20 percent) or private sources (23 percent).[2]

In light of these findings, we recommended more funding of mass communication research, but not so much reliance on government as in the other social sciences. Instead, we regarded the diversity of funding sources for mass communication research as healthy, especially in light of the long-standing tensions between government and journalism in this country, and the need for an independent media system in a democratic society. I still regard such diversity as healthy, but it is a bit disappointing to see a drop in government and private funding for mass communication research in the 1980s.

1982

In early November 1982, the Department of Telecommunications at Indiana University organized a research symposium entitled ''Directions for Communication Theory and Research in the 1980s.'' I was invited to speak along with Steve Chaffee of Stanford, James Anderson of Utah (who was a visiting professor at Indiana then) and Dolf Zillmann of the Telecommunications Department at Indiana.

In my remarks, I reviewed a few recommendations from my 1979 report with Richard Gray, and invoked Jay Blumler's "three-legged stool" metaphor to argue that communication research needs to be concerned with sources, messages and audiences jointly if we are to gain more insights into the communication process, whether it be interpersonal, group or mass (Blumler, 1981, p. 44). I called for more programmatic research on the effects of society on the media to complement all the audience research that had been done on the effects of media on society.

I also pointed out a number of trends in mass communication research that had begun to emerge in the late 1970s and early 1980s, especially in the first three volumes of the *Mass Communication Review Yearbook*. These included:

1. More concern about the development, control, support and institutional context of mass communication, especially from European scholars interested in broader social theories and a more critical approach to communication research in general.

2. A shift in emphasis among effects researchers from attitudes and opinions to knowledge acquisition and agenda setting, accompanied by more compelling evidence of important media effects that, in turn, had led to more concern about who controls the messages produced by these media.

3. A growing acceptance of the idea that multiple methods often provide more complete and more valid answers to many of the questions about communication than do the commonly used single methods such as content analysis, experiments and surveys.

4. More concern with the implications of communication research for policy making, especially in countries where the government plays a more active role in the formation of rules, laws and policies regarding communication media and messages.

I concluded that we needed more studies *over time* that collected information simultaneously on sources, messages and receivers to understand more fully communication processes, whether they be interpersonal, group or mass.

1985

Three years later, in December 1985, I presented a longer, more detailed paper on problems and promises in mass communication research at a conference on communication research at Syracuse University (Weaver, 1988). In this paper, I argued once again for more research on the producers of media messages, and I also asserted that the fundamental problems of communication research were mainly those of substance (or lack of it) rather than methods.

To me, the debates over quantitative versus qualitative methods, or over theoretical versus applied research, were—and are—pseudodebates, because we all need good theories and whatever evidence we can collect to test them.

As has been said before, there is nothing so practical as a good theory—a theory that accurately predicts and explains. But no study's findings are likely to be seen as significant, by practitioners or scholars, unless interesting and important questions are asked, regardless of the sophistication of methods or the statistical significance of the findings.

Agreeing on what questions are interesting or important is no easy task of course, but we must keep trying. The classic studies in communication are recognized by most of us as addressing important questions or issues of their time, regardless of their different methods.

I identified what I considered to be examples of fundamental problems in communication research in the mid-1980s (Weaver, 1988). These included:

1. A lack of application to important social and scholarly issues, or the "so what" question. In Peter Clarke's words, we might make "more profound contributions to human understanding if we paused now and then to ask whether the results of a proposed inquiry—any of its results—would make a difference if known" (Clarke, 1973, p. 5).

2. A lack of cumulative programs of research where the individual studies build upon each other. Here I quoted British scholar Jay Blumler's reaction in 1977 to recent American research as seeming to be "virtually unclassifiable." The image in Blumler's mind was of "a huge, in many respects impressive, but nevertheless rather rambling, exposed and vulnerable giant" (Blumler, 1978, p. 225). He did identify two strands of work where studies seemed to be related—one dealing with equality of opportunity in communication and one concerned with journalistic performance—but much of our research seemed to him to be without any clear purpose. This criticism is still valid today, I think.

3. An unwillingness among many communication researchers to speculate upon the implications of their work for policy or practice—especially as compared with scholars in other countries such as England or Germany.

4. A confusion of statistical significance with practical significance, especially by those doing experimental studies where average scores of different groups are compared.

5. A lack of a forum for researchers, communicators and policy makers to reach and influence each other. To illustrate this problem, I drew on our national survey of 1,001 U.S. journalists in 1982–83 to show that very few regularly read any of the research journals in our field (not surprisingly) or even the trade and industry publications (more surprising to me).

In addition to these problems, I saw some promise in mass communication research by the mid-1980s, including the following:

1. More and better research on journalists and media organizations, including studies by Stephen Hess, Herbert Gans, Cleve Wilhoit and myself, the *Los Angeles Times* and the Associated Press Managing Editors.

2. More concern with the implications of research for communications policy and practice, including studies of science writers and their work, news

coverage of the U.S. Senate, media competition and diversity of ideas and views in a community, the effects of television programming on children and the coverage of elections by television and newspapers.

3. More programs of research where studies build upon each other over time, including agenda setting, cultivation effects of television, televised violence and aggressive behavior, international news coverage, newspaper readership and circulation, and media uses and gratifications.

4. More studies employing multiple methods and covering longer periods of time. One example cited was Peter Clarke and Susan Evans's study of 1978 congressional campaign coverage, which included surveys of journalists and the public, as well as content analysis of the journalists' newspaper coverage. Another was the study by Gladys Lang and Kurt Lang of how Watergate became a highly salient national issue, which used a variety of evidence from various sources. Another agenda-setting study by Michael MacKuen used content analysis and survey research over a seventeen-year time period to study the relationship between media agendas and public agendas, as well as various "real-world" measures of unemployment, inflation, crime rates, heating fuel prices and troop levels in Vietnam.

5. More debate over research approaches and methods, as illustrated by the publication of the Sage Mass Communication Review Yearbooks, beginning in 1980, the summer 1983 "Ferment in the Field" issue of the *Journal of Communication,* and the emergence of new journals outside the United States such as *Media, Culture and Society,* the *European Journal of Communication Research,* the *Canadian Journal of Communication* and the *Keio Communication Review* in Japan. As a result of the articles carried in these and other new publications, debates over critical versus administrative research, policy versus policy-oriented studies, structuralist versus positivist approaches, and communication theory versus social theory became more familiar to American scholars by the mid-1980s.

I concluded this 1985 conference paper by urging communication researchers to put aside some of the old debates over theoretical versus applied research and quantitative versus qualitative methods, and to focus instead on what kinds of questions should be asked in future studies (see Table 13.2). I also expressed hope that more academic researchers would take a greater interest in the implications of their studies for communication policy and practice without becoming overly committed to certain causes, and that they would not rely so much on measures of statistical significance as substitutes for informed judgments about practical significance.

I called for more opportunities for researchers, communicators and policy makers to reach each other so that the findings of research might inform practices and policies. And I quoted my colleague at Indiana, David Nord, in urging scholars to avoid what he called "the two great errors of communication research"—defining communication so broadly that it loses any special mean-

Table 13.2
1985 Recommendations for New Directions in Mass Communication Research

Recommendation	Would make in 1992? YES	NO
1. More research on the producers and the production of media messages		X
2. More research that addresses truly important questions that make a difference in society	X	
3. More cumulative programs of research over time, such as agenda-setting and media performance	X	
4. More concern with implications of research findings for communication practice and policy	X	
5. More use of multiple methods and longer time periods	X	
6. More debate over research approaches and methods		X
7. More opportunities for researchers, practitioners and policy makers to talk and listen to each other	X	
8. More "middle-range" research that avoids the "two great errors" of defining communication too broadly or too narrowly	X	
9. More support for programs of research from communication industries	X	

ing and trivializing communication so that an obsession with measurement and the precise specification of contingent conditions leads to "evermore narrow studies that proclaim more and more about less and less" (Nord, 1985, p. 1).

Finally, I called for more support from the communication industry for programs of research that would last more than a few weeks or months and would lead to more informed and farsighted leadership and practice in journalism and mass communication.

1986

The following autumn I was given the opportunity to respond to a research agenda advanced by Jay Blumler, Michael Gurevitch and Mark Levy of the University of Maryland's Center for Research in Public Communication (Weaver, 1987). In that brief response, published with those of ten other scholars, I argued in favor of trying to come to some kind of agreement on the most important questions and areas of research, in the hope of stimulating more systematic and cumulative programs of research. I also suggested that there be more study of the influences on, and the relations between, mass communication sources, messages, and receivers to reinforce the Maryland group's basic assumption "that the public (or mass) communication process ought to be viewed as an integrated whole in which the various actors and institutions are linked and interdependent" (Gurevitch and Levy, 1985, p. 15).

I concluded this brief essay by arguing that one of the most significant questions for research is the power of mass media—the power to shape political agendas, to determine which versions of reality are acceptable on a widespread basis and to influence the values of a society. Whether one is most concerned with the influences of society upon the media, or vice versa, once this concern with power is made more explicit and is more carefully defined, the study of the public communication process stands a good chance of becoming less fragmented and more integrated within various social, cultural and political contexts.

1988

The last time I spoke about directions in research was some four years ago, when I was a candidate for the Roy W. Howard Chair at Indiana. Not surprisingly, I reviewed many of my earlier ideas and conclusions about past trends and problems in mass communication research. During my presentation to the faculty, I also reviewed more recent examples of some of the directions in research that I had identified three years prior for the Syracuse conference, and I commented more specifically on my personal research priorities.

I advocated more research on the effects of society upon the media, as I've been doing since 1979, but at the same time, I noted that I didn't want to abandon media effects research, because such research still has important and

Table 13.3
Summary of Key Recommendations for New Directions in Mass Communication Research, 1979–88

Recommendations	1979	1982	1985	1986	1988
More research on producers of media messages and effects of society on media	X	X	X		X
More cumulative programs of research over time	X		X	X	
More simultaneous study of sources, messages and audiences			X		X
More external funding for programs of research over time	X		X		
More attention to research questions that are significant for communication policy and practice			X	X	X

interesting things to tell us, especially those of us who try to educate the journalists and communicators of the future (see Table 13.3).

I pointed out that while I remained interested in studies of media agenda setting, I have become involved in studying what some have called agenda building, or how the media agenda gets set. Although those studies have been mostly concerned with mass communication, the role of direct personal experience and interpersonal communication is beginning to be recognized as increasingly important in agenda-setting processes (Weaver, Zhu, and Willnat, 1992).

I argued that the agenda-setting approach is fruitful in studying communication, whether at the personal, group or societal levels, because it offers hope of bringing together a variety of different kinds of communication studies, including those of sources, messages, uses and effects. I still think that it is one of the few middle-range conceptual approaches that has value for many different kinds of communication research, whether interpersonal, small group, organizational or mass, although the survey of key scholars mentioned earlier indicates that it is cited almost exclusively by those working in mass and political communication (So and Chan, 1991, pp. 45–47).

I concluded that my main concern in communication research is with the nature and quality of the messages that are produced, including the influences *on,* and the influences *of,* these messages. Although past research efforts, especially quantitative content analyses, have focused more on the structure of messages than on their meanings, I argued in favor of more fine-grained content analysis techniques to explore the meanings of various media messages if we want to move beyond *what* is reported to *how* different people, events, issues and processes are framed or portrayed.

These have been my thoughts on directions in journalism and mass communication research from 1979 to 1988, briefly described. Despite the changes in the practice of communication and in research about communication in the past four years, I still regard many of these ideas and recommendations as sound. But there have been some developments in our communication environment in the past few years that suggest the need for some new directions in communication research. Let me briefly review some of these newer developments and then make some recommendations for future directions in communication research.

RECENT COMMUNICATION DEVELOPMENTS

Since the early 1980s, there have been several important developments in communication that have implications for our research. First, new media have become more common, including computer bulletin boards, fax machines, satellite networks, videocassette recorders, and compact discs and the interfaces between these media. And still more loom on the horizon, including high definition television (HDTV), liquid display tubes, more sophisticated satellite technology, fiber-optic and two-way cable, and signal compression technology.

Second, new kinds of communication services have developed within existing media, including an explosion of cable TV channels, radio talk shows, televised talk and "infotainment" shows, and various telephone talk services. Many of these new services are characterized by greater feedback opportunities for receivers. In other words, they are more interactive than previous communication services and thus they blur the functions of sender and receiver that were more clearly defined in previous mass communication offerings.

Third, there is increasing competition for the time and attention of people by new media and new channels, and increasing economic competition among media and channels for advertising and user revenue. This has led to increasing specialization of communication content, but not necessarily to more diversity of ideas or points of view.

Fourth, in addition to specialization of content, there has been a convergence of the technologies of communication that makes it more difficult to study the uses and effects of particular media, as well as the production of the overlapping content of these media. This convergence also makes the old print-electronic, or verbal-nonverbal, distinctions so long of interest to communication researchers less relevant in light of messages that combine various modes of communication (writing, still and moving visual images, speaking and other sounds).

And, as Denis McQuail (1992) has noted, the more recent advances in distribution by cable and satellite have allowed more alternative organizations to have access to TV and radio channels as suppliers of information and culture. But these advances also make the media more international in character and lead to an international "media culture," where the same content forms, genres and substance are found in a variety of media, including books, newspapers, films, television, radio and sound recordings of various kinds.

Fifth, a "tiered" communication system is emerging, with some messages reaching the masses (important presidential speeches, the Gulf War coverage), others reaching significant segments of society (business news, some sporting events) and still others reaching relatively small, special interest groups (certain types of music, hobbies such as quilting or model railroading, matters of special interest to different minority groups).

What are the implications of these new developments for communication research? This question can be addressed in at least two ways—the first is to consider *what* is communicated (the communication agenda) and the second is more concerned with *how* information is communicated. In the research literature itself, we can also make a distinction between what is studied (the research agenda) and how certain subjects are studied (our paradigms, approaches and methods).

The title of this book invites us to go "beyond agendas" in considering new directions in communication research, a request that I interpret as meaning that we should focus on approaches and methods more than on topics. As mentioned earlier, it is difficult, perhaps impossible, to separate completely how we study communication from what we consider worth studying, or how information is communicated from what is communicated, but it is possible to emphasize approaches and methods that may cut across different topical areas such as political communication, organizational communication, mass communication, interpersonal influence, and so forth.

NEW DIRECTIONS IN COMMUNICATION RESEARCH

Along with the changes in our communication environment just described, I think there are already several healthy changes underway in our research approaches and methods. The first is a shift from quantitative to qualitative methods or, perhaps more accurately, a shift from reliance on solely quantitative surveys, experiments and content analyses to a tendency to use what once were considered "softer" methods (in-depth interviews, direct observations, focus groups and more impressionistic ways of analyzing communication content, some borrowed from semiotics). This trend is not confined to academic research. As an example, the European Society for Opinion and Marketing Research (ESOMAR) held a conference in Rome in February 1993 on qualitative research, including a major session on the relationship between qualitative and quantitative methods.

This trend, which has been going on for at least the past decade, may be primarily motivated by a recognition of the limits of quantitative methods, which are generally better at describing broader patterns and relationships than at providing explanations for why these patterns and relationships exist. It may also be motivated by a reaction against overly complicated and elaborate quantitative methods (LISREL, two-stage and three-stage least squares, logistic regression) that are very difficult to learn without advanced mathematical training and that take great amounts of time to employ, especially given the often small returns in additional knowledge gained.

And, finally, this trend of more use of qualitative methods is also due, I think, to the increasing familiarity of communication scholars with the literature and approaches of anthropology, feminist studies, literary studies and semiotics, in addition to psychology, sociology and political science.

Whatever the reasons for this shift toward more qualitative approaches, I think it comes at an opportune time. As our communication environment becomes more complex and multilevel, we need to use a variety of approaches and methods to analyze and understand it more fully. In doing so, we are returning full circle to some of the earliest social research by the Chicago School, which made extensive use of direct observation and extended interviews (Frazier and Gaziano, 1979).

The second change in how we study communication is a growing recognition that people get their information and ideas and opinions from a variety of sources, not just from the traditional media of newspapers, radio and television news, and the news magazines.

This was made especially clear to me in a 1989 paper by Diana Mutz that focused on the impact of direct personal experience, interpersonal discussion, and news media exposure on people's perceptions of unemployment as both a personal and a social problem. I was intrigued by this approach because of my interest in research on the role of mass media in agenda setting. Since then, two doctoral students and I have replicated this study using the issue of drug abuse, and we've found a "bridging function" of interpersonal discussion similar to what Mutz found. That is, increased discussion of drug abuse predicts increased concern over it as both a personal and a larger societal problem, whereas exposure to media reporting tends to predict to only one level of concern, but not to both (Weaver, Zhu, and Willnat, 1992).

This realization that our studies need to take account of influences other than the traditional news media is reinforced by developments in the 1992 presidential election campaign, where the so-called "new media" of talk shows, tabloids, "800" toll-free telephone numbers, computer bulletin boards and satellite networks were in many cases the main agenda setters, rather than the "old media" of the elite newspapers, news magazines and network television news programs (Alter, 1992; Balz, 1992; Harwood, 1992).

This inclusion of multiple sources of ideas and opinions in communication studies also implies a more interdisciplinary approach in our research—a cutting across the boundaries of journalism, telecommunications and speech communication at a minimum, and in some cases crossing the boundaries of other fields, such as anthropology, sociology, political science, psychology, semiotics and literary studies. Such an interdisciplinary approach fits well with the increasing complexity of our mediated communication environment.

A third trend in communication research is the movement away from studying direct effects of media messages to studying how people construct meanings from these messages, as evidenced in the numerous studies of information processing, interpretation of texts, and to a lesser extent, uses and gratifications, in the past decade or so.

There is a growing realization among communication researchers that the meaning of a media message lies not only in the text, but also in the reader, viewer or listener—and that any effects of a message depend also on the amount of attention paid to that message (McLeod and McDonald, 1985; Chaffee and Schleuder, 1986; Drew and Weaver, 1990).

The receiver of a text, or message, is surely limited in his or her interpretation of the meaning by the message itself, as semiotician and author Umberto Eco has recently argued in his critique of what he calls "unlimited semiosis," or the idea of "a free reading in which the will of the interpreters . . . beats the texts into a shape which will serve their own purposes" (Eco, 1990, pp. 15–16). But because any given message is open to at least several interpretations, this makes studying media effects more difficult and places a greater premium on the use of open-ended questions and observation than in the past, while also giving us a more accurate measure of how people really respond to mediated messages. This may trade some external validity for internal, but it also helps us deal with the increasing complexity of the combinations of media messages to which people are exposed, and to which they respond, in this information age.

Still another shift in how we study communication is a trend toward more fine-grained, or microlevel, analysis of communication content, especially in studies of discourse or framing (van Dijk, 1988; Pan and Kosicki, 1992). The popularity of macrolevel content analysis approaches that look for broader patterns of subjects, issues and themes (*what* is communicated) is giving way to more microlevel analyses of *how* certain issues or events are covered. This approach includes more impressionistic approaches to content analysis as well as more systematic ones.

In a sense, this is coming full circle to the early content analysis studies of the 1920s, 1930s and 1940s that used smaller units of analysis such as the assertion or the sentence or even the individual word (Lasswell, 1927; Lasswell and Leites, 1949). But these early content analysis studies grew out of concerns about wartime propaganda and were largely concerned with how favorable or unfavorable (or positive or negative) media messages were, not with the more extensive range of meanings that are of concern to those who study discourse or framing.

This kind of content analysis can tell us more about the individual trees than the forest, but the more general approaches so common to agenda-setting research are still needed to tell us about the contours of the larger forest—the larger patterns of subjects and issues that are covered (and not covered) by the various communication media. Another problem with the content analyses that focus on how certain subjects are covered is the tremendous time and effort needed to code individual assertions and phrases—and the extreme difficulty of doing so with nonverbal messages such as television and film images.

In spite of these difficulties, there seems to be an increase in studies that focus on *how* things are portrayed in various communication media, as well as on *what* subjects are emphasized, to gain a richer understanding of communication meanings and possible effects.

CONCLUSIONS

What conclusions can be drawn from these past and present trends in communication and communication research?

First, I hope that the tendency to use more qualitative, impressionistic approaches in studying communication content and effects will not result in throwing the baby out with the bath water. We in communication research have spent decades learning to apply quantitative methods and statistical analysis to our research. These methods can tell us a great deal about general patterns, trends and relationships—and they can enable us to generalize with far more accuracy than can our own personal experiences and impressions. So I hope the swing of the pendulum toward more qualitative, impressionistic approaches will not mean abandoning the strengths of quantitative approaches.

I'm concerned about this, because I don't see many examples of studies in communication that combine quantitative and qualitative approaches—or that employ more than one method of any kind. In their analysis of 2,284 mass communication research articles published from 1944–64, Wayne Danielson and G. Cleveland Wilhoit (1967) found no studies using more than one method. In our study of 122 journalism and mass communication articles published between 1954 and 1978, Gray and I found only 2.5 percent using some combination of methods (Weaver and Gray, 1979). In a study of 815 entries in *Communication Abstracts* from 1978–80, Wilhoit (1981, p. 14) found 4.5 percent employing multiple methods. And, in the unpublished 1983–92 study of four mass communication journals mentioned earlier, I found only 2.4 percent using more than one method.

These findings support my impression that most of the published research in mass communication is of one kind or another—either mostly quantitative or mostly qualitative. In fact, the dominant methods found in the study of four journals from 1983 to 1992 were content analysis (30 percent) and surveys (21 percent) on the quantitative side, and historical-philosophical (30 percent) on the qualitative side, just as was true from 1954 to 1978 (although the percentage of surveys has declined from 30 to 20 percent, and the percentage of content analysis studies had increased from 16 to 30 percent).

Even among the 2.4 percent that employed more than one method, the combinations were quantitative (survey and content analysis, and survey and experiment), suggesting that researchers in our field tend to favor either a quantitative or a nonquantitative approach, but not a combination of the two.

I hope that we will learn how to combine both approaches in single studies, and that our publications will welcome this multimethod approach. Otherwise, the findings of quantitative studies will not be directly connected with those of more qualitative approaches, and our understanding of communication processes will be less complete. A nice example of how to do this is found in Hallin (1992), where quantitative measures are used to demonstrate how the ''sound bite'' in television political news has shrunk in length from forty-three seconds in 1968 to nine seconds in 1988, and actual scripts from TV news over the years are used to give the reader a sense of the changing nature and tone of these reports.

Second, and following from the first conclusion, I hope that we will not abandon the forest for the trees in communication research, whether it involves the study of communicators, technologies, messages, audiences or some combination thereof. We still need a broad view of the contours of the forest as well as a closer examination of the individual trees. In other words, we need to keep working across different levels of analysis in communication research—from cultural to societal to organizational to small group to individual.

Third, I hope that more of us who study communication will make a greater effort to analyze the communication process more holistically by including measures of sources, communicators, messages and receivers simultaneously in single studies, along with their cultural and social contexts. I am surely one of the worst offenders in relying upon single methods (mainly surveys) and measures of only one dimension of the public communication process (usually media audiences), but I'm trying to do better.

This leads to my fourth point, which is that we need to study communication processes over longer periods of time—if not in single studies, then in studies that do more careful replicating of earlier research while at the same time adding some creative new elements. We need to try to build on previous research, not just through obligatory literature reviews that often don't connect directly with our present studies, but through careful replications that try to control for differences in sampling, question wording and social/cultural settings.

Table 13.4
1992 Recommendations for New Directions in Mass Communication Research

Recommendation

1.   Qualitative, impressionistic approaches to communication research need to be joined with more quantitative, systematic approaches. We should not "throw the baby out with the bath water" in terms of quantitative methods.

2.   We need to work across different levels of analysis (individual, small group, organizational, societal, and cultural) to gain a more complete understanding of communication processes and effects. This also requires more use of multiple methods in single studies.

3.   We need to study communication more holistically by including measures of sources, communicators, messages and receivers simultaneously in single studies, along with larger social and cultural frameworks.

4.   We need to study communication processes over longer periods of time, either in single studies or in creative replications of earlier studies that take account of changes in communication methods and technologies.

5.   We need to develop useful new concepts and theories to build on those that have done their work, such as systems theory, dependency theory, symbolic interactionism, uncertainty reduction, agenda-setting, knowledge gap, and diffusion of innovations.

6.   We need to keep paying attention to other fields, even though they often don't pay enough attention to us. What seems to be fragmentation or disarray in our field is also a sign of healthy interdisciplinary diversity.

7.   We have a number of new directions in communication research already — perhaps too many — but not a surplus of good ideas that are likely to prove fruitful for increasing our understanding of communication. Our task in the next decade and into the next millennium will be to determine which of these new directions are really useful and which are simply new bottles for old wine.

    Whatever our research agendas are, we need to pursue them over time—over years, rather than weeks or months—if we hope to extend our knowledge of communication. But in doing so, we need to keep new developments in our communication environment in mind and to modify our research designs and approaches when necessary to account for these new developments (see Table 13.4).

In our recent survey of journalists, for example, Cleve Wilhoit and I (1992) changed an open-ended question on the impact of new technology on journalists' work from one that asked about VDTs (video display terminals) and electronic news gathering in 1982 (Weaver and Wilhoit, 1986) to one that asked about the use of computerized databases such as NEXIS, DIALOG and VU/TEXT in 1992 because of the changes in communication technology. But we also left many of the questions unchanged so that direct comparisons could be made from 1971 to 1982 to 1992.

My point is that we must take account of changes in communication methods and technologies in our research, but we should not necessarily let new developments in communication set our research agendas in terms of which questions we consider important, even though these new developments may influence our research designs and methods.

Finally, I hope that during the next decade and into the next century, we will develop useful new concepts and theories in communication research to build on those that have done their work for us. It's not that I think approaches such as systems theory, dependency theory, information processing, symbolic interactionism, cultural studies, uncertainty reduction, social exchange, agenda setting, uses and gratifications, cultivation, knowledge gap and diffusion of innovations are irrelevant or no longer useful in our brave new information society. It's just that I think we need some new concepts, approaches and directions to reenergize and stimulate communication research, especially in light of the tremendous changes occurring in our communication environments.

Where will we find these new ideas? From our own experiences with the changing, converging technologies of communication. From our own thinking about how communication is taking place in this decade and on into the next millennium. From meetings such as the Wichita Symposium. From the new scholars entering our field with diverse academic and professional backgrounds. And, finally, from reading in fields other than our own while at the same time keeping in mind the puzzles of communication that still remain to be solved.

It's no secret that we tend to cite ourselves in communication research, just as those in other fields do, but in the past we have done better than those in other fields in referring to sources outside communication. In a citation analysis of nine core communication journals from 1975 to 1979, Byron Reeves and Christine Borgman (1983) found that while the average percentage of citations to core journals in communication was only 13 percent, the majority of citations in most other social sciences were to journals in the same discipline. As they put it, "communication research still remains very much an interdisciplinary activity dependent on a wide range of information bases" (Reeves and Borgman, 1983, p. 135). William Paisley (1984) also found that communication journals were more likely to cite major journals in other social sciences, but not vice versa.

More recently, a 1991 survey of twenty-nine top scholars published in nine journalism or mass communication journals found "considerable fragmentation and a lack of consensus about core works in the field,'' as well as little overlap in the lists of core books in the field (Leichty, Springston, and Huff, 1991).

These findings can be interpreted as evidence that communication is a field in disarray, with little disciplinary development (So, 1988), but they can also be seen as a sign of healthy interdisciplinary diversity. In view of the eclecticism of the communication field described in these studies and the acceleration of technological changes in communication, it is likely that there will be no shortage of new directions in communication research in this decade and beyond. Our field is simply too dynamic and too diverse not to produce new concepts, theories and paradigms.

In addition, as David Nord (1992) notes, ''the 'linguistic turn' in many other fields has pushed communication to center stage in all the social sciences and humanities. Everywhere, the interest is in language, signs, representations.'' Nord argues that it is our special task to study ''the *mediation* of language, signs, representations—and especially the formal organizations and structures that do the mediating.''

In a recent issue of one of our newest journals, *Communication Theory*, Wendy Leeds-Hurwitz (1992) also argues that there is a revolution occurring in all of the fields that study human behavior, including communication. She writes that within communication it has most frequently been called an ''interpretive approach,'' and it includes such labels as cultural studies, critical theory, postmodernism, semiotics, phenomenology, structuralism, hermeneutics, naturalistic enquiry, ethnography and social communication, among others (p. 131). I have tended to lump most of these approaches under the label ''qualitative studies'' in this chapter, undoubtedly without doing justice to their differences.

But the point is that we do have a number of new directions in communication research emerging—perhaps too many—even if they originated outside of our field and even if they concern broader issues of social theory, as Leeds-Hurwitz argues. Not all will prove useful or survive for long.

One of our main tasks in this decade and into the next century will be to determine which are useful for furthering our understanding of different kinds of communication and which are simply new bottles for old wine. Given the increasing complexity of our field and the heightened interest in communication among the social sciences and humanities generally, this will not be an easy job. But it should be interesting.

NOTES

1. This finding is based on an analysis of all the research articles in one randomly selected issue each of *Journalism Quarterly, Public Opinion Quarterly, Journal of Communication* and *Journal of Broadcasting and Electronic Media* for the years 1983, 1988 and 1992 (N = 126). Only those articles dealing directly with mass communication were coded from *Public Opinion Quarterly*. The same categories were used as in the

1954–78 study reported in Weaver and Gray (1979). In this earlier study, only *Journalism Quarterly* and *Public Opinion Quarterly* were analyzed from the mass communication field (in addition to three other journals from political science, psychology and sociology). We analyzed all the major articles in one randomly selected issue of each of these journals for each of the years 1954, 1958, 1963, 1968, 1973 and 1978 (N = 122 for the mass communication articles). See Weaver and Gray (1979) for more details on methods.

2. The remaining 14 percent of the funded studies from 1983 to 1992 were supported by a combination of university, government and private sources, compared with 18 percent of such studies from 1954 to 1978.

REFERENCES

AEJMC. (1992). *Journalism & mass communication directory, 10.* Columbia, SC: Association for Education in Journalism and Mass Communication.

Alter, J. (1992, June 8). Why the old media's losing control. *Newsweek,* p. 28.

Balz, D. (1992, May 25–31). In media res: If you can't beat 'em, bypass 'em. *Washington Post National Weekly Edition,* p. 12.

Blumler, J. G. (1978). Purposes of mass communications research: A transatlantic perspective. *Journalism Quarterly, 55*(2), 219–230. Also published in G. C. Wilhoit & H. de Bock (Eds.) (1980), *Mass communication review yearbook,* vol. 1 (pp. 33–44). Beverly Hills, CA: Sage.

Blumler, J. G. (1981). Mass communication research in Europe: Some origins and prospects. In G. C. Wilhoit & H. de Bock (Eds.), *Mass communication review yearbook,* vol. 2 (pp. 37–49). Beverly Hills, CA: Sage.

Chaffee, S. H., & Schleuder, J. (1986). Measurement and effects of attention to media news. *Human Communication Research, 13,* 76–107.

Clarke, P. (1973, December). How much of communication research is worth knowing about? *T & M Newsletter.* Association for Education in Journalism, Communication Theory & Methodology Division.

Danielson, W. A., & Wilhoit, G. C. (1967). *A computerized bibliography of mass communication research, 1944–1964.* New York: Magazine Publishers Association.

Drew, D., & Weaver, D. (1990). Media attention, media exposure, and media effects. *Journalism Quarterly, 67,* 740–748.

Eco, U. (1990). Drift and unlimited semiosis. *Institute for Advanced Study Distinguished Lecturer Series 1.* Bloomington: Indiana University.

Frazier, P. J., & Gaziano, C. (1979). Robert Ezra Park's theory of news, public opinion, and social control. *Journalism Monographs,* no. 64.

Gurevitch, M., & Levy, M. R. (1985). Introduction. *Mass communication review yearbook,* vol. 5 (pp. 11–22). Beverly Hills, CA: Sage.

Hallin, D. C. (1992). Sound bite news: television coverage of elections, 1968–1988. *Journal of Communication, 42*(2), 5–24.

Hampton Press. (1992). *Communication series.* Cresskill, NJ: Hampton Press.

Harwood, R. (1992, July 5). We may be witnessing the dawn of a new media order. *Sunday (Bloomington, IN) Herald-Times,* p. A11.

ICA. (1992, May). *Communication and new worlds: Official program for the 42nd annual conference of the International Communication Association.* Austin, TX: ICA.

Lasswell, H. D. (1927). *Propaganda technique in the World War*. London: Kegan Paul, Trench, Trubner & Co. Reprinted in 1971 as *Propaganda technique in World War I*. Cambridge, MA: MIT Press.

Lasswell, H. D., & Leites, N. (1949). *Language of politics: Studies in quantitative semantics*. George W. Stewart. Reprinted in 1965. Cambridge, MA: MIT Press.

Leeds-Hurwitz, W. (1992). Social approaches to interpersonal communication. *Communication Theory, 2*(2), 131–139.

Leichty, G., Springston, J., & Huff, W. A. (1991). *Core works in journalism and mass communication: Views from the top scholars in the field*. Unpublished paper.

McLeod, J., & McDonald, D. (1985). Beyond simple exposure: Media orientations and their impact on political processes. *Communication Research, 12*, 3–34.

McQuail, D. (1992). *Media performance: Mass communication and the public interest*. Newbury Park, CA: Sage.

Mutz, D. C. (1989, May). *Yours, mine and ours: Information sources, perceptions of unemployment and their political consequences*. Paper presented to the annual meeting of the International Communication Association, San Francisco, CA. Revised and published as Mutz, D. C. (1992). Mass media and the depoliticization of personal experience. *American Journal of Political Science, 36*, 483–508.

Nord, D. P. (1985). *Career narrative*. Unpublished memo. Bloomington: School of Journalism, Indiana University.

Nord, D. P. (1992, July 14). Personal memo. Bloomington: School of Journalism, Indiana University.

Paisley, W. (1984). Communication in the communication sciences. In B. Dervin & M. J. Voigt (Eds.), *Progress in the communication sciences* (pp. 1–43). Norwood, NJ: Ablex.

Pan, Z., & Kosicki, G. M. (1992, May). *Framing analysis: An approach to news discourse*. Paper presented to the annual meeting of the International Communication Association, Miami, FL.

Reeves, B., & Borgman, C. L. (1983). A bibliometric evaluation of core journals in communication research. *Human Communication Research, 10*(1), 119–136.

So, C.Y.K. (1988). Citation patterns of core communication journals: An assessment of the developmental status of communication. *Human Communication Research, 15*, 236–255.

So, C.Y.K., & Chan, J. M. (1991, August). *Evaluating and conceptualizing the field of communication: A survey of the core scholars*. Paper presented to the annual meeting of the Association for Education in Journalism and Mass Communication, Boston, MA.

van Dijk, T. (1988). *News as discourse*. Hillsdale, NJ: Lawrence Erlbaum Associates.

Weaver, D. (1987). Thoughts on an agenda for mass communication research. In M. Gurevitch & M. R. Levy (Eds.), *Mass communication review yearbook*, vol. 6 (pp. 60–64). Newbury Park, CA: Sage.

Weaver, D. H. (1988). Mass communication research problems and promises. In N. W. Sharp (Ed.), *Communications research: The challenge of the Information Age* (pp. 21–38). Syracuse, NY: Syracuse University Press.

Weaver, D. H., & Gray, R. G. (1979, August). *Journalism and mass communication research in the United States: Past, present and future*. Paper presented to the annual meeting of the Association for Education in Journalism, Houston, TX.

Also published in G. C. Wilhoit & H. de Bock (Eds.) (1980), *Mass communication review yearbook,* vol. 1 (pp. 124–151). Beverly Hills, CA: Sage.

Weaver, D., & Wilhoit, G. C. (1986). *The American journalist: A portrait of U.S. news people and their work.* Bloomington: Indiana University Press.

Weaver, D., & Wilhoit, G. C. (1992, November). Journalists: Who are they, really? In E. E. Dennis (Ed.), *Media Studies Journal,* 6 (pp. 63–79). New York: Freedom Forum Media Studies Center.

Weaver, D., Zhu, J., & Willnat, L. (1992, May). *Information sources and agenda-setting: Testing a theory of bridging.* Paper presented to the annual meeting of the American Association for Public Opinion Research, St. Petersburg, FL. In press, *Journalism Quarterly.*

Wilhoit, G. C. (1981). Introduction. In G. C. Wilhoit & H. de Bock (Eds.), *Mass communication review yearbook,* vol. 2 (pp. 13–33). Beverly Hills, CA: Sage.

Index

Social interaction, 42, 43
Social organization, 191
Social science, 19, 30, 86
Society, fragmentation of, 2
Sociology, 22–36. *See also* Chicago
    School; Phenomenological sociology
Spatial diversity, 180
Speech communication, 3, 146
Spencer, Herbert, 24
Sperry, S. L., 82
Spiral of silence theory, 132
Sreberny-Mohammadi, Annabelle, 182
Standard Oil Company, 21
Stimulus-interpretation-response model,
    27
Stimulus-response theory, 27
Stratification of informational welfare,
    197. *See also* Information
Stroh, P., 80
Strong, Josiah, 41
Symbolic interactionism, 4, 14, 19, 24,
    179; meaning as the core of, 158
Syracuse University, 203

Technical dialogue, 61
Technologies of communication, 14. *See
    also* National cultures: technologies,
    cultures, and communication
Technology transfer theory, 161
"Teenage Mutant Ninja Turtles," 142
Teilhard de Chardin, Pierre, 171
Telecommunications, 45, 48, 154, 157
Telecommunications theory, 151
Television: children viewers, 139;
    educational, 144; effects of, 139;
    violence, 140. *See also* Educational
    programming
*Television and America's Children: A
    Crisis of Neglect* (Palmer), 141
Television producers and genres in the
    United Kingdom and United States, 6,
    91–92; edinfotainment, 95–96; factual
    programming, 93–95; genre-based
    cross-national comparisons, 99–100;
    genre segregation, 98–99; nonfactual
    program producers, 96–97; producers
    of specific genres, 92–93; specific
    genres (fiction, comedy, documentary,

game shows, chat shows), 98; work
    schedules, 97
Temporal diversity, 180
Thomas, W. I., 23
Thompson, Robert L., 93
Thought News, 29
Tichenor, P. J., 5
Time Warner, 183
Tixier, Maud, 7
Tojo, Hideki, 130
"Tongues Untied," 143
Tracey, Michael, 143
Transmission model, 157
Trenaman, J., 191
Tripolar model of communication, 7,
    121–124
Tse-tung, Mao, 130
Tsujimura, A., 63
Tunstall, Jeremy, 6, 7, 126
Tuskegee Institute, 29
Two-way interaction, 4

Urban communication, 49–54
Urban communication systems, 41
Urban ideology, 52
USA Today, 84
Use of the Mass Media by the Urban Poor
    (Greenberg and Dervin), 50

van Dijk, T., 80, 212
*Vested Interests: Cross-dressing and
    Cultural Anxiety* (Garber), 173
Video teleconferences, 159–160
Vrdoljak, Anton, 84

Wahlke, J., 80
Wartella, Ellen, 8, 161, 164
Washington, Booker T., 29
Weaver, David H., 11, 203, 212, 213,
    216, 218
Weaver, W., 157
Weber, Max, 21
Western Europe and managerial culture,
    7, 101; attitudes toward risk, 110–111;
    attitudes toward work, 103;
    communication styles, 104–108;
    education, 104; formal versus informal
    communication, 106–107; hierarchy,

About the Contributors

JENNINGS BRYANT is professor of communication, holder of the Ronald Reagan–endowed Chair of Broadcasting and director of the Institute for Communication Research at the University of Alabama. He has written more than 75 articles, 35 book chapters and 80 convention papers. He has also authored or co-authored about a dozen books, mainly devoted to the effects of television.

JAMES W. CAREY is visiting professor at Columbia University's Graduate School of Journalism. Prior to this position, he was dean of the College of Communications and research professor of communications at the University of Illinois, Urbana-Champaign. He has written extensively on culture and communication, mass media and popular culture and communication research. His books include *Media, Myths and Narratives* (1988) and *Communication as Culture: Essays on Media and Society* (1989).

PHILIP GAUNT is currently director of research at The Wichita State University's Elliott School of Communication. Before returning to the academy, he worked for many years as a journalist, broadcaster, film maker and writer in a number of different countries. He also spent six years as a media specialist with UNESCO in Paris. He is the author of several books and textbooks, as well as articles in *Journalism Quarterly, Media, Culture and Society, Gazette* and other journals. His recent publications include *Choosing the News: The Profit Factor in News Selection* (1990) and *Making the Newsmakers: International Handbook of Journalism Training* (1992), both published by Greenwood Press.

DORIS A. GRABER is professor of political science at the University of Illinois at Chicago and a faculty associate in the Department of Communication. She is the author of many articles and books dealing with political communication, including *Verbal Behavior and Politics* (1976), *Processing the News: How People Tame the Information Tide* (1988), *Public Sector Communication: How Organizations Manage Information* (1992) and *Mass Media and American Politics,* 4th ed. (1993).

YOUICHI ITO is professor in the Faculty of Policy Management at Keio University, Fujisawa, and associate director of the university's Institute for Communication Research. He has published widely on a variety of communication topics in Asia, Europe and the United States. His recent English-language publications include *Communication and Culture: A Comparative Approach* (1989) and major articles in *Media, Culture and Society* and *Communication Yearbook,* as well as a chapter in *Cultures, Politics and Research Programs: An International Assessment of Practical Problems in Field Research,* edited by Narula and Pearce (1990).

GARTH S. JOWETT is currently professor of communication at the University of Houston. He has served as director for social research for the Canadian government's Department of Communication. He has also been a consultant to various international communications agencies. He was appointed a Gannett Center fellow in 1988–89 and has published widely in the area of popular culture and the history of communications. His book, *Film: The Democratic Art* (1976), is considered to be a benchmark in film history. It has now been completely revised and will reappear as *Moviegoing in America: A Social History.*

DENIS MCQUAIL is currently professor of mass communication at the University of Amsterdam. He was formerly professor of sociology at the University of Southampton in the United Kingdom. He has also taught at the Annenberg School at the University of Pennsylvania and was a senior fellow of the Gannett Center for Media Studies at Columbia University in New York in 1989. His research interests cover a broad range of areas: political communication and election campaigns; audience research; media theory and communication models; and media policy, with particular reference to the impact and policy implications of new communications technology in Europe. He is the author or co-author of a dozen books, including his influential *Mass Communication Theory* (1983, 1987) and his latest major work, *Media Performance: Mass Communication and the Public Interest* (1992).

W. BARNETT PEARCE is professor and chair of the Department of Communication at Loyola University Chicago. Previous to this appointment, he taught at the universities of Massachusetts, Kentucky and North Dakota. His interests are sharply focused on "social constructionism" as a way of thinking about communication, and his research wanders widely among the traditional topics within the discipline. He has written numerous journal articles, book chapters and convention papers and has lectured in many parts of the world on communication theory, communication and society and development communication. His most recent books include: (with Michael Weiler) *Reagan and American Public Discourse* (1992); (with Uma Narula) *Cultures, Politics and Research Programs: An International Assessment of Practical Problems in Field Research* (1990); and *Communication and the Human Condition* (1989).

EVERETT M. ROGERS is currently professor and chair of the Department of Communication and Journalism at the University of New Mexico. Prior to this appointment, he was the Walter H. Annenberg Professor of Communications at the University of Southern California and the Janet M. Peck Professor of International Communication at Stanford University. A prolific researcher, Rogers has authored or co-authored more than twenty-five books, including his influential *Diffusion of Innovations* (1962) and *Communication Technology: The New Media in Society* (1986). His latest book, *A Century of Communication Study* (1993), from which his chapter in this book draws extensively, was written in 1991–92 when Rogers was a fellow at the Center for Advanced Study in the Behavioral Sciences at Stanford.

MAUD TIXIER holds the Chair of Corporate Communication at ESSEC (the Advanced School of Economic and Commercial Sciences) in Cergy, just outside Paris. She has traveled widely and much of her research and consulting is international in nature. Her recent books include *Travailler en Europe: Mobilité, Recrutement, Culture* (1992), *La Communication de Crise: Enjeux et Stratégies* (1991) and (with Alain Jolibert) *La Négotiation Commerciale* (1988), which was awarded the 1989 prize of the French Academy of Commercial Sciences. She has taught in Canada, Britain and the United States and is much in demand as a consultant and speaker on business communication.

JEREMY TUNSTALL is professor of sociology at City University in London. His early work, in the British sociological tradition of studies of manual occupations, produced *The Fishermen* (1962) and *Old and Alone* (1966). He has also written extensively about journalists and the media in general. His books on U.S. communications include *The Media Are American* (1977) and *Communications Deregulation* (1986). In recent years, he has studied communications policy, resulting first in *The Media in Britain* (1983). He has also co-authored (with Michael Palmer of University of Paris III) two books on European communications policy, *Liberating Communications* (1990) and *Media Moguls* (1991). He plans to write a book on the world media industry with the projected title of *The Media Are No Longer American*.

ELLEN WARTELLA is dean of the College of Communications at the University of Texas at Austin. She serves on the editorial boards of seven journals and book series and is the author or editor of six books and dozens of book chapters and articles on mass media effects on children and other audiences. As a consultant to the Federal Communications Commission, Federal Trade Commission and congressional investigations on children and television, she has been an advocate for better programming for children. She has been a visiting professor at the universities of Munich and California-Santa Barbara, and has lectured at various other universities in the United States, Canada, Western Europe, Taiwan and Australia.

DAVID H. WEAVER is the Roy W. Howard Professor of Journalism and Mass Communication Research at Indiana University. He is author or co-author of *The Formation of Campaign Agendas* (1991), *Contemporary Public Opinion* (1991), *The American Journalist: A Portrait of U.S. News People and Their Work* (1986, 1991), *Videotex Journalism* (1983), *Media Agenda-Setting in a Presidential Election* (1981) and *Newsroom Guide to Polls and Surveys* (1980). He has also written numerous book chapters, articles and reports on U.S. journalists, media agenda setting, newspaper readership, foreign news coverage and journalism education. Weaver serves on the editorial boards of *Political Communication* and the *Newspaper Research Journal*. He was the 1987–88 president of the Association for Education in Journalism and Mass Communication and the 1986–87 president of the Midwest Association for Public Opinion Research.